FIRST ENCOUNTERS

FIRST ENCOUNTERS

Native Voices on the Coming of the Europeans

Howard B. Leavitt, Editor

 GREENWOOD

AN IMPRINT OF ABC-CLIO, LLC
Santa Barbara, California • Denver, Colorado • Oxford, England

Copyright 2010 by Howard B. Leavitt

Library of Congress Cataloging-in-Publication Data

First encounters : native voices on the coming of the Europeans / [edited by] Howard B. Leavitt.
   p. cm.
Includes bibliographical references and index.
   ISBN 978–0–313–35131–0 (hard copy : alk. paper) — ISBN 978–0–313–35132–7 (ebook)
1. First contact of aboriginal peoples with Westerners—Sources.   2. Colonies—History—Sources.
3. Acculturation—History—Sources.   4. Indigenous peoples—History—Sources.   5. Indigenous peoples—
Biography.   6. Europeans—History—Sources.   7. Colonists—History—Sources.   8. Conquerors—
History—Sources. I. Leavitt, Howard B.
GN368.F57   2010
303.48′2172201724—dc22   2009053671

ISBN: 978–0–313–35131–0
EISBN: 978–0–313–35132–7

14 13 12 11 10   1 2 3 4 5

This book is also available on the World Wide Web as an eBook.
Visit www.abc-clio.com for details.

Greenwood
An Imprint of ABC-CLIO, LLC

ABC-CLIO, LLC
130 Cremona Drive, P.O. Box 1911
Santa Barbara, California 93116-1911

This book is printed on acid-free paper ∞

Manufactured in the United States of America

This anthology is dedicated to Chinua Achebe,
Africa's preeminent twentieth-century writer,
whose classic novel *Things Fall Apart*
was the inspiration for this anthology.

CONTENTS

LIST OF SIDEBARS

PREFACE

History, since it is written by the conqueror, inevitably tends to glorify the victor and ignore the defeated. The voices of the conquered, the overwhelmed, and the subjugated are nearly always absent. *First Encounters: Native Voices on the Coming of the Europeans* seeks to redress this imbalance. In these 42 selections, native witnesses describe their initial contacts with Europeans who came into their lands as explorers, slavers, missionaries, soldiers, settlers, and governors. This anthology covers five continents and five centuries. These accounts, some long, some short, bear witness to the dark side of colonial history which has usually been ignored.

Many of the selections also throw light on the process of social change in its early stages when traditional indigenous societies, many of them thousands of years old, started to unravel under the impact of European culture and technology. These first-hand reports of the moment of impact, and the events that followed, provide insight into the painful steps that stable, traditional societies have had to take in order to participate in the modern world.

The overall effect of these accounts is decidedly negative. Slave-traders steal children, colonists steal land, and missionaries undermine traditional beliefs, customs, and rituals. But the conclusion that the European and his civilization have brought nothing but harm to indigenous populations is, of course, incorrect. There have been important benefits. However, native voices are usually angry and often full of despair, as they describe a darker side of the intruders' activities: deceit, force, intimidation, and destruction.

The selections were chosen for the quality of their writing and for their insight into how their societies were being changed. I found them in archives, libraries, and bookstores on three continents over a period of 25 years. Some of them were originally published in mid-twentieth century when it was still possible to locate and interview people who had actually witnessed the events. They are drawn from a variety of sources: autobiographies, novels, historical documents, and journals. On the questions of validity of translation and the transcription of oral history, I have relied on the work of other scholars and publishers. For each entry I have supplied background material, biographical information about the author, when available, and my own comments.

The selections in this anthology are organized into five geographical areas, one for each continent. Some sections are longer than others because of an abundance of interesting material. Each has an introduction to provide historical context for the voices and a timeline to give them a chronological structure. Sidebars are interspersed to give useful and sometimes dramatic information. A number of pictures depict incidents being related, and some even show the speakers themselves. Inevitably most of the voices are male, though there are two women, and even a group of five girls.

Several terms which may need clarification appear in the anthology. First of all, there is the need to explain the term *white man*. To some it is inflammatory, but this is the term used by indigenous people throughout the four or five hundred years of the colonial era. History cannot be erased, but the term can be used with sensitivity and accuracy. This anthology uses the term *white man* not to denote race but to label the intruding group, with its advanced technology, with the same label used by the peoples they were intending to dominate, the label which focused on their most immediate distinguishing characteristic, their strange and sometimes frightening pallor.

There is no consensus as to the appropriate name for the original inhabitants of the Americas. The term *American Indian* derives from the name of an Italian explorer and from Columbus's geographical error. Although I use such terms as *Native American* and *Indian* interchangeably, neither is satisfactory.

Even the term *first encounter* is sometimes used very broadly. Some of the selections deal with the long term effects of the first encounter, including the effect of new technology. In a number of selections, the term denotes first encounter with surrogates of the white man, for example the native catechist who has been trained in a hurry to teach elementary school grades in the newly established missionary schools.

In the case of Asia, a very broad use of the term is necessary. Europeans first arrived there slowly and almost imperceptibly over hundreds of years, discernable only after a critical mass appeared in the 1800s. Scholars were among the first to comment on the European incursions, and a number of their criticisms are included.

This anthology will be of interest to teachers of courses in sociology, anthropology, and history. It would be of general interest to all who are interested in the history of and elevation of minority voices. It should be of special interest to university and high school students who are enrolled in African American or Native American studies programs and/or those whose ancestors were victims of European colonization. But in addition, those who have European ancestors will want to learn about the other, the negative, side of the process of colonization put into place by their forebears.

The idea for this anthology was born at the convergence of three aspects of my life. In the first place, my father at one time was a missionary assigned to Tripoli, Syria (now Lebanon), as principal of a mission school. After four years, he either resigned or was pressured to leave. He had become a critic of his Church's injunction to all missionaries that their primary duty was to make Jesus Christ known as *Savior, Lord, and Master*. He had come to believe in the then-heretical idea that a good Muslim could be just as good a person as could a good Christian. My father was deeply disturbed when he learned that at the mission hospital in Tripoli, patients could be admitted only after they had attended a Christian religious service. As I grew up, I was constantly made aware of the good works, the selfless, altruistic, and dedicated behavior of missionaries who proselytized by example. This was balanced later, however, by my awareness of the manipulative and cruel extremes to which some missionaries would go in the name of proselytizing for Christ.

Second, my graduate studies at Columbia University exposed me to the literature on social change and the disruption of traditional societies caused by the introduction of modern technology. Later, I was able to apply this knowledge when working for foreign aid agencies in analyzing the success or failure of educational development projects abroad. Many trips to Africa and Latin America countries gave me a close look at social change brought about by Western development projects. As a professor at several universities, I have tried out some of these vivid accounts in both undergraduate and graduate courses. Students have invariably shown great interest and enthusiasm.

Third, Chinua Achebe's 1959 novel, *Things Fall Apart*, arguably the first African novel to deal with the impact of the arrival of the white man, served as a catalyst. Achebe was one of the first to describe the missionary's use of modern technology as proof that his God was more powerful than local tribal gods.

I resolved to seek other native accounts of the disruption of societies by white missionaries, colonists, soldiers, or businessmen. I have brought them together in this book.

ACKNOWLEDGMENTS

I wish to express my deep appreciation to the following people who provided much welcomed assistance in the production of this anthology.

Elaine Buller, consultant
Joan Leavitt, permissions editor
John Leavitt, technical support
Michael Thelwell, professor of Afro-American Studies, University of Massachusetts
Veronica Towers, editor, Greenwood Press

INTRODUCTION

In 1492 Europeans burst out of their continent, bent on exploring, conquering, and colonizing the world. During the next four centuries, Europeans achieved domination of one kind or another over most of the rest of the world. To explain how and why this happened, is both complex and speculative. Obviously it was the result of the fortuitous combination of many factors. Population and economic development were on the rise in Europe. Its long coastlines were an invitation to maritime exploration. Europeans discovered how to use the scientific method to understand nature, invent new things, and processes. This application of technology to the range of human activity revolutionized all aspects of life.

Advances in ship building resulted in specialized vessels for specific purposes. During Columbus's time, the heavy carrack was designed for trade; the lighter caravel for exploration. A century later, the English and Dutch built the formidable man-of-war naval ship. Redesigned sails and rigging permitted making headway against an adverse wind. More accurate and deadly cannons were developed to ensure the winning of sea battles and the conquest of foreign ports. New tools of navigation speeded up maritime discoveries.

Sometimes overlooked is the European development of the business side of exploration for new markets and sources of wealth. The first steps in creating maritime venture capital were in place. Bank loans, insurance, and joint stock companies provided vigorous support for the launching of voyages of exploration and commerce.

These accomplishments and the prospect of more advances produced a general atmosphere of confidence and even arrogance among Europeans. A feeling of exceptionalism spread. European culture was *civilized* and should be spread around the world for the benefit of the less fortunate. By the early twentieth century, this had become rationalized as the *White Man's Burden*. Christianity was the one true religion and should be vigorously exported; proselytizing among the *heathen* was made a priority. Missionaries accompanied voyagers and took up residence in colonies and foreign lands for this purpose.

There are some striking aspects of European expansion as it proceeded around the world over the course of five centuries. Real colonization in Africa only began 350 years after it had arrived in South America, and 275 years after the founding of Jamestown and Plymouth in North America. This delay was caused by the nature of European economic relations with Africa. European countries had established numbers of trading posts and forts along the coast of Africa. To these ports, came African traders from the interior with slaves, minerals, and agricultural products. For roughly 300 years, an estimated ten million slaves were shipped from these ports to markets in North America, the Caribbean, Brazil, and Europe. The African coastal trade was so profitable, that Europeans delayed the colonization of the interior for almost 400 years.

The paramount objective of colonization was to make money. But colonization did not take the same form in all places. In South America, colonists intermarried with the indigenous people to create blended societies. In North America, the Indians were pushed further and further west until, much reduced in numbers; they occupied a tiny percent of a continent which used to be theirs. In Asia, there was no large settlement of Europeans; they made money by wringing trade concessions from old disintegrating empires in India and China.

Most of the native voices in this anthology are voices protesting the destruction of their culture by the European intruders. It should be kept in mind that at one time, all our ancestors belonged to a traditional, pre-literate tribal society stretching back in time for thousands of years. Most of the peoples who were colonized still belonged to such societies. Life for them was often a struggle for survival, since people were unable to exert much control over threats to life such as famine, disease, natural disasters, and predators. Survival mechanisms had developed. They tried to placate gods with rituals and sacrifices. Extended kinship ties provided a strong system of social security. They practiced a subsistence mode of life, not commercial, where just enough food was produced or found. Generally land was not privately held. The absence of writing placed great emphasis on the need for accurate oral history to preserve the identity of a tribe. These tribal characteristics had been tested over time and had proven to be efficient in preserving the society. Colonizing Europeans were ignorant of the value of these basic and historic tribal ways, and in their haste to make money, spread *civilization* and convert souls to Christianity; they often behaved in very destructive ways.

For example, they gave the indigenous people the impression that their advanced technology was the result of their having a more powerful God, reason enough to convert. They introduced, by force, the private ownership of land. Although they promoted such things as better food, clothing, housing, and medicine, in the process, they disrupted tribal government and custom, religion, and family ties. They ignored the social consequences of substituting cash for barter and the accompanying loss of control over one's life. They indirectly encouraged the abandonment of tribal villages and promoted the rush to the cities. They introduced formal education at the expense of close family ties.

These negative aspects of colonization, often the subject of the anthology's native voices, need to be placed in context. Settlers and missionaries also did an enormous amount of good work in building hospitals, schools, and printing presses, as well as assisting native people in adopting the beneficial aspects of modernization and finding ways to adjust to the new society.

The reader is left with the puzzling question: historically, was colonization, on the whole, good or bad? The answer must rely heavily on the answer to another question. What is the best way for societies to make the difficult change from the traditional to the modern, since it is inevitable?

But this is the way things happened. Here, seen through the eyes of the indigenous peoples, is the record of European colonization.

Part One

FIRST ENCOUNTERS IN AFRICA

INTRODUCTION

In 1450, Portuguese explorers were the first Europeans to sail down the coast of Africa, more than 40 years before Christopher Columbus set out for the West across the Atlantic Ocean. A surprising 430 years would pass before the colonization of Africa would start. These early voyages of discovery resulted in the establishment of a string of coastal settlements or forts, used for the collection of goods to be loaded aboard ships and sent back to European ports. As long as the European merchants could count on the delivery of goods to these coastal ports by local traders, there was no need for them to penetrate the unknown and forbidding African continent. The lucrative nature of this trade, gold, spices, ivory, and slaves, soon brought the Dutch, English, French, Spanish, and Danish into the competition. The result was an international patchwork of rival trading posts scattered along the coast of Africa. Originally, slaves in small numbers were transported to North Africa, largely for domestic purposes. However, following the beginning of colonization in South and North America in the sixteenth and seventeenth centuries, the growing demand for large numbers of agricultural and mining workers brought about a great expansion of the slave trade at African ports. Eventually, the slave trade was ended by Britain in 1807 and in the following year, the United States banned the importation of new slaves.

In the 1880s, this centuries old system of coastal trading posts came to an end in what was called the *scramble for Africa*. Europeans countries vied with each other to grab territory and establish colonies in the African interior. It began in 1879, when King Leopold II of Belgium sent the foremost explorer of Africa, Henry M. Stanley, back to the central part of the continent, the Congo, which he had explored before. His task was to persuade local chieftains to cede land to the king. Stanley's efforts were so successful that within one year, Leopold claimed an area of Africa equal in size to all of Western Europe. Then the agents of Otto von Bismarck, chancellor of the German Empire, carved out territories in what is now Tanzania, South-West Africa, Togo, and Cameroon. These successes on the part of the Belgians and Germans were alarming to other European powers that feared that opportunities for wealth and power were escaping them. The scramble for Africa had begun in earnest.

In order to regularize this race, Bismarck convened an international conference to divide up the African continent among the European powers. The Berlin Conference in 1885 established a number of rules: actual occupation was necessary to claim a territory, countries would respect each other's colonies, and the slave trade was banned. By the early twentieth century, colonization in Africa was under way. European colonial powers quickly exploited newly found resources for transport back to Europe: minerals, cotton, cocoa, rubber, palm oil, and diamonds.

By 1902, the scramble for colonies in sub-Saharan Africa was over. Only two states, Liberia and Ethiopia, remained independent. The newly colonized people of Africa reacted in predictable ways. On the one hand, they were outraged and angered at the indignities, oppression, and exploitation which accompanied colonization. On the other hand, there was hope and the anticipation that European education and technology would benefit their lives. This contradiction has been present ever since that time, as developing countries, even today, continue to be resentful of the intrusions of the Europeans, while at the same time avidly seeking the benefits of European knowledge.

Although explorers and missionaries had visited Africa before its division into colonies, the establishment of a colony was the signal for numbers of Europeans to emigrate to the new lands to run the farms, schools, mines, and businesses and, in the case of missionaries, to save the souls of the indigenous people. The confrontation between European culture and values and those of the tribal societies brought about enormous and sometimes devastating changes in Africa.

This was the moment in the history of Africa, roughly at the end of the nineteenth century and the beginning of the twentieth, when native voices were first raised in protest over the arrival of the European intruders. In most ex-colonial countries in the world it is difficult to find accounts, in English, of first encounters with Europeans. This is not so with Africa, where publications of all kinds, written in or translated into English, abound. This is especially true in the English-speaking former colonies of Britain.

Two reasons may explain this proliferation. The first is that Britain was a strong supporter of both local education, as well as higher education, in England, for top students. This emphasis on education may account for the greater number of highly trained successful writers available to write and publish on the coming of the Europeans, as well as other subjects.

A second reason may be the unique activities of the Heinemann Educational Publishers in London. Through the creation of its African Writers Series, it played an extraordinary role in the identification of promising writers, encouragement for them to write, and then the publication of their books. Chinua Achebe, one of Africa's preeminent writers and the person to whom this anthology is dedicated, was the first general editor of the series. Over the second half of the twentieth century, Heinemann published over 330 titles of African writing. The impact on African intellectual life is not measurable, but it may be safe to assume that this form of assistance to a developing country is unique around the world and, without doubt, of tremendous value.

1

PRINCE MODUPE
I Was a Savage
Guinea

Editor's Notes: Prince Modupe has written an account of one of the more dramatic missionary confrontations in the literature by native writers. Its main theme is the strategy of some missionaries to lure natives to view the material products of Western technology as proof that their God was the more powerful. This was a strategy for conversion. The title of his book, from which this boyhood account is taken, I Was a Savage *(later published as* A Royal African*), is deliberately ironic, for Modupe describes his boyhood as happy, family-oriented, and in harmony with nature.*

Prince Modupe was born in 1901 in French Guinea, and he was educated in Freetown, Sierra Leone. In 1922, he immigrated to the United States where he studied anthropology. He then had a long career in Hollywood as an actor and technical consultant. His account of growing up in Africa was published in 1957.

Everyone was agog about the expected arrival of the white man with the powerful *juju*. If his magic was more powerful than ours, then we must have it. That was Grandfather's decree. Grandfather wanted our people to have the best of everything. I doubt now that he had the slightest notion of the sweeping changes the new *juju* would bring with it. He probably thought of it as similar to the *juju* with which we were familiar, only more potent.

We believed in the existence of a demon who was said to be white in colour. But of course this man we were expecting could not be an ogre or Grandfather would not receive him. There were a few other white or nearly white things in our lives—cotton, white chickens, white cola, grubs in rotten stumps, white ants.

These seemed natural and everyday enough, but a white human was beyond simple imagining.

As I listened to the wild speculation among the villagers, the image which formed in my mind was that of a white ant or termite queen. After she has been fertilized, she is sealed in a clay cyst in the termite mound and her abdomen becomes hugely distended, several inches long. If this cyst is dug out and cracked open, the amazing abdomen, egg-swollen, can be seen softly palpitating. I wondered whether white human skin was soft as a swollen termite belly and whether the coursing of blood and processes of digestion could be seen through a milkily transparent outer covering, unpleasantly soft to the touch.

My father could have dispelled my grotesque notions and those of the other villagers if he had wished because he had been at the coast and had seen white men, both French and English. I did not voice my private imaginings, and as to the others, perhaps it gave him some secret satisfaction to listen without comment to the naive ideas of the untravelled.

In Dubréka, a foreigner was a black man from another tribe, even an adjoining tribe. Within a tribe, the sense of brotherhood was strong beyond the ability of the non-tribal part of the world to understand, but our sense of brotherhood ended abruptly at tribal bounds. We extended courtesies to neighbouring tribes but not the feeling of brotherliness. Paul Boolama had told us that the new white *juju* made of all men, everywhere, brothers. The very compactness within a tribe was what made this new notion so appallingly radical. It seemed highly impractical. How could the close-clutched be large? Who then would be left for us to hold ourselves at the ready against? Perhaps we had misunderstood Paul Boolama? Surely, sameness was necessary to oneness!

These heated discussions went on at age-levels above me. I was more interested in the appearance of the white man and the things it was said he would bring to demonstrate his *juju*—sticks that roared and spat fire, killing anything at which they were pointed, something which looked like water but was solid rather than flowing and would give a man back his face, just like a quiet pool. There were to be images of canoes that crossed water for days without end, images of huts made of stone and as tall as all the houses of Dubréka stacked one on top of the other. Drummers kept us informed of the progress of the white man and his carriers. I was so excited that I could not sleep the night before he arrived.

The only person I saw in the village who was not excited and pleasantly expectant was my grandfather's brother, D'gba. Grand-uncle D'gba never wanted anything changed in the least. He was sure that anything different or new was automatically bad and to be condemned. He was in the difficult position of not being able to voice his protest. Had he been chief, the white man would not have been allowed so much as to pause in the town. But Grandfather had spoken and D'gba could not do a thing about it. To object to the chief's decree would have been treason. If found guilty of treason after a trial by the elders, he would have been banished or else the executioner's long curved blade would have severed his head, just as it had severed Santigi's.

D'gba was fond of me and sometimes he would talk to me. At rare intervals he would even let me talk to him, quite a different matter in tribal Africa. Younger ones do not express unsolicited opinions to elders. Although D'gba seemed fond of me, I feared him greatly. When he asked me questions about Grandfather's household which I felt should not be answered, I was acutely uncomfortable and tried to be evasive without loss of politeness in my replies. When he questioned me about plans for receiving the white man, I could see rage working over his face as he formed the questions.

Finally, the white man arrived. My first sight of him was a delightful relief. He did not appear to have demon quality and although his belly was large, it was not out of proportion to his head like the termite queen's. The only part of him that was much out of scale was his feet, which were encased in leather. For some reason, I had believed from childhood that to be a real man one had to have a large belly and big feet. This fellow had both and he looked human besides. Furthermore, he was not really white as milk is white, not the portion of him which showed, at least; he was more the colour of leather. Most of him was covered; the black coat hung down past his knees, and the short sturdy neck was bound with a band of cloth which was really white. His lips appeared like nothing more than a faintly red slit in his face and his nose seemed bird-beakish long and thin. His wife and a little girl-child were with him, and they too were encased in clothing. The child had hair which hung to her shoulders and was the colour of gold. It was in curls like shavings from the chisels of our wood-carvers, not springy and crisp like mine. The three were led across the clearing to the royal stool where my grandfather sat waiting for them. The elders, the witchdoctors, and the head warriors moved forward with them as they advanced to stand before the chief. The rest of us, out of custom, remained in the background, not pressing too close. I longed to hear what was being said and I had a great desire to touch the golden curls of the little girl. I could see from the gestures and various groupings that the traditional courtesies were being exchanged. Grandfather sat on his stool with grave dignity. There was a waiting-to-see in his posture as the missionary placed gifts at his feet. Everyone gaped in wide-mouthed wonder. Some of the little boys scrambled up trees and perched on branches for a better view. Much as I would have liked to do the same, I was too mature for that kind of behaviour. All I could do was quietly and slowly to edge my way toward a more advantageous position.

Finally, stools were brought for the man and his family. If the stools had not been fetched, it would have meant lack of approval of the missionary's manners and lack of further interest on Grandfather's part. The interview would have been over. Although I did not know it, my future hung on that nod of my grandfather's head. If he had not approved the seating of our guests, I would not now be writing this story. I would not be writing anything, anywhere, nor reading either. All I knew of writing was that the small group of Moslems who lived in one quarter of our town had symbols for their beliefs marked on paper, but they did not read these; they had them sewed into leather packets which they wore as good-fortune amulets. All that interested me at this moment was getting closer to the heap of gifts at Grandfather's feet. When I had wormed my way into view of them, the objects seemed to be new things and there was glitter among them. They did not have the earth quality of our own artifacts. I later came to know these things as a Bible, a camera, a mirror, a kaleidoscope, shoes, a high hat, cigarettes, matches, tinned goods, shiny trinkets, and cotton goods. There was something else which may need a bit of explanation—a keg of whisky. We had palm wine to drink, a mild fermented brew of palm sap, but we had never heard of distilled liquor. In time I was to learn that the particular missionary who visited us belonged to a denomination which makes a distinction between temperance and abstinence. Their ministers are allowed to drink and to smoke, but not to excess. I suppose our visitor thought that mellowing our minds toward his words was a worthy use of whisky.

The photographs which the man brought showing bridges and cities, trains, boats, big buildings, were not impressive to us even when we were allowed to view them at close range. Having had no experience with the diminished scale of things in a photograph, we gained no concept of magnitude. But there were other pictures which disturbed me deeply. They were bright depictions of heaven and hell, which I later learned were made expressly for mission use. In them all the bright angels hovering over the golden streets had white faces. The tortured creatures in hell with the orange-red flames licking over agonized, contorted bodies all had black faces! Some of the fire-seared damned seemed little boys about the age I had been when Tango and I broke the Foula pot.

The missionary spoke to us through his interpreter. He denounced our old ceremonious life, the rituals, especially sacrifice. He said that we worshipped wood and stone and carved images. This was not accurate, but no one was impolite enough to contradict him. Anyway, it would have been too difficult to make a stranger understand. For a moment there was deep silence. Someone coughed. An old man shuffled his feet. An elder next to me rumbled in his throat. I turned my head and saw that it was Grand-uncle D'gba. I switched my attention back to the missionary; wondering why Grandfather allowed him to go on insulting everything we held sacred and valuable. I could see that Grandfather was trying his best to follow the spirited ranting of the white man. His expression was puzzled and he was trying his best to understand. Perhaps the *juju* would be clearer to us than the speech.

The crowd became restless. All this talk-talk! Their politeness held out, but they shifted their weight on their feet, squirmed a little, rustled quietly. Finally, the harangue ended.

The missionary picked up the mirror, made a few twists of his wrist as though gathering up the invisible power in the vicinity of it, and gazed into the glass. Grandfather leaned forward, watching closely. The white man proffered the shiny handle to Grandfather. My grandfather, who had always been considered a brave man by his people, jerked back away from it. Then, warily, he accepted it.

He did not gaze into it at once. It was plain that he feared the thing. The missionary spoke reassurance.

The crowd tensed. Grandfather had to go through with what he had started or forfeit pride. He looked into the mirror. A cry of surprise escaped from his throat. He turned the handle, looking at the back, and saw his reflection disappear. When he turned it to the front side, there he was again! He spoke to his brother D'gba. I do not know whether he did this because he knew his brother was opposed secretly to these goings-on and hoped to convince him by the new wonders, or whether the mirror simply seemed a wondrous thing to show one's brother.

D'gba reluctantly approached, his face contorted with scorn. An order from the chief was an order, brother or not. Every muscle in his body spoke of his aversion to the command but he dared not speak against it. Grandfather handed D'gba the mirror, pointed at the image. D'gba howled and fell to the ground, the mirror in his hand. He laid the fearful thing in the dust and smashed it with his fist. Perhaps he thought to liberate his trapped self from it, to get his face back. The thing broke, cutting his hand. Blood dripped from him as he stood up.

Blood has mystic significance to an African. Blood is lifestuff; life drips away with blood. A tribesman will endure enormous welts and bruises without a whimper if the skin is not broken, but let someone draw blood, even a bead of blood from a faint scratch, and the matter takes on enormous proportions and gravity.

While an excited murmur ran through the crowd and D'gba examined his red-dripping hand, the missionary spoke quickly and emphatically to Grandfather. Grandfather nodded and gave us the verdict. What had happened was due to D'gba's resentment of the white man's god. D'gba had been punished, as we had all seen. The white man's god was capable of punishments far beyond this. What was the loss of a little blood compared to having to spend all of the time not yet come rolling in the hot flames of hell? A black devil with horns kept the fires tended. D'gba disappeared, holding his wounded hand at the wrist.

The missionary followed up his initial triumph with a tin opener. With great flourishes he opened a tin of beans and ate some of the contents to show they were not poisoned. He offered some to Grandfather, who tasted a small portion and then larger portions, approving the flavour of this wonderful *ewa*, beans not cooked, yet ready to eat, coming all together from a shining "pod" which was hard like iron. The other articles were shown, demonstrated, explained. Grandfather was enchanted with the kaleidoscope, reluctant to put it down.

The missionary preached while the portions of whisky were doled out, first to the chief and the elders, then to each villager in turn as they formed in line. Grandfather jerked his head at the first taste and coughed, but after the second attempt he was smacking his lips and requesting more.

A long time was required for the end section of the queue to come abreast of the keg. The young men had to defer to the elder ones in this as in all things, and many of the elders, after downing their allotments, would slip back into line with their age-group for second helpings. Probably the missionary was too busy working up to the mass conversion to notice this. In any case, as many as drank and drew away and returned found themselves mellowed and ready to give themselves up to the new faith.

I noticed that Grandfather's eyes became bloodshot. When he stood up to walk he no longer moved with slow dignified royal steps. Uncertainty swayed him from side to side, but he wavered toward the diminishing keg. His purpose was certain even if his feet were not. I did not know what drunkenness was so I attributed Grandfather's condition to his body's being possessed with the power of the new *juju*. I saw him waving the Bible in the air as he announced that we accepted the new religion for our own. It was true, then, I concluded, that the white *juju* was superior to our own. Its power had caught D'gba and drawn blood, its power had transformed Grandfather, its power produced the wonderful objects the missionary had brought, its power warmed the belly, so the men said who had swallowed the sacred elixir from the keg. The only one of the older men who could not testify to that was D'gba. He did not take part in the drinking, nor was he to be seen in the throng.

Grandfather invited the white man to stay to dinner and for the night. The invitation was accepted. The women and children retreated to start the cooking and evening tasks. Great fires were lighted in the compound and the warriors gathered around them. Good food was brought, steaming hot. I stayed as close to the missionary and his family as I dared. My eyes lingered on the little girl with the golden curls. I reasoned that she must be immensely wealthy to have gold stuff for hair. It was because of her father's *juju*, of course, that this wealth had come to her and to her family.

Grandfather and the missionary came by the tree where I was standing in shadow. The missionary cleared his throat, hawked, and spat. They passed on. The spittle lay in the dust almost at my feet. It had been part of the body of this powerful, wealthy, celestial being. Would not the essence of these attributes be in this part of him, now separated from his body? I kneeled reverently beside the damp spot in the dust and touched it with a stick. No sound nor smoke came from it as I half feared. This gave me confidence to touch the dampness with my finger. I picked it up, cupping it in my hands. I was sure that some of the white man's power now belonged to me. But how to keep it? The answer to that was to swallow it. It would then become part of my body just as the body-stuff of the leopard became part and one with the initiate into the Pende-Pende society. Glowing with anticipation of wonderful things to come after absorbing this small portion of power essence, I swallowed it. Perhaps if enough of this potion were obtainable, my hair would turn to gleaming gold-stuff like the little girl's. I stood up, waiting tremulously for some change to work within me. I had felt as a leopard when its blood flowed with mine. Now I waited to feel as a god. Nothing happened. Had my skin lightened a shade? I could not tell in the dark. I felt at my hair. No, nothing had changed except this one thing: for the first time in my life I felt doubt about the desirability of a brown skin and kinky hair. Why did gold grow above the faces of little white girls, who according to the pictures sprouted shining wings as soon as they went to live in the glorious compound of worthy Deads, a compound glowing with gold under their pale little feet? How could they smile with what seemed a mother-love delight as they peered down over the edge of the golden compound into a fiery pit, deep and wide enough to hold all the *doomboos* [chimpanzees] the Yolos had ever consumed? But the fiery pit did not hold *doomboos* waiting to be caged. It was filled with black people who might have been Sousous. Why did the horned demon who banked the fires of hell have a black face like us? Why did he twist his mouth with laughter while he seared the flesh of small boys who were as black as himself?

Perhaps the real reason why my limbs trembled and my hands shook was that a little of the pride and glory which I had felt in being a Sousou youth had gone out with the light of this eventful day!

2

MONGO BETI
BACK TO MY VILLAGE
Cameroon

Editor's Notes: A slightly different type of encounter is the theme of Mongo Beti's novel. Medza, the protagonist, writes his account of returning to his village in the Cameroons, West Africa, from Paris, as a failed scholar from the Sorbonne (University of Paris). To his surprise, instead of disgrace, he is met with fame and is questioned day and night about what he had learned. The near total incomprehension of his listeners and his own inability to enjoy the freedoms of his boyhood friends, illustrate the dislocation brought about by Western education in a tribal society.

Mongo Beti, born in 1930, became a well-known Francophone novelist and political essayist who examined closely the on-going transition from a traditional to a modern Africa. He died in 2001.

Everyone in the village was paying court to me, especially my uncle, who went to great and obvious trouble to do me little services. He showed me a good deal more respect than an elderly man should show a youth—certainly more than was sanctioned by custom. Yet, unlike the usual unkind comments which such behavior normally provokes, in this case nothing at all was said by those who came to the house. Everyone seemed to think it was a favor simply to talk with me. As soon as I realized this I got into an agony of embarrassment.

I had become a pet or mascot for the whole of Kala: not only a strange animal, but an animal that they liked to examine at close quarters, to hear roar, or howl, or bray, or whatever. The women used to turn up in droves, too, and look me over with that greedy up-and-down stripping expression common to

From *Mission to Kala* by Mongo Beti (London: Heinemann, 1958): pp. 47–48, 58–59, 60–65.

women the world over. Never in my life have I been examined so minutely or with so little shame.

In the afternoon one woman, hardly bothering to conceal her feelings, put her cards—more or less—on the table.

"Young man," she said, "you shouldn't take offense at people being so interested in you. We don't see a college-educated boy like you here every day of the week—*and* a city dweller into the bargain!" Heavens, I had forgotten that. Educated *and* a city dweller. She's right, damn it, I thought, after a moment's stunned silence. As an educated city boy, my uppermost thought was that I had made a stupid nonsense of my exams. But never mind; a diploma, even by default, was a rare enough commodity in the Kala market. So that was it: educated *and* a city dweller. Why hadn't I thought of it earlier?

Now the woman began to ask me questions. She was about the same age as my mother, but prematurely aged by the heavy manual labor that all these up-country people undertake.

"What do they teach you at school?" she demanded.

"Who?"

"The Whites, of course, boy! What do they teach you?" The room was crowded, so I couldn't laugh, which was what I wanted to do.

"What do they teach me? Oh, heaps of things," I said unconvincingly.

The whole thing embarrassed me horribly. I wanted to be kind to this woman; she meant well enough, but how on earth was I to give her the most elementary notion of such things as geography, advanced mathematics, or the social sciences? Nevertheless, I had a shot at it; with gestures and stumbling, awkward, vague phrases I did my best. . . .

If only they wouldn't treat me just as a "scholar" and nothing else! I'd have given all the diplomas in the world to swim like Duckfoot Johnny, or to dance like the Boneless Wonder, or to have the sexual experience of Petrus Son-of-God, or to throw an assegai (spear) like Zambo. I wanted desperately to eat, drink, and be happy without having to bother my head about next term, or such depressing things as revision-work and orals. The very least I could do was to conquer my fear of women—even divorcées. I would soon learn how to respond to their advances. I would make up to this girl who was gone on me. I was forgetting, however, that afterward there would be no reason for her to go on pining for me. . . .

"Are there many White children at your school?" my hostess inquired.

I said, yes, there were a lot.

"More White than Colored?"

"No, not nearly so many."

"What are they *like*, these White children? Tell us what they're like," she persisted.

"Heavens—just like children anywhere, the world over—"

"*Really*? Just like ordinary children?"

"Exactly," I said. "They have rows, and fights; and are insubordinate—there's no difference at all."

A man's voice broke in. "And in class," he said loudly. "Are they cleverer than you in class?"

"No. They aren't either more clever or more stupid than we are. They're just the same as—as—a mixed bunch."

"Will the learned gentleman please explain, then," the same voice went on, in astonished tones, "how it is that their minds work faster than ours?"

"They don't. They grasp a point no faster and no slower than we do. "

"Well, well. That's really surprising. They *ought* to be quicker on the uptake, though, shouldn't they?"

"Why should they?" another man's voice broke in. "Why are you so determined that they should be quicker than our children? We don't breed young animals, do we? What are you thinking of?"

"How can you ask such a question?" the first man replied. "It's perfectly reasonable to suppose that White children should learn faster than Black. What are they being taught? *Their* ancestral wisdom, not ours, isn't that so? Who invented airplanes and trains and cars and steamships? The Whites. Very well then. Now if it was *our* ancestral wisdom that was taught in this school, it would be normal to expect Colored children to learn faster than Whites, wouldn't it. . . . ?"

"Listen to me, all of you. Here's my personal opinion, for what it's worth. It's by no means certain that it *was* the Whites who invented cars and airplanes and all that. When you talk about Colored folk, you mean us, don't you? All right, we're nobodies. But what about all the other Colored people, all over the world? How can you be sure that they don't make planes and trains and cars?"

To judge by the approving murmur which greeted it, this argument was a popular one. Finally the first man admitted that its proposer was probably right, yes, he might very well be right. . . .

Then they all got down to it and interrogated me non-stop. As there was a great number of them, they were often all asking me questions at once. This embarrassed me horribly, because I didn't know which ones to answer first. They varied in subject but were all of equal interest. I was utterly disconcerted, and one thing embarrassed me in particular: the attitude of the women and young girls. They absolutely devoured me with their eyes, and the expressions they wore were so unequivocal that I could not help recognizing them for what they were at once, despite my natural modesty. It was like reading a young peasant girl's passionate love letter.

Sometimes I glanced at Zambo, who squatted in a corner miserably, indifferent to the atmosphere of enthusiasm permeating the room, perhaps even hating it, but in any case the disregarded odd man out. Occasionally I caught my uncle's eye, too; he looked strangely complacent, rather like an old French peasant who has just married off his daughter to the richest, best-looking young man in the district. He was gay and pleased, and obviously willing me to make a success of the occasion.

But I was thinking that I shouldn't see Eliza (that, I had found out, was her name); not tonight, anyway, I told myself. Looking back, I suspect Eliza had become my symbol of absolute liberty, the freedom enjoyed by country boys like Duckfoot Johnny, the Boneless Wonder, Son-of-God, and the rest. I saw this freedom as the most precious possession I could acquire, and realized at the same time that in all likelihood I should never have it. Without being aware of it, I was no more than a sacrifice on the altar of Progress and Civilization. My youth was slipping away, and I was paying a terrible price for—well, for *what*? Having gone to school, at the decree of my all-powerful father? Having been chained to my books when most children of my age were out playing games? I did not exactly feel "in love" with Eliza, but I certainly desired her. My desire was the kind most characteristic of the inexperienced male; I hardly dared admit it even to myself.

And now missing this meeting with her showed me in a vague yet compulsive fashion that if I went on as I was doing, against my natural bent, I should never be truly myself, or have any real individuality. I should never be anything but a point of view, a myth, a zero-like abstraction with which my fellow human beings could play at will, indifferent to my own desires or pleasures.

Soon Zambo got up and left, abandoning me to my unhappy dilemma, rather as though I were a drowning man being sucked under by the current and beyond any hope of rescue. I was the most unlucky man in the world, I thought.

Apart from anything else, I was stifling. The room was far too hot and very small; the air was thick with smoke, and smelt of palm wine, tobacco, and chewing-gum. I made a tremendous effort, which pushed me sluggishly, like a sack of coconuts, onto the platform of benevolent resignation and cordiality reserved for scapegoats such as myself. I no longer felt any desire to discourage the attentions of my audience; I abandoned my useless and egotistic attempts at revolt. I began to chew the local gum myself, and certainly nothing I could have done would have pleased them more.

"Look at him!" they exclaimed, audibly. "Look, he's not snobbish, for all his learning. He's chewing gum *just like us*."

At such moments, conscious of all those staring eyes converging on me like so many rays, I got the feeling that the atmospheric gravity had at least doubled its pressure. There was a hurricane lamp burning on the table, its glass bulging and rounded like an old man's belly. The light it gave out was in fact not very strong, but to me it seemed as blinding as a searchlight set up at the same distance at pointblank range. As a result, they all saw me very clearly, and I could hardly make them out at all.

I sat there wondering to what extremes of idiocy the whole business could go. Lucky for me, I thought, that my friends couldn't see me pontificating in this half-witted fashion—and anyway, what did it matter? I realized that my affection for these people outweighed any resentment I felt at my own ridiculous position. It was certainly a serious occasion as far as they were concerned.

"And what *do* the whites teach you?" my hostess was still inquiring mercilessly.

"Oh—heaps of things—"

"Come on, then: tell us them."

"Would you understand if I did?" I snapped.

The remark was greeted with a murmur of disappointment. God, what a clanger, I thought. If I'm going to stay—and I must—I've got to behave myself.

"Listen to me, my boy," said an old man, getting to his feet and interspersing his remarks with placatory gestures, as though he were soothing a baby. "Listen: it doesn't matter if we don't understand. Tell us all the same. For you the Whites are the real people, the people who matter, because you know their language. But we can't speak French and we never went to school. For us *you* are the white man—you are the only person who can explain these mysteries to us. If you care for us at all, my son, do this thing for us. If you refuse, we've probably lost our only chance of ever being able to learn the white man's wisdom. Tell us, my son."

He has a point there, I thought. These people were all so damnably persuasive.

"All right, then," I said. "They teach us—let's see—well, geography."

"Geography?" exclaimed someone, fumbling over the unfamiliar syllables. "What's that?"

I gave them what must have been the most feeble, certainly the most arguable definition of geography ever presented to any audience. I had never tried to formulate such a definition in my native tongue before, and now the thing had to be done for an audience who hung on my every word. Then, to make my ideas more intelligible, I decided to illustrate them with an example I found myself (somewhat to my surprise) telling these simple people about New York—an inconceivable city to them, with its more than seven million inhabitants and skyscrapers of anything up to seventy-five floors, soaring up for a thousand feet. It was child's play to describe New York, probably because my only knowledge of it derived from the cinema. There was no longer any question of my drying up. I warmed to the theme, losing myself in an intoxicating sea of details. I imagined that my audience would be galvanized by the picture I conjured up; but in fact I went to all this trouble for nothing. (Still anxious to avoid giving them complexes, I omitted to tell them that Americans were in the habit of lynching Negroes in the street, simply because of the color of their skin.) No; the really astonishing thing, which still bothers me in retrospect, was that America left these simple-minded people stone-cold indifferent.

3

CAMERON DUODU
BEATINGS AT THE MISSION SCHOOL
Ghana

Editor's Notes: The encounter depicted here is an indirect one; that of native school children in class with a surrogate of the missionary, a native village school teacher. Some missionaries, in order to spread the gospel as quickly as possible, recruited and trained native catechists who were rushed into elementary schools with little or no training in teaching. In this passage from his novel, Cameron Duodu vividly depicts how the schoolchildren were treated by an untrained, sadistic teacher, an employee of the missionaries.

Duodu was born and educated in Ghana and began his career as a journalist and author in the capital city of Accra. He is now a freelance journalist and broadcaster in London.

I found my mind again and again choosing to take me right back to the same time eight years ago when I first made my acquaintance with that classroom, when I was in Class Three. . . .

[My] mind moved to our Class Three teacher, Mr. Mante Yaw. He was one of the most wicked people I ever came across when I was a child. Every morning, the first two or three periods in the classroom were devoted to multiplication tables, hymns, or passages from the Presbyterian Church Catechism. The previous day Mr. Mante Yaw would have told us that we should learn "Seven Times" or "Eight Times" as the case might be, or a particular passage from the Catechism or Hymn Book. I was the class prefect and he would ask me to go and cut a stick and bring it to him. There was always a large stock of raffia canes in the school store, ostensibly cut from the bush to be used in weaving

From *The Gab Boys* by Cameron Duodu (London: Deutsch, 1967), pp. 56–62. Reprinted by permission of the author.

baskets but in reality used mainly in whipping us. (Each time I went to the store to cut a cane for our teacher, I met other class prefects busily engaged on the same mission.)

Whenever I brought him a stick, Mr. Mante Yaw would get hold of me and give me two or three lashes. His explanation was that he wanted to test the stick and see whether it was strong. I didn't like being whipped at all and so took great pains to memorise all the tables and recitations he gave us. And yet I got whipped all the same. I wept bitterly whenever he whipped me like that, for I had no answer for the wickedness of the thing. If I didn't go when he asked me to cut a stick for him, he would whip me. And yet when I brought it to him, he whipped me with it. Why? Did I ask him to send me?

We were a miserable lot in that classroom. You would hear us shouting in unison, morning after morning: "Seven times one, seven; seven times two, fourteen; seven times three, twenty-one . . . " until we reached seven times twelve. Then we would go on to eight. When we reached twelve times twelve, we would start again at two times. Our most precious book was the small book of tables we called "Times." When we finished the multiplication, tables, we would go on to the "Pence" table. "Thirteen pence, one shilling, one penny; fourteen pence, one shilling, two pence; fifteen pence . . . " until we reached "one hundred and eight pence, nine shillings"; all this was "practice." After that would begin the "singles" in which we had to recite the tables and passages individually. The teacher would stand by with his stick ready as each child recited the tables, and the moment hear she faltered, the cane would descend, "Pah-Pah-Pah!" on the back. While he or she would be wailing aloud, calling on both parents to come and see what murder was being done, Mr. Mante Yaw would be bellowing out: "FOOLS. YOU SAY YOU WON'T LEARN. YOU'LL SEE! NEXT!" And another frightened child would try to rid his or her small mind of the confusion that filled it and sort out the shillings and pence. So much terror was attached to this job that even if one had been able to memorise the tables, one was likely to forget them when the crucial time came for reciting them.

How much we hated that man was demonstrated by the interpretation we placed upon an incident concerning him that might have been of a completely innocent nature. One day, a School Inspector came to our school. At that time, Education Officers were clever people who stole into schools without allowing themselves to be seen and this chap just walked into our classroom when our teacher was at his best, raining lashes on us. Practically every child was moaning, yet the "Pah-Pah!" continued. So when the Inspector walked in, we didn't even say the customary "Good-mooorr-ning sir" but just continued crying. The teacher also continued whipping us and shouting threats from his frothy mouth.

The Inspector looked at the scene for some time and went away. Absorbed completely in our thoughts of hatred, none of us bothered to tell the teacher that somebody had entered the room and gone back. Shortly after the Inspector had gone away, we saw our head-teacher come running—a man with a big head whom we called Koo-tipoh which, freely translated, meant something like "the man whose head looks as if were tied into a knot" . . .

He came running towards our classroom. Now, when he walked, his head seemed to roll from side to side, for his legs were not straight but crooked, and they wobbled slightly, making his head move in the same way. That was when he walked. Imagine then what he would have looked like as his hose-encased legs ran. It was a beautiful sight and those of us who sat near the windows forgot our pains and called our friends to come and look.

The head-teacher was really agitated, for ignoring his dignity, he did not reach the classroom at all before shouting out: "Mr. Mante Yaw! Mr. Mante Yaw! (pant . . . pant . . .) What do you think you are doing? (pant . . . pant . . .) Don't you know that there is an Inspector in the school? (sniff . . . sniff . . . pant)."

Our teacher jumped like a cat, his eyes wide open. "Come to the office, AT ONCE!" the head-teacher bellowed and began to retrace his steps, not running now but going at such a fast rate that he looked even more ridiculous than when he ran.

The word "Inspector" had brought absolute silence to the classroom. We looked at our teacher, whose face was as aghast as if he had been told that the earth had opened up and swallowed his wife. He didn't say a word to us but went out quietly towards the office.

He didn't come back for over one and a half hours. Then his eyes were very red and almost swollen. He "closed" us as soon as the bell rang and we went home. On the way one bright lad suggested that the Inspector had caned Mr. Mante Yaw. "Otherwise, why would his eyes look so red?" the boy asked. "The Inspector wanted to show him what a cane feels like on the skin so that he wouldn't beat us so much."

Nobody wanted to argue with the boy. And to this day all the members of that class believe that the teacher was really given a taste of the lash by the Inspector.

It was after that happy episode that one of our mates, Kwabena 'Nkyi, summoned courage to walk out of the class whenever the beating became unbearable. He was bigger than most of us, having failed about twice in Class Two before he was able to reach Class Three. He had a temper like that of a blood-hound; whenever Mr. Mante Yaw beat him, he would howl at the top of his voice and try to hold the stick so that the lashes wouldn't reach him. In the past that was the farthest he went, for like the rest of us he thought Mr. Mante Yaw was all-powerful.

But when the Inspector came and "caned" Mante Yaw, Kwabena 'Nkyi got an idea. He would run home and bring his grandmother and his step-mother.

The grandmother was soft-spoken and gentle, whereas the step-mother was loud-mouthed and was endowed with more of the fighting spirit than was good for one of her sex.

"Teacher," she would begin; "were you brought here from your town in Akuapem to beat our children or to teach them?" She wouldn't wait for a reply for she wasn't asking a question at all, but in true Akyem Abuakwa invective was making a statement. "Have you ever had a child? Do you know how it is to sit at home and labour in the agony of childbirth? There is no money in your town and you have come here to seek some. And yet when we pay school fees to pay you to *teach* our children, it is kill that you want to kill them. Why do you hate Kwabena 'Nkyi like that? What has he done to you? Has he gone to make love to your wife? Every day, you beat him. Why? Why? Why? Why? When you went to school, what was your position in your class? . . . "

At this stage the grandmother would put a restraining hand on her and say, "Akosua stop; it's all right. Heh, Kwabena go and sit down."

"Oh, Mother, I won't stop anything," the step-mother would say, brushing off the grandmother's hand. "This teacher thinks the people of this town are fools."

All this time Kwabena 'Nkyi would be standing behind her, whimpering. The grandmother would try again: "Kwabena, stop crying and go and sit down. Here, get a penny and stop crying."

"All right, we shall leave him now," the step-mother would look appeased, "but you, Mante Yaw, beat him again and you will see. I will get his school fees from you—mind you, he has paid for the whole year."

They would then go, and Kwabena 'Nyki would go and sit down.

Mr. Mante Yaw would then make a congregation of us and preach us a sermon whose main theme was his own righteousness. "I want to make it clear to you that I don't hate any of you. Even Yirenkyi, I don't hate him. It's for his own future good that I whip him. I want you all to learn hard so that you can become people of importance in the future. Would you prefer that I don't whip you and leave your heads to die or would you like me to beat you so that you will become clever?"

We would have preferred that our backs and buttocks should be freed of the stabbing pain of the cane, but not all of us had step-mothers with sharp tongues and we would say in unison: "Teacher, whip us!"

He would ask again: "Shall I whip you or leave your heads to die?"

And again, we would say: "Teacher, whip us!"

"All right," Mr. Mante Yaw would say. "All those who want to learn hard, hands up!" And up would shoot every hand except that of Kwabena 'Nkyi, who knew too well that the whole show was for his benefit.

"All right," Mr. Mante Yaw would say again, "you who want to learn, I'll do my best for you. But as for those who will go and call their mothers and aunts to abuse their own teacher, you will see what will happen to them. When the rest of you have become important people who have large cars and a lot of money, those people will be working as PWD labourers on the roads."

We would all laugh at this, for we thought, from what we saw of PWD labourers, that only very poor people did that kind of work-standing in the sun for so long and repairing roads with shovels and pick-axes, or weeding the grass that grew underneath telephone poles.

4

CHIEF MOJIMBA
AND H. M. STANLEY

Confrontations

Congo

Editor's Notes: First encounters have often turned deadly as a result of extreme differences of perception of the situation at hand. Chief Mojimba, a local tribal chief in what is now the Congo, with his tribesmen in canoes, saw white brothers approaching. Henry Morton Stanley, the famous British journalist and explorer, and his soldiers saw vicious warriors. The results of the ensuing battle illustrate the well-known saying that the victors write history. Stanley's victory is well-recorded in the history books. Mojimba's loser's account appears as an obscure footnote.

CHIEF MOJIMBA'S ACCOUNT

When we heard that the man with the white flesh was journeying down the Lualaba (Lualaba-Congo) we were open-mouthed with astonishment. We stood still. All night long the drums announced the strange news—a man with white flesh! That man, we said to ourselves, has a white skin. He must have got that from the river-kingdom. He will be one of our brothers who were drowned in the river. All life comes from the water, and in the water he has found life. Now he is coming back to us, he is coming home . . .

We will prepare a feast, I ordered, we will go to meet our brother and escort him into the village with rejoicing! We donned our ceremonial garb. We assembled the great canoes. We listened for the gong which would announce our brother's presence on the Lualaba. Presently the cry was heard: He is

---

Chief Mojimba's account as told to Father Joseph Frässle. Reprinted from *The Quest for Africa: Two Thousand Years of Exploration*, by Heinrich Schiffers, tr. by Diana Pyke (New York: G. P. Putnam, 1957), pp. 196–197, and *Through the Dark Continent*, by H. M. Stanley, Vol. II (New York: Harper & Brothers, 1878), pp. 268–273.

An 1878 engraving depicting the battle that erupted on the Congo River between the warriors led by Chief Mojimba and Henry Morton Stanley's British forces. (*Source*: H. M. Stanley, *Through the Dark Continent*. [London: Sampson Low, Marston, Searle & Rivington, 1878].)

approaching the Lohali! Now he enters the river! Halloh! We swept forward, my canoe leading, the others following, with songs of joy and with dancing, to meet the first white man our eyes had beheld, and to do him honor.

But as we drew near his canoes there were loud reports, bang! bang! and fire-staves spat bits of iron at us. We were paralyzed with fright; our mouths hung wide open and we could not shut them. Things such as we had never seen, never heard of, never dreamed of—they were the work of evil spirits! Several of my men plunged into the water . . . What for? Did they fly to safety? No—for others fell down also, in the canoes. Some screamed dreadfully, others were silent—they were dead, and blood flowed from little holes in their bodies. "War! that is war!" I yelled. "Go back!" The canoes sped back to our village with all the strength our spirits could impart to our arms.

That was no brother! That was the worst enemy our country had ever seen.

And still those bangs went on; the long staves spat fire, flying pieces of iron whistled around us, fell into the water with a hissing sound, and our brothers continued to fall. We fled into our village—they came after us. We fled into the forest and flung ourselves on the ground. When we returned that evening our eyes beheld fearful things: our brothers, dead, bleeding, our village plundered and burned, and the water full of dead bodies.

The robbers and murderers had disappeared.

H. M. STANLEY'S ACCOUNT

About 8 A.M. we came in view of a marketplace, near which there were scores of small canoes. The men at once rushed into them and advanced all round us. We refrained a long time, but finally, as they became emboldened by our stillness and began to launch their wooden spears, which they proceeded to do all together as soon as somebody cried out "Mutti" (sticks), we were obliged to reply to them with a few shots, which compelled them to scamper away ahead of us. Drums then awakened the whole country, and horns blew deafening blasts. Some canoes boldly followed us.

We came, about 10 A.M., to another market green. Here, too, warriors were ready, and again we had recourse to our weapons. The little canoes with loud threats disappeared quickly down river: the land warriors rushed away into the woods. We did not wish to hurry, because the faster we proceeded the quicker we found we were involved in trouble. We therefore loitered indifferently: rest was so rare that it became precious when we obtained it.

At noon . . . we resumed our journey, rowing at a steady though not a fast pace. We had descended the river for about an hour when we came again in sight of those waspish little canoes, and from the left bank, 3,000 yards off, canoes were seen heading across the river at a terrific pace, while horns blew and drums bear. We heard shouts of defiance, or threats, we knew not which, we had become indifferent to the incessant noise and continued fury.

In these wild regions our mere presence excited the most furious passions of hate and murder, just as in shallow waters a deep vessel stirs up muddy sediments. It appeared to be a necessity, then why should we regret it? Could a man contend with the inevitable?

At 2 P.M. heralded by savage shouts from the wasp swarm, which from some cause or other are unusually exultant, we emerged out of the shelter of the deeply wooded banks and came into a vast stream, nearly 2,000 yards across at the mouth. As soon as we entered its waters, we saw a great fleet of canoes hovering about in the middle of the stream. The canoe-men, standing up, gave a loud shout when they saw us and blew their horns louder than ever. We pulled briskly on to gain the right bank when, looking upstream, we saw a sight that sent the blood tingling through every nerve and fiber of our bodies: a flotilla of gigantic canoes bearing down upon us, which both in size and numbers utterly eclipse anything encountered hitherto!

Instead of aiming for the right bank, we formed a line and kept straight downriver, the boat taking position behind. Yet after a moment's reflection, as I noted the numbers of the savages, the daring manner of the pursuit, and the apparent desire of our canoes to abandon the steady compact line, I gave the order to drop anchor. Four of our canoes made believe not to listen, until I chased them to return to the line, which was formed of eleven double canoes, anchored ten yards apart. The boat moved up to the front and took position 50 yards above them. The shields were next lifted by the noncombatants, men, women and children in the bows, and along the outer lines, as well as astern, and from behind these the muskets and rifles were aimed.

We had sufficient time to take a view of the mighty force bearing down on us and to count the number of the war vessels. There were 54 of them! A monster canoe led the way, with two rows of upstanding paddles, 40 men on a side, their bodies bending and swaying in unison as with a swelling barbarous chorus they drove her down toward us.

In the bow, standing on what appeared to be a platform, were ten prime young warriors, their heads gay with red feathers: at the stern, eight men with long paddles, whose tops were decorated with ivory balls, guided the monster vessel; and dancing up and down from stem to stern were ten men, who appeared to be chiefs. All the paddles are headed with ivory balls, every head bears a feather crown, every arm shows gleaming white ivory armlets. From the bow of the canoe streams a thick fringe of the long white fibre of the Hyphen palm.

The crashing sound of large drums, a hundred blasts from ivory horns, and a thrilling chant from 2,000 human throats did not tend to soothe our nerves or to increase our confidence. However, it was "neck or nothing." We had no time to pray or to take sentimental looks at the savage world, or even to breathe a sad farewell to it. So many other things had to be done speedily and well.

As the foremost canoe came rushing down, its consorts on either side beating the water into foam and raising their jets of water with their sharp prows, I turned to take a last look at our people and said to them:

Boys, be firm as iron; wait until you see the first spear, and then take good aim. Don't fire all at once. Keep aiming until you are sure of your man. Don't think of running away, for only your guns can save you.

The monster canoe aimed straight for my boat, as though it would run us down; but when within fifty yards off, it swerved aside and, when nearly opposite, the warriors above the manned prow let fly their spears and on either side there was a noise of rushing bodies. But every sound was soon lost in the ripping, crackling musketry. For five minutes we were so absorbed in firing that we took no note of anything else; but at the end of that time we were made aware that the enemy was reforming about 200 yards above us.

Our blood was up now. It was a murderous world, and we felt for the first time that we hated the filthy, vulturous ghouls who inhabited it. We therefore lifted our anchors and pursued them upstream along the right bank until, rounding a point, we saw their villages. We made straight for the banks and continued the fight in the village streets with those who had landed, hunting them out into the woods, and there only sounded the retreat, having returned the daring cannibals the compliment of a visit.

A PORTRAIT OF CHIEF MOJIMBA

This cannibal king, covered with tattoo-marks, gave me the shudders with his glistening face, his bleary drunkard's eyes and bloated, mutilated nose! The lobes of his ears were weighted down with eight small ivory pegs. Little flat pieces of ivory were inserted in the protruding lips, making his speech very indistinct. I had to fill his pipe for him. He rammed a further lot in, muttering: "More, more! Not nearly enough!" I had time to admire his wonderful necklace of choicest leopards' teeth. On his head he wore a cap of leopard-skin, adorned with the creature's grinning bloodthirsty looking muzzle as well as with red parrots' feathers. Add to these a reddish-brown loincloth with white stripes and a similar scarf suspended from the shoulders, made from the skin of the okapi, whose habitat is confined entirely to the Lohali.

Father Joseph Frässle as quoted in Heinrich Schiffers, *The Quest for Africa*, New York: G. P. Putnam's Sons, 1957, p. 196.

5

CONGO REFUGEES

RUBBER FOREST ATROCITIES, PART I
Congo

Editor's Notes: During the last half of the nineteenth century, Leopold II, the king of Belgium, owned the Congo Free State as a personal possession. His administration there had one goal—to exploit its natural resources, especially rubber. Regard for the welfare of the Congolese people was totally ignored. In 1903, Roger Casement, the British Consul for the Congo Free State, conducted an investigation into widespread rumors of mistreatment there. After a stay of nearly three months, he returned to write one of the most damning and accusatory reports in all of colonial history. The publication of this report shocked the world and helped to bring about an end to Leopold's personal rule in the Congo.

In his report are direct quotations from the local people he interviewed; these are the native voices. These excerpts reveal the brutal effects of colonization—forced resettlement, taxation, forced labor, torture, and the destruction of villages.

Hearing of the Basengele refugees from Lake Leopold II, I decided to visit the nearest Settlement of these fugitives, some 20 miles away to see them for myself. . . .

At Mpoko found large town of Batende, and scattered through it many small settlements of Basengele refugees. The town of Mpoko consists approximately of seventy one Batende houses and seventy-three occupied by Basengele. These latter seemed industrious, simple folk, many weaving the Mpusu palm fibre into mats or native cloth; others had smithies, working brass wire into bracelets, chains, and anklets; some iron workers making knives. Sitting down

Séamas Ó. Síocháin and Michael O'Sullivan, eds., *The Eyes of Another Race: Roger Casement's Congo Report and 1903 Diary* (Dublin: University College Dublin Press, 2003), pp. 118–124.

in one of these blacksmith's sheds, the five men at work ceased and came over to talk to us. 1 counted ten women, six grown-up men, and eight lads and women in this one shed of Basengeles. I then asked them through Scrivener and Lusala—the native interpreter—to tell me why they had left their homes. Three of the men sat down in front of me, and told a tale which I cannot think can be true, but it seemed to come straight from their hearts. It was translated to me almost word for word by Scrivener and Lusala, and I repeatedly asked certain parts to be gone over again while I wrote in my note book. The fact of my writing down and asking for names, &c., seemed to impress them, and they spoke with what certainly impressed me as being great sincerity.

I asked, first, why they had left their homes around Lake Leopold II, and to come to live in a strange far-off country among the Batende, where they owned nothing, and were little better than servitors? All, when this question was put, women as well, shouted out, "On account of the rubber tax levied by the Government posts around the Lake and along the Mfini."

I asked particularly the names of the places whence they had come. They answered they were from Bangongo. Other Basengele refugees here at Mpoko were Bakutu, others again were Bateto, but all had fled from their homes for the same reason—it was the "rubber tax."

I asked then how this tax was imposed. The chief of them, who had been hammering out an iron neck collar on my arrival, spoke first. He said:

"I am Moyo. These other two beside me are Wankaki and Nkwabali, all of us Bandongo [*sic*]. From our country each village had to take twenty loads of rubber. These loads were big: they were as big as this" (Producing an empty basket which came nearly up to the handle of my walking-stick.) "That was the first size. We had to fill that up, but as rubber got scarcer the white man reduced the amount. We had to take these loads in four times a-month."

Q: "How much pay did you get for this?"
A: (Entire audience). "We got no pay! We got nothing!"

And then Moyo, whom I asked, again said: "Our village got cloth and a little salt, but not the people who did the work. Our Chiefs eat up the cloth, the workers get nothing. The pay was a fathom of cloth and a little salt for every big basket full, but it was given to the Chief, never to the men. It used to take ten days to get the twenty baskets of rubber—we were always in the forest and then when we were late we were killed. We had to go further and further into the forest to find the rubber vines, to go without food, and our women had to give up cultivating the fields and gardens. Then we starved. Wild beasts—the leopards—killed some of us when we were working away in the forest, and others got lost or died from exposure and starvation, and we begged the white man to leave us alone, saying we could get no more rubber, but the white men and their soldiers said: 'Go! You are only beasts yourselves, you are nyama (meat).' We tried, always going further into the forest, and when we failed and our rubber was short, the soldiers came to our towns and killed us. Many were shot, some had their ears cut off; others were tied up with ropes around their necks and bodies and taken away. The white men sometimes at the posts did not know of the bad things the soldiers did to us, but it was the white men who sent the soldiers to punish us for not bringing in enough rubber."

Here Nkwabali took up the tale from Moyo:

"We said to the white men, 'We are not enough people now to do what you want us. Our country has not many people in it and we are dying fast. We are killed by the work you make us do, by the stoppage of our plantations and the breaking up of our homes.'

The white man looked at us and said: 'There are lots of people in Mputu' (Europe, the white man's country). 'If there are lots of people in the white man's country there must be many people in the black man's country.' The white man who said this was the chief white man at Ibale, his name was Kwango, he was a very bad man. Other white men of Bula Matadi [Congo Free State] who had been bad and wicked were Mfuami Bonginda, Malu Maiu (Quick! Quick!), Mpampi. These had killed us often, and killed us by their own hands as well as by their soldiers. Some white men were good. These were Nkango, Bako Mobili, Nyambi, Nyeli, and Fuashi."

These ones told them to stay in their homes and did not hunt and chase them as the others had done, but after what they had suffered they did not trust more any one's word, and they had fled from their country and were now going to stay here, far from their homes, in this country where there was no rubber.

Q: "How long is it since you left your homes, since the big trouble you speak of?"

A: "It lasted for three full seasons, and it is now four seasons since we fled and came into the Batende country."

Q: "How many days is it from Mpoko to your own country?"

A: "Six days of quick marching. We fled because we could not endure the things done to us. Our Chiefs were hanged, and we were killed and starved and worked beyond endurance to get rubber."

Q: "How do you know it was the white men themselves who ordered these cruel things to be done to you? These things must have been done without the white man's knowledge by the black soldiers."

A. (Nkwabali): "The white men told their soldiers: 'You kill only women; you cannot kill men. You must prove that you kill men.' So then the soldiers when they killed us" (here he stopped and hesitated, and then pointing to the private parts of my bulldog—it was lying asleep at my feet), he said: "then they cut off those things and took them to the white men, who said: 'It is true, you have killed men.' "

Consul: "You mean to tell me that any white man ordered your bodies to be mutilated like that, and those parts of you carried to him?"

Nkwabali, Wankaki, and all (shouting): "Yes! many white men. Malu Malu did it."

Consul: "You say this is true? Were many of you so treated after being shot?"

All (shouting out): "Nkoto! Nkoto!" (Very many! Very many!).

There was no doubt that these people were not inventing. Their vehemence, their flashing eyes, their excitement, was not simulated. Doubtless they exaggerated the numbers, but they were clearly telling what they knew and loathed. Scrivener, beside me, said that these stories had been told to him before when he had first found these Basengele refugees ten months previously in the back country behind Bolobu. They often became so furious at the recollection of what had been done to them that they lost control over themselves, and he had ceased to question them. One of the men before me (Wankaki) was getting into this state now. I asked whether Basengele tribes were still running from their country, or whether they now stayed at home and worked voluntarily.

Moyo answered "They cannot run away now—not easily, there are sentries in the country there between the Lake and this; besides, there are few people left."

Nkwabali said: "We heard that letters came to the white men on the Lake to say that the people were to be well treated. We heard that these letters had been sent by the big white men in Mputu (Europe), but our white men tore up these letters, laughing, saying 'We are the 'basango' and 'banyanga' (fathers and mothers, i.e., elders). Those who write to us are only 'bana' (children).' Since we left our homes the white men now around the Lake have asked us to go home again. We have heard that they want us to go back, but we will not go. We are not warriors, and do not want to fight. We only want to live in peace with our wives and children, and so we stay here among the Batende, who are kind to us, and will not return to our homes."

Q: "Would you not like to go back to your homes? Would you not, in your hearts, all wish to return?"

A: (By many.) "We loved our country, but we will not trust ourselves to go back."

Nkwabali: "Go, you white men, with the steamer to Lake Leopold and see what we have told you is true. Perhaps if other white men, who do not hate us, go there, Bula Matadi may stop from hating us, and we may be able to go home again."

I asked to be pointed out any refugees from other tribes, if there were such, and they brought forward a lad who was a Bateto, and a man of the Baboma, on the Kasai, Mfini. These two, answering me, said there were many with them from their tribes who had fled from their country.

Went on about fifteen minutes to another Basengele group of houses in the midst of the Batende town. Found here mostly Bakuti, the old Chief sitting in the open village Council-house with a Baboma man and two lads. An old woman soon came and joined, and another man. The woman began talking with much earnestness. She said the Government had worked them so hard they had had no time to attend their fields and gardens, and they had starved to death. Her children had died; her sons had been killed. The two men, as she spoke, muttered murmurs of assent.

The old Chief said: "We used to hunt elephants long ago, there were plenty in our forests, and we got much meat; but Bula Matadi killed the elephant hunters because they could not get rubber, and so we starved. We were sent out to get rubber, and when we came back with little rubber we were shot."

Q: "Who shot you?"

A: "The white men, Malu Malu, Mpampi, Fuami, sent their soldiers out to kill us."

Q: "How do you know it was the white man who sent the soldiers? It might be only these savage soldiers themselves."

A: "No, no. Sometimes we brought rubber into the white man's stations. We took rubber to Malu Malu's station, Mbongo, and to Ibali and to Fuami's station. When it was not enough rubber the white man would put some of us in lines, one behind another, and would shoot through all our bodies. Sometimes he would shoot us like that with his own hand; sometimes his soldiers would do it."

Q: "You mean to say you were killed in the Government posts themselves by the Government white men themselves, or under their eyes?"

A: (Emphatically.) "We were killed in the stations of the white men themselves. We were killed by the white man himself. We were shot before his eyes."

[At another place] the chief speaker [was] a young man named Bakotembesi, who lives at Bwonzola. He seems about 22 or 23, and speaks with an air of frankness. He says: "The Basengele here and others who come to Lukolela, come from a place near Lake Leopold II, called Mbelo. It is connected with the lake by a stream. His own town in the district of Mbelo is Mpenge. Mbele is a big district and had many people. They now bring the Government india-rubber, kwanga (cassava bread), and fowls, and work on broad paths connecting each village. His own village has to take 300 baskets of india-rubber. They get one piece of cotton cloth, called locally a sanza, and no more" (Note. - This cannot be true. He is doubtless exaggerating.) Four other men with him were wearing the rough palm-fibre cloth of the country looms, and they pointed to this as proof that they got no cloth for their labours. Bakotambesi continuing said: "We were then killed for not bringing in enough rubber."

Q: "You say you were killed for not bringing in rubber. Were you ever mutilated as proof that the soldiers had killed you?"

A: "When we were killed the white man was there himself. No proof was needed. Men and women were put in a line with a palm tree and were shot."

Here he took three of the four men sitting down and put them one in line behind the other, and said: "The white men used to put us like that and shoot all with one cartridge. That was often done, and worse things."

Q: "But how, if you now have to work so hard, are you yourselves able to come here to Lukolela to see your friends?"

A: "We came away without the sentries or soldiers knowing, but when we get home we may have trouble."

Q: "Do you know the Basengele who are now at Mpoko, near Bolobo?" (Here I gave the names of Moyo, Wankaki, and Nkwabali.)

A: "Yes; many Basengele fled to that country. Moyo we know ran away on account of the things done to them by the Government white men. The Batende and Basengele have always been friends. That is why the Basengele fled to them for refuge."

Q: "Are there sentries or soldiers in your villages now?"

A: "In the chief villages there are always four soldiers with rifles. When natives go out into the forest to collect rubber they would leave one of their number behind to stay and protect the women. Sometimes the soldiers finding him thus refused to believe what he said, and killed him for shirking his work. This often happens."

Asked how far it was from Lukolela to their country they say three days' journey, and then about two days more on to Lake Leopold by water, or three if by land. They begged us to go to their country, they said: "We will show you the road, we will take you there, and you will see how things are, and that our country has been spoiled, and we are speaking the truth."

6

FIVE CONGOLESE GIRLS
RUBBER FOREST ATROCITIES, PART II
Congo

Editor's Notes: In August 1903, Roger Casement went to the American Baptist Mission School where he took statements from five girl students who, as small children, had survived the bloody massacres of the mid-1890s when the agents of King Leopold II of Belgium were viciously punishing the natives for not producing enough rubber. Their horrifying accounts, which he recorded very carefully, formed part of his report from the Congo.

(Pebe is their name for Rev. Mr. Clark who ran the school and helped Casement with his investigations.)

BIKELA'S STATEMENT

I was born at Ehanga. After my father died my mother and I went to Mokili. When we returned to Ehanga soon after that, Lokokwa of Bikoro (Swanson) came to fight with us because of rubber. Ehanga did not want to take rubber to the white man. We and our mothers ran away very far into the bush. The . . . soldiers are very strong and they fought hard. One soldier was killed and they killed one Ehanga man. Then the white man said let us go home and they went home, and then we, too, came out of the bush. This was the first fight. After that another fighting [*sic*] took place. I, my mother, grandmother, and my sister Nzaibiaka, we ran away into the bush. The soldiers came and fought us, and left the town and followed us into the bush. When the soldiers came into the

Séamas Ó. Síocháin and Michael O'Sullivan, eds., *The Eyes of Another Race: Roger Casement's Congo Report and 1903 Diary* (Dublin: University College Dublin Press, 2003), pp. 148–158.

bush near us they were calling my mother by name, and I was going to answer, but my mother put her hand to my mouth to stop me. Then they went to another side, and then we left that place and went to another. When they called my mother, if she had not stopped me from answering, we would all have been killed then. A great number of our people were killed by the soldiers. The friends who were left buried the dead bodies and there was very much weeping. After that there was not any fighting for some time. Then the soldiers came again to fight with us and we ran into the bush, but they really came to fight with Iyembe. They killed a lot of Iyembe people and then one soldier came out to Ehanga, and the Ehanga people killed him with a spear. And when the other soldiers heard that their friend was killed they came in a large number and followed us into the bush. Then the soldiers fired a gun and some people were killed. After that they saw a little bit of my mother's head, and the soldiers ran quickly towards the place where we were and caught my grandmother, my mother, Nzaibaika, and another little one, younger than us.

Several of the soldiers argued about my mother, because each wanted her for a wife, so they finally decided to kill her. They killed her with a gun—they shot her through the stomach—and she fell and when I saw that I cried very much, because they killed my mother and grandmother— and I was left alone. My mother was near to the time of her confinement at that time. And they killed my grandmother too, and I saw it all done. They took hold of Nzaibiaka and asked her where her older sister was and she said: "She has just run away." They said, "Call her." She called me, but I was too frightened and would not answer, and I ran and went away and came out at another place and I could not speak much because my throat was very sore. I saw a little bit [of] "kwanga" [cassava bread] lying on the ground and I picked it up to eat. At that place there used to be a lot of people, but when I got there there were none. Nzaibiaka was taken to Bikolo, and I was at this place alone. One day I saw a man coming from the back country. He was going to kill me but afterwards he took me to a place where there were people, and I saw my step-father, Nzaibiaka's father. He asked to buy me from this man, but the man would not let him. He said, "She is my slave now; I found her." One day the men went out fishing and when I looked I saw the soldiers coming, so I ran away, but a string caught my foot and I fell, and a soldier named Lombola caught me. He handed me over to another soldier and as we went away we saw some Ikoko people fishing, and soldiers took a lot of fish from them and an Ikoko woman and we went to Bikoro, and they took me to the white man.

The white man set me to work. The white man's woman called me to cook some bananas for her, and when I had finished she was eating, and the white man was there too, we saw some of Pebe's men coming, so he called four of us small folks, NzaibIaka, Bikela, and Mongo, and told us to go with Pebe's men to the Mission at Ikoko. I had a very bad headache when I was in the canoe. Evening school was going on when we arrived at the Mission. Mama Monkasa

(Mrs. Clark) and Pebe gave us some bananas and corn to eat. At first we did not know that the white people of God were so kind to people—we thought that they were bad like the white people we had seen in the State, but we found out it was not so, but they are quite different. The soldiers told us that when a missionary died we should be buried with him, but they only told us so to frighten us.

(Signed) BIKELA,

Signed by Bikcla before me, after the foregoing statements had been translated by Miss Lena Clark to her before me, at Ikoko, this 12th day of August, 1903.

(Signed) ROGER CASEMENT,

His Britannic Majesty's Consul

SEKOLO'S STATEMENT (EXCERPTS)

Ntange sent some Ikoko men to tell the Nkoho people to send people to go and work for him and also to send goats. The Nkoho people would not do it, so he went to fight our town. When we were told by the men that the soldiers were coming, we began to run away. My mother told me to wait for her until she got some things ready to take with us, but I told her we must go now, as the soldiers were coming.

I ran away and left my mother and went with two old people who were running away, but we were caught, and the old people were killed, and the soldiers made me carry the baskets with the things these dead people had and the hands they cut off. I went on with the soldiers. Then we came to another town, and they asked me the way and the name of the place, and I said: "I do not know;" but they said, "If you do not tell us we will kill you," so I told them the name of the town. Then we went into the bush to look for people, and we heard children crying, and a soldier went quickly over to the place and killed a mother and four children, and then we left off looking for the people in the bush, and they asked me again to show them the way out, and if I did not they would kill me, so I showed them the way. They took me to Ntange, and he told me to go and stay with the soldier who caught me. They tied up six people, but I cannot tell how many people were killed, because there were too many for me to count. They got my little sister and killed her and threw her into a house and set fire to the house. . . .

My father was killed in the same fight as I was captured, my mother was killed by a sentry stationed at Nkoho after I left.

ELIMA'S STATEMENT (EXCERPTS)

After she had reached the outside of the town she stood still, and remembered that she would be scolded by her father and mother for leaving her sister, so she went back at night. She came upon a house where the white man was sleeping; she saw the sentry on a deck chair outside in front of the house, apparently asleep, because he did not see her slip past him. Then she came to the house where her sister was, and took her and she started to run away again. They slept in a deserted house at the very end of the town. Early in the morning the white man sent out the soldiers to go and look for people all over the town and in the houses. Elima was standing outside in front of the house, trying to make her sister walk some, as she was very tired, but the little sister could not run away through weakness. While they were both standing outside the soldiers came upon them and took them both. One of the soldiers said: "We might keep them both, the little one is not bad-looking;" but the others said "No, we are not going to carry her all the way; we must kill the youngest girl." So they put a knife through the child's stomach, and left the body lying there where they had killed it. They took Elima to the next town, where the white man had told them to go and fight. They did not go back to the house where the white man was, but went straight on to the next town. The white man's name was Bonginda (Lieutenant Durieux). The soldiers gave Elima something to eat on the way. When they came to this next town they found that all the people had run away.

In the morning the soldiers wanted Elima to go and look for manioc for them, but she was afraid to go out as they looked to her as if they wanted to kill her. The soldiers thrashed her very much, and began to drag her outside, but the Corporal (Lambola) came and took her by the hand and said, "We must not kill her; we must take her to the white man." Then they went back to the town where Bonginda was, and they showed him Elima. Bonginda handed her over to the care of a soldier. At this town she found that they had caught three people, and among them was a very old woman, and the cannibal soldiers asked Bonginda to give them the old woman to eat, and Bonginda told them to take her. Those soldiers took the woman and cut her throat, and then divided her and ate her. Elima saw all this done. In the morning the soldier who was looking after her was sent on some duty by Bonginda, and before the soldier went out he had told Elima to get some manioc leaves not far from the house and to cook them. After he left she went to do as he had told her, and those cannibal soldiers went to Bonginda and said that Elima was trying to run away, so they wanted to kill her; but he told them to tie her, so the soldiers tied her to a tree, and she had to stand in the sun nearly all day. When the soldier who had charge of her came back he found her tied up. Bonginda called to him to ask about Elima, so he explained to Bonginda what he had told Elima to do, so he was allowed to untie her. They stayed several days at this place, then Bonginda asked Elima if she knew all the towns round about, and she said yes, then he told her to show them the way, so that they could go and catch people.

They came to a town and found only one woman, who was dying of sickness, and the soldiers killed her with a knife. At several towns they found no people, but at last they came to a town where several people had run to, as they did not know where else to go, because the soldiers were fighting everywhere. At this town they killed a lot of people men, women, and children—and took some as prisoners. They cut the hands off those they had killed, and brought them to Bonginda; they spread out the hands in a row for Bonginda to see. After that they left to return to Bikoro. They took a lot of prisoners with them. The hands which they had cut off they just left lying, because the white man had seen them, so they did not need to take them to Bikoro. Some of the soldiers were sent to Bikoro with the prisoners, but Bonginda himself and the other soldiers went to Bofiji, where there was another white man. The prisoners were sent to Misolo (M. Muller). Elima was about two weeks at Bikoro, and then she ran away into the bush at Bikoro for three days, and when she was found she was brought back to Misolo and he asked her why she had run away. She said because the soldiers had thrashed her.

Mr. Clark happened to be at Bikoro the day that Elima was found and brought back to Misolo. Misolo told her to go and work in the garden, but Mr. Clark asked to take her over to the Mission station at Ikoko. She came here about January of 1896.

Elima's mother was killed by soldiers and her father died of starvation, or rather he refused to eat because he was bereaved of his wife and all his children.

BONSONDO'S STATEMENT (EXCERPTS)

When they were all killed she waited in the grass for two nights. She was very frightened, and her throat was sore with thirst, and she looked about and at last she found some water in a pot. She stayed on in the grass a third night, and buffaloes came near her and she was very frightened and they went away. When the morning came she thought she would be better to move, and went away and got up a tree. She was three days without food, and was very hungry. In the tree she was near her grandmother's house, and she looked around and, seeing no soldiers, she crept to her grandmother's house and got some food and got up the tree again. The soldiers had gone away hunting for buffaloes, and it was then she was able to get down from the tree. The soldiers came back, and they came towards the trees and bushes calling out: "Now we see you; come down, come down!" This they used to do, so that people, thinking they were really discovered, should give themselves up; but she thought she would stay on, and so she stayed up the tree. Soon afterwards the soldiers went, but she was still afraid to come down. Presently she heard her grandmother calling out to know if she was alive, and when she heard her grandmother's voice she knew the soldiers were gone, and she answered, but her voice was very small—and she came down and her grandmother took her home.

That was the first time. Soon afterwards she and her grandmother went away to another town called Ngandi, near Nko, and they were there some days together, when one night the soldiers came. The white man sent the soldiers there because the Ngandi people had not taken to the State what they were told to take. Neither her own people nor the Ngandi people knew there was any trouble with the Government, so they were surprised. She was asleep. Her grandmother—her mother's mother—tried to awaken her, but she did not know. She felt the shaking, but she did not mind because she was very sleepy.

The soldiers came quickly into the house—her grandmother rushed out just before. When she heard the noise of the soldiers around the house, and looked and saw her grandmother not there, she ran out and called for her grandmother; and as she ran her brass anklets made a noise, and some one ran after her and caught her by the leg, and she fell and the soldiers took her.

NCONGO'S STATEMENT

Statement made to His Majesty's Consul at Ikoko on the 12th August, 1903. She is a young female scholar of the Mission.

When we began to run away from the fight, we ran away many times. They did not catch me because I was with mother and father. Afterwards mother died; four days passed, father died also. I and an older sister were left with two younger children, and then the fighting came where I had run to.

Then my elder sister called me: "Ncongo, come here." I went. She said: "Let us run away, because we have not any one to take care of us." When we were running away we saw a lot of Nkundu people coming towards us. We told them to run away, war was coming. They said: "Is it true?" We said: "It is true; they are coming." The Nkundu people said: "We will not run away; we did not see the soldiers." Only a little while they saw the soldiers, and they were killed. We stayed in a town named Nkombe. A male relative called me: "Ncongo, let us go;" but I did not want to. The soldiers came there; I ran away by myself: when I ran away I hid in the bush. While I was running I met with an old man who was running from a soldier. He (the soldier) fired a gun. I was not hit, but the old man died. Afterwards they caught me and two men. The soldiers asked: "Have you a father and mother?" I answered, "No." They said to me, "If you do not tell us we will kill you." I said: "Father and mother are dead." After that my oldest sister was caught, too, in the bush, and they left my little brother and sister alone in the bush to die, because heavy rain came on, and they had not had anything to eat for days and days. At night they tied my hands and feet for fear that I should run away. In the morning they caught three people—two had children; they killed the children. Afterwards I was standing outside, and a soldier asked me, "Where are you going?" I said, "I am going home." He said, "Come on." He took his gun; he put me in the house; he wanted to kill me. Then another soldier came and took me. We heard a big noise; they told us that the fighting was over, but it was not so. When we were going on the way they killed ten children because they were very, very small; they killed them in the water. Then they killed a lot of people, and they cut off their hands and put them into a basket and took them to the white man. He counted out the hands—200 in all; they left the hands lying. The white man's name was (Lieutenant Durieux) "Bonginda." After that Bonginda sent us prisoners with soldiers to Bikoro to Misolo. Misolo told me to weed grass. When I was working outside a soldier came and said: "Come here;" and when I went he wanted to cut my hand off, and so I went to the white man to tell him and he thrashed the soldier.

On our way, when we were coming to Bikoro, the soldiers saw a little child, and when they went to kill it the child laughed so the soldier took the butt of the gun and struck the child with it, and then cut off its head. One day they killed my half-sister and cut off her head, hands and feet because she had on rings. Her name was Mobe. Then they caught another sister, and they sold her to the Ngundu people, and now she is a slave there. When we came to Bikoro the white man said to send word to the friends of the prisoners to come with goats to buy off some of their relatives. A lot were bought off, but I had no one to come and buy me off because father was dead. The white man said to me, "You shall go to the English." The white man (Misolo) gave me a small boy to care for, but I thought he would be killed, so I helped to get him away. Misolo asked me to bring the boy to him, but I said: "He has run away." He said he would kill me, but Pebe came to Bikoro and took me away.
Note—Ncongo came to the Mission at Ikoko in December of 1895.

(Signed) NCONGO

Signed by Ncongo before me after the foregoing statements had been translated by Miss Lena Clark to her before me at Ikoko, this 12th day of August, 1903

(Signed) ROGER CASEMENT,

His Britannic Majesty's Consul

7

OLAUDAH EQUIANO
I SURVIVED THE MIDDLE PASSAGE
Nigeria

Editor's Notes: Olaudah Equiano's first encounter with the white man was when his black slave traders deposited him aboard a slave ship bound for Barbados. He had been captured in eastern Nigeria by local black raiders in search of slaves to transport across Nigeria to a waiting slave ship. One estimate of the number of victims of this trade during the seventeenth and eighteenth centuries is ten million men, women, and children. At the port, the first encounter occurred with English seamen whom Equiano ironically described as savages and possibly cannibals. The shipboard technology, totally new to Equiano, he ascribed to magical powers of the white man. The firsthand account of the passage to the West Indies is shocking. He was taken from Barbados to Virginia where he was purchased by a British naval officer and taken to England. He served in the British navy and was resold in the West Indies to a Quaker merchant. At the age of 31, he was able to purchase his own freedom. What distinguishes Equiano from all other slaves, was that his master, living outside of the American colonies where there were strict laws to prohibit the education of slaves, taught him how to read and write. Thus, at the age of 41, he wrote and published his own autobiography in 1788, an immediate bestseller. Later, he played an important role in establishing the African country of Sierra Leone as a British haven for slaves liberated by its Navy following the 1807 anti-slavery proclamation.

In his autobiography, he makes brief reference to a little-known fact about life in eastern Nigeria. Slaves among the Ibo tribes were common but were treated extraordinarily well and in some cases, slaves owned their own slaves.

Olaudah Equiano, *The Interesting Narrative of the Life of Olaudah Equiano* (Boston: Bedford/ St. Martin's, 1995), pp. 46–58.

Olaudah Equiano
or
GUSTAVUS VASSA,
the African

Olaudah Equiano depicted in the frontispiece of the first American edition of *The Interesting Narrative of Olaudah Equiano* (1791). (*Source*: Olaudah Equiano, *The Interesting Narrative of the Life of Olaudah Equiano, or Gustavus Vassa, the African*, 2 vols [New York: W. Durell, 1789, 1791]; first American edition.)

My father, besides many slaves, had a numerous family of which seven lived to grow up, including myself and a sister who was the only daughter. As I was the youngest of the sons I became, of course, the greatest favourite with my mother and was always with her; and she used to take particular pains to form my mind. I was trained up from my earliest years in the art of war, my daily exercise was shooting and throwing javelins, and my mother adorned me with emblems after the manner of our greatest warriors. In this way I grew up till I was turned the age of 11 when an end was put to my happiness in the following manner. Generally when the grown people in the neighbourhood were gone far in the fields to labour, the children assembled together in some of the neighbours' premises to play, and commonly some of us used to get up a tree to look out for any assailant or kidnapper that might come upon us, for they sometimes took those opportunities of our parents' absence to attack and carry off as many as they could seize. One day, as I was watching at the top of a tree in our yard. I saw one of those people come into the yard of our next neighbour but one to kidnap, there being many stout young people in it. Immediately on this I gave the alarm of the rogue and he was surrounded by the stoutest of them, who entangled him with cords so that he could not escape till some of the grown people came and secured him. But alas! ere long it was my fate to be thus attacked and to be carried off when none of the grown people were nigh. One day, when all our people were gone out to their works as usual and only I and my dear sister were left to mind the house, two men and a woman got over our walls, and in a moment seized us both, and without giving us time to cry out or make resistance they stopped our mouths and ran off with us into the nearest wood. Here they tied our hands and continued to carry us as far as they could till night came on, when we reached a small house where the robbers halted for refreshment and spent the night. We were then unbound but were unable to take any food, and being quite overpowered by fatigue and grief, our only relief was some sleep, which allayed our misfortune for a short time. The next morning we left the house and continued travelling all the day. . . .

When we went to rest the following night they offered us some victuals, but we refused it, and the only comfort we had was in being in one another's arms all that night and bathing each other with our tears. But alas! we were soon deprived of even the small comfort of weeping together. The next day proved a day of greater sorrow than I had yet experienced, for my sister and I were then separated while we lay clasped in each other's arms. It was in vain that we besought them not to part us; she was torn from me and immediately carried away, while I was left in a state of distraction not to be described. I cried and grieved continually, and for several days I did not eat anything but what they forced into my mouth. At length, after many days' travelling, during which I had often changed masters, I got into the hands of a chieftain in a very pleasant country. This man had two wives and some children, and they all used me extremely well and did all they could to comfort me, particularly the first wife, who was something like my mother. . . .

I was again sold. I was now carried to the left of the sun's rising, through many different countries and a number of large woods. The people I was sold to used to carry me very often when I was tired either on their shoulders or on their backs. I saw many convenient well-built sheds along the roads at proper distances, to accommodate the merchants and travellers who lay in those buildings along with their wives, who often accompany them; and they always go well armed. . . .

I was again sold and carried through a number of places till, after travelling a considerable time, I came to a town called Tinmah in the most beautiful country I had yet seen in Africa. It was extremely rich, and there were many rivulets which flowed through it and supplied a large pond in the centre of the town, where the people washed. Here I first saw and tasted coconuts, which I thought

Some Africans captured members of enemy tribes and enslaved them or sold them to Europeans. (*Source*: John Langdon Davies, comp., *The Slave Trade and Its Abolition* [London: Jackdaw Publications/New York: Grossman Publishers, 1971, c. 1965].)

superior to any nuts I had ever tasted before; and the trees, which were loaded, were also interspersed amongst the houses, which had commodious shades adjoining and were in the same manner as are ours, the insides being neatly plastered and whitewashed. Here I also saw and tasted for the first time sugar-cane. Their money consisted of little white shells the size of the finger-nail. I was sold here for 172 of them by a merchant who lived and brought me there. I had been about two or three days at his house when a wealthy widow, a neighbour of his, came there one evening, and brought with her an only son, a young gentleman about my own age and size. Here they saw me; and, having taken a fancy to me, I was bought of the merchant, and went home with them. Her house and premises were situated close to one of those rivulets I have mentioned, and were the finest I ever saw in Africa: they were very extensive, and she had a number of slaves to attend her. The next day I was washed and perfumed and when meal-time came I was led into the presence of my mistress, and ate and drank before her with her son. This filled me with astonishment; and I could scarce help expressing my surprise that the young gentleman should suffer me, who was bound, to eat with him who was free; and not only so, but that he would not at any time either eat or drink till I had taken first, because I was the eldest, which was agreeable to our custom. Indeed everything here, and all their treatment of me, made me forget that I was a slave. The language of these people resembled ours so nearly that we understood each other perfectly. They had also the very same customs as we. There were likewise slaves daily to attend us, while my young master and I with other boys sported with our darts and bows and arrows, as I had been used to do at home. In this resemblance to my former happy state I passed about two months; and I now began to think I was to be adopted into the family, and was beginning to be reconciled to my situation, and to forget by degrees my misfortunes, when all at once the delusion vanished; for without the least previous knowledge, one morning early, while my dear master and companion was still asleep, I was wakened out of my reverie to fresh sorrow, and hurried away even amongst the uncircumcised. . . .

All the nations and people I had hitherto passed through resembled our own in their manner, customs, and language: but I came at length to a country the inhabitants of which differed from us in all those particulars. I was very much struck with this difference, especially when I came among a people who did not circumcise and ate without washing their hands. They cooked also in iron pots and had European cutlasses and crossbows, which were unknown to us, and fought with their fists amongst themselves. Their women were not so modest as ours, for they ate and drank and slept with their men. But above all, I was amazed to see no sacrifices or offerings among them. In some of those places the people ornamented themselves with scars, and likewise filed their teeth very sharp. They wanted sometimes to ornament me in the same manner, but I would not suffer them, hoping that I might some time be among a people who did not thus disfigure themselves, as I thought they did. At last I came to the banks of a large river, which was covered with canoes in which the people appeared to live with their household utensils and provisions of all kinds. I was beyond measure astonished at this, as I had never before seen any water larger than a pond or a rivulet: and my surprise was mingled with no small fear when I was put into one of these canoes and we began to paddle and move along the river. We continued going on thus till night, and when we came to land and made fires on the banks, each family by themselves, some dragged their canoes on shore, others stayed and cooked in theirs and laid in them all night. Those on the land had mats of which they made tents, some in the shape of little houses: in these we slept, and after the morning meal we embarked again and proceeded as before. I was often very much astonished to see some of the women, as well as the men, jump into the water, dive to the bottom, come up again, and swim about. Thus I continued to travel, sometimes by land, sometimes by water, through different countries and various nations, till at the end of six or seven months after I had been kidnapped I arrived at the sea coast. . . .

The first object which saluted my eyes when I arrived on the coast was the sea, and a slave ship which was then riding at anchor and waiting for its cargo. These filled me with astonishment, which was soon converted into terror when I was carried on board. I was immediately handled and tossed up to see if I were sound by some of the crew, and I was now persuaded that I had gotten into a world of bad spirits and that they were going to kill me. Their complexions too differing so much from ours, their long hair and the language they spoke (which was very different from any I had ever heard) united to confirm me in this belief. Indeed such were the horrors of my views and fears at the moment that, if ten thousand worlds had been my own, I would have freely parted with them all to have exchanged my condition with that of the meanest slave in my own country. When I looked round the ship too and saw a large furnace or copper boiling and a multitude of black people of every description chained together, every one of their countenances expressing dejection and sorrow, I no longer doubted of my fate; and quite overpowered with horror and anguish, I fell motionless on the deck and fainted. When I recovered a little I found some black people about me, who I believed were some of those who had brought me on board and had been receiving their pay; they talked to me in order to cheer me, but all in vain. I asked them if we were not to be eaten by those white men with horrible looks, red faces, and loose hair. They told me I was not, and one of the crew brought me a small portion of spirituous liquor in a wine glass, but being afraid of him I would not take it out of his hand. One of the blacks therefore took it from him and gave it to me, and I took a little down my palate, which instead of reviving me, as they thought it would, threw me into the greatest consternation at the strange feeling it produced, having never tasted such any liquor before. Soon after this the blacks who brought me on board went off, and left me abandoned to despair.

I now saw myself deprived of all chance of returning to my native country or even the least glimpse of hope of gaining the shore, which I now considered as friendly; and I even wished for my former slavery in preference to my present situation, which was filled with horrors of every kind, still heightened by my ignorance of what I was to undergo. I was not long suffered to indulge my grief; I was soon put down under the decks, and there I received such a salutation in my nostrils as I had never experienced in my life: so that with the loathsomeness of the stench and crying together, I became so sick and low that I was not able to eat, nor had I the least desire to taste anything. I now wished for the last friend, death, to relieve me; but soon, to my grief, two of the white men offered me eatables, and on my refusing to eat, one of them held me fast by the hands and laid me across I think the windlass, and tied my feet while the other flogged me severely. I had never experienced anything of this kind before, and although, not being used to the water, I naturally feared that element the first time I saw it, yet nevertheless could I have got over the nettings I would have jumped over the side, but I could not; and besides, the crew used to watch us very closely who were not chained down to the decks, lest we should leap into the water: and I have seen some of these poor African prisoners most severely cut for attempting to do so, and hourly whipped for not eating. This indeed was often the case with myself. In a little time after, amongst the poor chained men I found some of my own nation, which in a small degree gave ease to my mind. I inquired of these what was to be done with us; they gave me to understand we were to be carried to these white people's country to work for them. I then was a little revived, and thought if it were no worse than working, my situation was not so desperate: but still I feared I should be put to death, the white people looked and acted, as I thought, in so savage a manner; for I had never seen among my people such instances of brutal cruelty, and this not only shown towards us blacks but also to some of the whites themselves. One white man in particular I saw, when we were permitted to be on deck, flogged so unmercifully with a large rope near the foremast that he died in consequence of it; and they tossed him over the side as they would have done a brute. This made me fear these people the more, and I expected nothing less than to be treated in the same manner. I could not help expressing my fears and apprehensions to some of my countrymen: I asked them if these people had no country but lived in this hollow place (the ship): they told me they did not, but came from a distant one.

"Then," said I, "how comes it in all our country we never heard of them?" They told me because they lived so very far off. I then asked where were their women? had they any like themselves? I was told they had: "And why," said I, "do we not see them?" They answered because they were left behind. I asked how the vessel could go? They told me they could not tell, but that there were cloths put upon the masts by the help of the ropes I saw, and then the vessel went on; and the white men had some spell or magic they put in the water when they liked in order to stop the vessel. I was exceedingly amazed at this account and really thought they were spirits. I therefore wished much to be from amongst them for I expected they would sacrifice me: but my wishes were vain, for we were so quartered that it was impossible for any of us to make our escape. While we stayed on the coast I was mostly on deck, and one day, to my great astonishment, I saw one of these vessels coming in with the sails up. As soon as the whites saw it they gave a great shout, at which we were amazed; and the more so as the vessel appeared larger by approaching nearer. At last she came to an anchor in my sight, and when the anchor was let go I and my countrymen who saw it were lost in astonishment to observe the vessel stop, and were now convinced it was done by magic. Soon after this the other ship got her boats out, and they came on board of us, and the people of both ships seemed very glad to see each other. Several of the strangers also shook hands with us black people, and made motions with their hands signifying I suppose we were to go to their country; but we did not understand them. At last, when the ship we were in had got in all her cargo, they made ready with many fearful noises, and we were all put under deck so that we could not see how they managed the vessel. But this disappointment was the last of my sorrow. The stench of the hold while we were on the coast was so intolerably loathsome that it was dangerous to remain there for any time, and some of us had been permitted to stay on the deck for the fresh air; but now that the whole ship's cargo were confined together it became absolutely pestilential. The closeness of the place and the heat of the climate, added to the number in the ship, which was so crowded that each had scarcely room to turn himself, almost suffocated us. This produced copious perspirations, so that the air soon became unfit for respiration from a variety of loathsome smells, and brought on a sickness among the slaves, of which many died, thus falling victims to the improvident avarice, as I may call it, of their purchasers. This wretched situation was again aggravated by the galling of the chains, now become insupportable, and the filth of the necessary tubs, into which the children often fell and were almost suffocated. The shrieks of the women and the groans of the dying rendered the whole a scene of horror almost inconceivable. Happily perhaps for myself I was soon reduced so low here that it was thought necessary to keep me almost always on deck, and from my extreme youth I was not put in fetters. In this situation I expected every hour to share the fate of my companions, some of whom were almost daily brought upon deck at the point of death, which I began to hope would soon put an end to my miseries. Often did I think many of the inhabitants of the deep much more happy than myself. I envied them the freedom they enjoyed, and as often wished I could change my condition for theirs. Every circumstance I met with served only to render my state more painful, and heighten my apprehensions and my opinion of the cruelty of the whites. One day they had taken a number of fishes, and when they had killed and satisfied themselves with as many as they thought fit, to our astonishment who were on the deck, rather than give any of them to us to eat as we expected, they tossed the remaining fish into the sea again, although we begged and prayed for some as well as we could, but in vain; and some of my countrymen, being pressed by hunger, took an opportunity when they thought no one saw them of trying to get a little privately; but they were discovered, and the attempt procured them some very severe floggings. One day, when we had a smooth-sea and moderate wind, two of my wearied countrymen who were chained together (I was near them at the time), preferring death to such a life of misery, somehow made through the nettings and jumped into the sea: immediately another quite dejected fellow, who on account of his illness was suffered to be out of irons, also followed their example; and I believe many more would very soon have done the same if they had not been prevented by the ship's crew, who were instantly alarmed. Those of us that were the most active were in a moment put down under the deck, and there was such a noise and confusion amongst the people of the ship as I never heard before, to stop her and get the boat out to go after the slaves. However two of the wretches were drowned, but they got the other and afterwards flogged him unmercifully for thus attempting to prefer death to slavery. In this manner we continued to undergo more hardships than I can now relate, hardships which are inseparable from this accursed trade. Many a time we were near suffocation from the want of fresh air, which we were often without for whole days together. This and the stench of the necessary tubs carried off many. During our passage I first saw flying fishes, which surprised me very much: they used frequently to fly across the ship and many of them fell on the deck. I also now first saw the use of the quadrant; I had often with astonishment seen the mariners make observations with it, and I could not think what it meant. They at last took notice of my surprise, and one of them, willing to increase it as well as to gratify my curiosity, made me one day look through it. The clouds appeared to me to be land, which disappeared as they passed along. This heightened my wonder, and I was now more persuaded than ever that I was in another world and that everything about me was magic. At last we came in sight of the island of Barbados, at which the whites on board gave a great shout and made many signs of joy to us. We did not know what to think of this, but as the vessel drew nearer we plainly saw the harbour and other ships of different kinds and sizes, and we soon anchored amongst them off Bridgetown. Many merchants and planters now came on board, though it was in the evening. They put us in separate parcels and examined us attentively. They also made us jump, and pointed to the land, signifying we were to go there. We thought by this we should be eaten by these ugly men, as they appeared to us; and when soon after we were all put down under the deck again, there was much dread and trembling among us, and nothing but bitter cries to be heard all the night from these apprehensions, insomuch that at last the white people got some old slaves from the land to pacify us. They told us we were not to be eaten but to work, and were soon to go on land where we should see many of our country people. This report eased us much; and sure enough soon after we were landed there came to us Africans of all languages. We were conducted immediately to the merchant's yard, where we were all pent up together like so many sheep in a fold without regard to sex or age. As every object was new to me everything I saw filled me with surprise. What struck me first was that the houses were built with storeys, and in every other respect different from those in Africa: but I was still more astonished on seeing people on horseback. I did not know what this could mean, and indeed I thought these people were full of nothing but magical arts. While I was in this astonishment one of my fellow prisoners spoke to a countryman of his about the horses, who said they were the same kind they had in their country. I understood them though they were from a distant part of Africa, and I thought it odd I had not seen any horses there; but afterwards when I came to converse with different Africans I found they had many horses amongst them, and much larger than those I then saw. We were not many days in the merchant's custody before we were sold after their usual manner, which is this: On a signal given, (as the beat of a drum) the buyers rush at once into the yard where the slaves are confined, and make choice of that parcel they like best. The noise and clamour with which this is attended and the eagerness visible in the countenances of the buyers serve not a little to increase the apprehensions of the terrified Africans, who may well be supposed to consider them as the ministers of that destruction to which they think themselves devoted. In this manner, without scruple, are relations and friends separated, most of them never to see each other again. I remember in the vessel in which I was brought over, in the men's apartment there were several brothers who, in the sale, were sold in different lots; and it was very moving on this occasion to see and hear their cries at parting. 0, ye nominal Christians! might not an African ask you, Learned you this from your God who says unto you, Do unto all men as you would men should do unto you? Is it not enough that we are torn from our country and friends to toil for your luxury and lust of gain? Must every tender feeling be likewise sacrificed to your avarice? Are the dearest friends and relations, now rendered more dear by their separation from their kindred, still to be parted from each other and thus prevented from cheering the gloom of slavery with the small comfort of being together and mingling their sufferings and sorrows? Why are parents to lose their children, brothers their sisters, or husbands their wives? Surely this is a new refinement in cruelty which, while it has no advantage to atone for it, thus aggravates distress and adds fresh horrors even to the wretchedness of slavery.

THE SLAVE MARCH

Here we met the notorious Tip-pu-Tib's annual caravan, which had been resting after the long march through Ugogo and the hot passes of Chunyo. As they filed past we noticed many chained together by the neck. Others had their necks fastened into the forks of poles six feet long, the ends of which were supported by the men who preceded them. The women, who were as numerous as the men, carried babies on their backs in addition to a tusk of ivory or other burden on their heads. They looked at us with suspicion and fear, having been told that white men always desired to release slaves in order to eat their flesh, like the Upper Congo cannibals.

It is difficult to describe the filthy state of their bodies; in many instances, not only scarred by the cut of the "chicote" [a piece of hide used to enforce obedience], but feet and shoulders were a mass of open sores, made more painful by the swarms of flies which followed the march and lived on the flowing blood. They presented a moving picture of utter misery, and one could not help wondering how many of them have survived the long tramp from the Upper Congo, at least 1,000 miles distant. Our own inconveniences sank into insignificance compared with the suffering of this crowd of half-starved, ill-treated creatures who, weary and friendless, must have longed for death.

Albert J. Swann, *Fighting the Slave Hunters in Central Africa*, Philadelphia: J. B. Lippincott Company, 1910, pp. 47–48.

8

CHINUA ACHEBE
THE WHITE MAN ARRIVES
Nigeria

Editor's Notes: Few writers have provided such an extended and detailed account of African tribal life as a background for recording the impact of white missionaries. Chinua Achebe's 1959 novel Things Fall Apart *has been translated into 50 languages and sold several million copies. The setting is a remote, traditional Nigerian village in the late nineteenth century about to be changed forever by the advent of European civilization. In these excerpts there is an ongoing argument about whose god is more powerful, the Christian God or the local tribal gods. Okonkwa is the main character in the novel and Obierika is his friend who begins these selections with a story.*

Achebe was born in 1930 in eastern Nigeria and is a graduate of University College in Ibadan. He worked for the Nigerian Broadcasting Co. and helped found the outstanding "African Writers Series," a project of Britain's Heinemann Publishing Co. with over 300 titles. Achebe has received 12 honorary doctorates and has taught in several U.S. colleges and universities, most recently at Bard College.

"Three moons ago," said Obierika, "on an Eke market day a little band of fugitives came into our town. Most of them were sons of our land whose mothers had been buried with us. But there were some too who came because they had friends in our town, and others who could think of nowhere else open to escape. And so they fled into Umuofia with a woeful story." He drank his palm-wine, and Okonkwo filled his horn again. He continued:

"During the last planting season a white man had appeared in their clan."

"An albino," suggested Okonkwo.

Reprinted from *Things Fall Apart*, by Chinua Achebe. Pearson Education Limited, © Chinua Achebe 1958. Reprinted by Heinemann Educational Publishers, 1996: pp. 97–128, selections.

"He was not an albino. He was quite different." He sipped his wine. "And he was riding an iron horse. The first people who saw him ran away, but he stood beckoning to them. In the end the fearless ones went near and even touched him. The elders consulted their Oracle and it told them that the strange man would break their clan and spread destruction among them."

Obierika again drank a little of his wine. "And so they killed the white man and tied his iron horse to their sacred tree because it looked as if it would run away to call the man's friends. I forgot to tell you another thing which the Oracle said. It said that other white men were on their way. They were locusts, it said, and that first man was their harbinger sent to explore the terrain. And so they killed him."

"What did the white man say before they killed him?" asked Uchendu.

"He said nothing," answered one of Obierika's companions.

"He said something, only they did not understand him," said Obierika. "He seemed to speak through his nose."

"One of the men told me," said Obierika's other companion, "that he repeated over and over again a word that resembled Mbaino. Perhaps he had been going to Mbaino and had lost his way."

"Anyway," resumed Obierika, "they killed him and tied up his iron horse. This was before the planting season began. For a long time nothing happened. The rains had come and yams had been sown. The iron horse was still tied to the sacred silk-cotton tree. And then one morning three white men led by a band of ordinary men like us came to the clan. They saw the iron horse and went away again. Most of the men and women of Abame had gone to their farms. Only a few of them saw these white men and their followers. For many market weeks nothing else happened. They have a big market in Abame on every other Afo day and, as you know, the whole clan gathers there. That was the day it happened. The three white men and a very large number of other men surrounded the market. They must have used a powerful medicine to make themselves invisible until the market was full. And they began to shoot. Everybody was killed, except the old and the sick who were at home and a handful of men and women whose *chi* [personal gods] were wide awake and brought them out of that market." He paused.

"Their clan is now completely empty. Even the sacred fish in their mysterious lake have fled and the lake has turned the color of blood. A great evil has come upon their land as the Oracle had warned."

There was a long silence. Uchendu ground his teeth together audibly. Then he burst out:

"Never kill a man who says nothing. Those men of Abame were fools. What did they know about the man?" He ground his teeth again and told a story to illustrate his point. "Mother Kite once sent her daughter to bring food. She went, and brought back a duckling. "You have done very well," said Mother Kite to her daughter, "but tell me, what did the mother of this duckling say when you swooped and carried its child away?" "It said nothing," replied the young kite. It just walked away." "You must return the duckling," said Mother Kite. "There is something ominous behind the silence." And so Daughter Kite returned the duckling and took a chick instead. "What did the mother of this chick do?" asked the old kite. "It cried and raved and cursed me," said the young kite. "Then we can eat the chick," said her mother. "There is nothing to fear from someone who shouts. Those men of Abame were fools."

"They were fools," said Okonkwo after a pause. "They had been warned that danger was ahead. They should have armed themselves with their guns and their machetes even when they went to market."

"They have paid for their foolishness," said Obierika. "But I am greatly afraid. We have heard stories about white men who made the powerful guns and the strong drinks and took slaves away across the seas, but no one thought the stories were true."

"There is no story that is not true," said Uchendu. "The world has no end, and what is good among one people is an abomination with others. We have albinos among us. Do you not think that they came to our clan by mistake, that they have strayed from their way to a land where everybody is like them?"

The arrival of the missionaries had caused a considerable stir in the village of Mbanta. There were six of them and one was a white man. Every man and woman came out to see the white man. Stories about these strange men had grown since one of them had been killed in Abame and his iron horse tied to the sacred silk-cotton tree. And so everybody came to see the white man. It was the time of the year when everybody was at home. The harvest was over.

When they had all gathered, the white man began to speak to them. He spoke through an interpreter who was an Ibo man, though his dialect was different and harsh to the ears of Mbanta. Many people laughed at his dialect and the way he used words strangely. Instead of saying "myself" he always said "my buttocks." But he was a man of commanding presence and the clansmen listened to him. He said he was one of them, as they could see from his color and his language. The other four black men were also their brothers, although one of them did not speak Ibo. The white man was also their brother because they were all sons of God. And he told them about this new God, the Creator of all the world and all the men and women. He told them that they worshipped false gods, gods of wood and stone. A deep murmur went through the crowd when he said this. He told them that the true God lived on high and that all men when they died went before Him for judgment. Evil men and all the heathen who in their blindness bowed to wood and stone were thrown into a fire that burned like palm-oil. But good men who worshipped the true God lived forever in His happy kingdom. "We have been sent by this great God to ask you to leave your wicked ways and false gods and turn to Him so that you may be saved when you die," he said.

"Your buttocks understand our language," said someone light-heartedly and the crowd laughed.

"What did he say?" the white man asked his interpreter. But before he could answer, another man asked a question: "Where is the white man's horse?"

he asked. The Ibo evangelists consulted among themselves and decided that the man probably meant bicycle. They told the white man and he smiled benevolently.

"Tell them," he said, "that I shall bring many iron horses when we have settled down among them. Some of them will even ride the iron horse themselves." This was interpreted to them but very few of them heard. They were talking excitedly among themselves because the white man had said he was going to live among them. They had not thought about that.

At this point an old man said he had a question. "Which is this god of yours," he asked, "the goddess of the earth, the god of the sky, Amadiora or the thunderbolt, or what?"

The interpreter spoke to the white man and he immediately gave his answer. "All the gods you have named are not gods at all. They are gods of deceit who tell you to kill your fellows and destroy innocent children. There is only one true God and He has the earth, the sky, you and me and all of us."

"If we leave our gods and follow your god," asked another man, "who will protect us from the anger of our neglected gods and ancestors?"

"Your gods are not alive and cannot do you any harm," replied the white man. "They are pieces of wood and stone."

When this was interpreted to the men of Mbanta they broke into derisive laughter. These men must be mad, they said to themselves. How else could they say that Ani and Amadiora were harmless? And Idemili and Ogwugwu too? And some of them began to go away.

Then the missionaries burst into song. It was one of those gay and rollicking tunes of evangelism which had the power of plucking at silent and dusty chords in the heart of an Ibo man. The interpreter explained each verse to the audience, some of whom now stood enthralled. It was a story of brothers who lived in darkness and in fear, ignorant of the love of God. It told of one sheep out on the hills, away from the gates of God and from the tender shepherd's care.

After the singing the interpreter spoke about the Son of God whose name was Jesu Kristi. Okonkwo, who only stayed in the hope that it might come to chasing the men out of the village or whipping them, now said:

"You told us with your own mouth that there was only one god. Now you talk about his son. He must have a wife, then." The crowd agreed.

"I did not say He had a wife," said the interpreter, somewhat lamely.

"Your buttocks said he had a son," said the joker. "So he must have a wife and all of them must have buttocks."

The missionary ignored him and went on to talk about the Holy Trinity. At the end of it Okonkwo was fully convinced that the man was mad. He shrugged his shoulders and went away to tap his afternoon palm-wine.

But there was a young lad who had been captivated. His name was Nwoye, Okonkwo's first son. It was not the mad logic of the Trinity that captivated him. He did not understand it. It was the poetry of the new religion, something felt in the marrow. The hymn about brothers who sat in darkness and in fear seemed to answer a vague and persistent question that haunted his young soul—the question of the twins crying in the bush and the question of Ikemefuna who was killed. He felt a relief within as the hymn poured into his parched soul. The words of the hymn were like the drops of frozen rain melting on the dry palate of the panting earth. Nwoye's callow mind was greatly puzzled.

The missionaries spend their first four or five nights in the marketplace, and went into the village in the morning to preach the gospel. They asked who the king of the village was, but the villagers told them that there was no king. "We have men of high title and the chief priests and the elders," they said.

It was not very easy getting the men of high title and the elders together after the excitement of the first day. But the missionaries persevered, and in the end they were received by the rulers of Mbanta. They asked for a plot of land to build their church.

Every clan and village had its "evil forest." In it were buried all those who died of the really evil diseases, like leprosy and smallpox. It was also the dumping ground for the potent fetishes of great medicine men when they died. An "evil forest" was, therefore, alive with sinister forces and powers of darkness. It was such a forest that the rulers of Mbanta gave to the missionaries. They did not really want them in their clan, and so they made them that offer which nobody in his right senses would accept.

"They want a piece of land to build their shrine," said Uchendu to his peers when they consulted among themselves. "We shall give them a piece of land." He paused, and there was a murmur of surprise and disagreement. "Let us give them a portion of the Evil Forest. They boast about victory over death. Let us give them a real battlefield in which to show their victory." They laughed and agreed, and sent for the missionaries, whom they had asked to leave them for a while so that they might "whisper together." They offered them as much of the Evil Forest as they cared to take. And to their greatest amazement the missionaries thanked them and burst into song.

"They do not understand," said some of the elders. "But they will understand when they go to their plot of land tomorrow morning." And they dispersed.

The next morning the crazy men actually began to clear a part of the forest and to build their house. The inhabitants of Mbanta expected them all to be dead within four days. The first day passed and the second and third and fourth, and none of them died. Everyone was puzzled. And then it became known that the white man's fetish had unbelievable power. It was said that he wore glasses on his eyes so that he could see and talk to evil spirits. Not long after, he won his first three converts.

Although Nwoye had been attracted to the new faith from the very first day, he kept it secret. He dared not go too near the missionaries for fear of his father. But whenever they came to preach in the open marketplace or the village playground, Nwoye was there. And he was already beginning to know some of the simple stories they told.

"We have now built a church," said Mr. Kiaga, the interpreter, who was now in charge of the infant congregation. The white man had gone back to Umuofia, where he built his headquarters and from where he paid regular visits to Mr. Kiaga's congregation at Mbanta.

"We have now built a church," said Mr. Kiaga, "and we want you all to come in every seventh day to worship the true God."

On the following Sunday, Nwoye passed and repassed the little red-earth and thatch building without summoning enough courage to enter. He heard the voice of singing and although it came from a handful of men it was loud and confident. Their church stood on a circular clearing that looked like the open mouth of the Evil Forest. Was it waiting to snap its teeth together? After passing and re-passing by the church, Nwoye returned home.

It was well known among the people of Mbanta that their gods and ancestors were sometimes long-suffering and would deliberately allow a man to go on defying them. But even in such cases they set their limit at seven market weeks or twenty-eight days. Beyond that limit no man was suffered to go. And so excitement mounted in the village as the seventh week approached since the impudent missionaries built their church in the Evil Forest. The villagers were so certain about the doom that awaited these men that one or two converts thought it wise to suspend their allegiance to the new faith.

At last the day came by which all the missionaries should have died. But they were still alive, building a new red-earth and thatch house for their teacher, Mr. Kiaga. That week they won a handful more converts. And for the first time they had a woman. Her name was Nneka, the wife of Amadi, who was a prosperous farmer. She was very heavy with child.

Nneka had had four previous pregnancies and childbirths. But each time she had borne twins, and they had been immediately thrown away. Her husband and his family were already becoming highly critical of such a woman and were not unduly perturbed when they found she had fled to join the Christians. It was a good riddance.

The young church in Mbanta had a few crises early in its life. At first the clan had assumed that it would not survive. But it had gone on living and gradually becoming stronger. The clan was worried, but not overmuch. If a gang of *ejulefu* decided to live in the Evil Forest it was their own affair. When one came to think of it, the Evil Forest was a fit home for such undesirable people. It was true they were rescuing twins from the bush, but they never brought them into the village. As far as the villagers were concerned, the twins still remained where they had been thrown away. Surely the earth goddess would not visit the sins of the missionaries on the innocent villagers?

But on one occasion the missionaries had tried to overstep the bounds. Three converts had gone into the village and boasted openly that all the gods were dead and impotent and that they were prepared to defy them by burning all their shrines.

"Go and burn your mothers' genitals," said one of the priests. The men were seized and beaten until they streamed with blood. After that nothing happened for a long time between the church and the clan.

But stories were already gaining ground that the white man had not only brought a religion but also a government. It was said that they had built a place of judgement in Umuofia to protect the followers of their religion. It was even said that they had hanged one man who killed a missionary.

Although such stories were now often told they looked like fairy-tales in Mbanta and did not as yet affect the relationship between the new church and the clan. There was no question of killing a missionary here, for Mr. Kiaga, despite his madness, was quite harmless. As for his converts, no one could kill them without having to flee from the clan, for in spite of their worthlessness they still belonged to the clan. And so nobody gave serious thought to the stories about the white man's government or the consequences of killing the Christians. If they became more troublesome than they already were they would simply be driven out of the clan.

And the little church was at that moment too deeply absorbed in its own troubles to annoy the clan. It all began over the question of admitting outcasts.

These outcasts, or *osu*, seeing that the new religion welcomed twins and such abominations, thought that it was possible that they would also be received. And so one Sunday two of them went into the church. There was an immediate stir; but so great was the work the new religion had done among the converts that they did not immediately leave the church when the outcasts came in. Those who found themselves nearest to them merely moved to another seat. It was a miracle. But it only lasted till the end of the service. The whole church raised a protest and was about to drive these people out, when Mr. Kiaga stopped them and began to explain.

"Before God," he said, "there is no slave or free. We are all children of God and we must receive these our brothers."

"You do not understand," said one of the converts. "What will the heathen say of us when they hear that we receive *osu* into our midst? They will laugh."

"Let them laugh," said Mr. Kiaga. "God will laugh at them on the judgment day. Why do the nations rage and the peoples imagine a vain thing? He that sitteth in the heavens shall laugh. The Lord shall have them in derision."

"You do not understand," the convert maintained. "You are our teacher, and you can teach us the things of the new faith. But this is a matter which we know." And he told him what an *osu* was.

He was a person dedicated to a god, a thing set apart—a taboo for ever, and his children after him. He could neither marry nor be married by the freeborn. He was in fact an outcast, living in a special area of the village, close to the Great Shrine. Wherever he went he carried with him the mark of his forbidden caste—long, tangled and dirty hair. A razor was taboo to him. An *osu* could not attend an assembly of the free-born, and they, in turn, could not shelter under his roof. He could not take any of the four titles of the clan, and when he died he was buried by his kind in the Evil Forest. How could such a man be a follower of Christ?

"He needs Christ more than you and I," said Mr. Kiaga.

"Then I shall go back to the clan," said the convert. And he went. Mr. Kiaga stood firm, and it was his firmness that saved the young church. The wavering converts drew inspiration and confidence from his unshakable faith. He ordered the outcasts to shave off their long, tangled hair. At first they were afraid they might die.

"Unless you shave off the mark of your heathen belief I will not admit you into the church," said Mr. Kiaga. "You fear that you will die. Why should that be? How are you different from other men who shave their hair? The same God created you and them. But they have cast you out like lepers. It is against the will of God, who has promised everlasting life to all who believe in His holy name. The heathen say you will die if you do this or that, and you are afraid. They also said I would die if I built my church on this ground. Am I dead? They said I would die if I took care of twins. I am still alive. The heathen speak nothing but falsehood. Only the word of our God is true.

Umuofia had indeed changed during the seven years Okonkwo had been in exile. The church had come and led many astray. Not only the low-born and the outcast but sometimes a worthy man had joined it. Such a man was Ogbuefi Ugonna, who had taken two titles, and who like a madman had cut the anklet of his titles and cast it away to join the Christians. The white missionary was very proud of him and he was one of the first men in Umuofia to receive the sacrament of Holy Communion, or Holy Feast as it was called in Ibo. Ogbuefi Ugonna had thought of the Feast in terms of eating and drinking, only more holy than the village variety. He had therefore put his drinking-horn into his goatskin bag for the occasion.

But apart from the church, the white men had also brought a government. They had built a court where the District Commissioner judged cases in ignorance. He had court messengers who brought men to him for trial. Many of these messengers came from Umuru on the bank of the Great River, where the white men first came many years before and where they had built the center of their religion and trade and government. These court messengers were greatly hated in Umuofia because they were foreigners and also arrogant and high-handed. They were called *kotma*, [court messengers] and because of their ash-colored shorts they earned the additional name of Ashy-Buttocks. They guarded the prison, which was full of men who had offended against the white man's law. Some of these prisoners had thrown away their twins and some had molested the Christians. They were beaten in the prison by the *kotma* and made to work every morning clearing the government compound and fetching wood for the white Commissioner and the court messengers. Some of these prisoners were men of title who should be above such mean occupation. They were grieved by the indignity and mourned for their neglected farms.

As they cut grass in the morning the younger men sang in time with the strokes of their machetes:

> *Kotma* of the ash buttocks,
> He is fit to be a slave.
> The white man has no sense,
> He is fit to be a slave.

The court messengers did not like to be called Ashy-Buttocks, and they beat the men. But the song spread in Umuofia.

Okonkwo's head was bowed in sadness as Obierika told him these things.

"Perhaps I have been away too long," Okonkwo said, almost to himself. "But I cannot understand these things you tell me. What is it that has happened to our people? Why have they lost the power to fight?"

"Have you not heard how the white man wiped out Abame?" asked Obierika.

"I have heard," said Okonkwo. "But I have also heard that Abame people were weak and foolish. Why did they not fight back? Had they no guns and machetes? We would be cowards to compare ourselves with the men of Abame. Their fathers had never dared to stand before our ancestors. We must fight these men and drive them from the land."

"It is already too late," said Obierika sadly. "Our own men and our sons have joined the ranks of the stranger. They have joined his religion and they help to uphold his government. If we should try to drive out the white men in Umuofia we should find it easy. There are only two of them. But what of our own people who are following their way and have been given power? They would go to Umuru and bring the soldiers, and we would be like Abame." He paused for a long time and then said: "I told you on my last visit to Mbanta how they hanged Aneto."

"What has happened to that piece of land in dispute?" asked Okonkwo.

"The white man's court has decided that it should belong to Nnama's family, who had given much money to the white man's messengers and interpreter."

"Does the white man understand our custom about land?

"How can he when he does not even speak our tongue? But he says that our customs are bad; and our own brothers who have taken up his religion also say that our customs are bad. How do you think we can fight when our own brothers have turned against us? The white man is very clever. He came quietly and peaceably with his religion. We were amused at his foolishness and allowed him to stay. Now he has won our brothers, and our clan can no longer act like one. He has put a knife on the things that held us together and we have fallen apart."

There were many men and women in Umuofia who did not feel as strongly as Okonkwo about the new dispensation. The white man had indeed brought a lunatic religion, but he had also built a trading store and for the first time palm-oil and kernel became things of great price, and much money flowed into Umuofia.

And even in the matter of religion there was a growing feeling that there might be something in it after all, something vaguely akin to method in the overwhelming madness.

This growing feeling was due to Mr. Brown, the white missionary, who was very firm in restraining his flock from provoking the wrath of the clan. One member in particular was very difficult to restrain. His name was Enoch and his father was the priest of the snake cult. The story went around that Enoch had killed and eaten the sacred python, and that his father had cursed him.

Mr. Brown preached against such excess of zeal. Everything was possible, he told his energetic flock, but everything was not expedient. And so Mr. Brown came to be respected even by the clan, because he trod softly on its faith. He made friends with some of the great men of the clan and on one of his frequent visits to the neighboring villages he had been presented with a carved elephant tusk, which was a sign of dignity and rank. One of the great men in that village was called Akunna and he had given one of his sons to be taught the white man's knowledge in Mr. Brown's school.

Whenever Mr. Brown went to that village he spent long hours with Akunna in his *obi* [living quarters] talking through an interpreter about religion. Neither of them succeeded in converting the other but they learned more about their different beliefs.

"You say that there is one supreme God who made heaven and earth," said Akunna on one of Mr. Brown's visits. "We also believe in Him and call Him Chukwu. He made all the world and the other gods."

"There are no other gods," said Mr. Brown. "Chukwu is the only God and all others are false. You carve a piece of wood—like that one (he pointed at the rafters from which Akunna's carved *Ikenga* hung), and you call it a god. But it is still a piece of wood."

"Yes," said Akunna. "It is indeed a piece of wood. The tree from which it came was made by Chukwu, as indeed all minor gods were. But He made them for His messengers so that we could approach Him through them. It is like yourself. You are the head of your church."

"No," protested Mr. Brown. "The head of my church is God Himself."

"I know," said Akunna, "but there must be a head in this world among men. Somebody like yourself must be the head here."

"The head of my church in that sense is in England."

"That is exactly what I am saying. The head of your church is in your country. He has sent you here as his messenger. And you have also appointed your own messengers and servants. Or let me take another example, the District Commissioner. He is sent by your king."

"They have a queen," said the interpreter on his own account.

"Your queen sends her messenger, the District Commissioner. He finds that he cannot do the work alone and so he appoints *kotma* to help him. It is the same with God, or Chukwu. He appoints the smaller gods to help Him because His work is too great for one person."

"You should not think of Him as a person," said Mr. Brown. "It is because you do so that you imagine He must need helpers. And the worst thing about it is that you give all the worship to the false gods you have created."

"That is not so. We make sacrifices to the little gods, but when they fail and there is no one else to turn to we go to Chukwu. It is right to do so. We approach a great man through his servants. But when his servants fail to help us, then we go to the last source of hope. We appear to pay greater attention to the little gods but that is not so. We worry them more because we are afraid to worry their Master. Our fathers knew that Chukwu was the Overlord and that is why many of them gave their children the name Chukwuka—'Chukwu is Supreme.'"

"You said one interesting thing," said Mr. Brown. "You are afraid of Chukwu. In my religion Chukwu is a loving Father and need not be feared by those who do His will."

"But we must fear Him when we are not doing His will," said Akunna. "And who is to tell His will? It is too great to be known."

In this way Mr. Brown learned a good deal about the religion of the clan and he came to the conclusion that a frontal attack on it would not succeed. And so he built a school and a little hospital in Umuofia. He went from family to family begging people to send their children to his school. But at first they only sent their slaves or sometimes their lazy children. Mr. Brown begged and argued and prophesied. He said that the leaders of the land in the future would be men and women who had learned to read and write. If Umuofia failed to send her children to the school, strangers would come from other places to rule them. They could already see that happening in the Native Court, where the D.C. was surrounded by strangers who spoke his tongue. Most of these strangers came from the distant town of Umuru on the bank of the Great River where the white man first went.

In the end Mr. Brown's arguments began to have an effect. More people came to learn in his school, and he encouraged them with gifts of singlets and towels. They were not all young, these people who came to learn. Some of them were thirty years old or more. They worked on their farms in the morning and went to school in the afternoon. And it was not long before the people began to say that the white man's medicine was quick in working. Mr. Brown's school produced quick results. A few months in it were enough to make one a court messenger or even a court clerk. Those who stayed longer became teachers; and from Umuofia laborers went forth into the Lord's vineyard. New churches were established in the surrounding villages and a few schools with them. From the very beginning religion and education went hand in hand.

Mr. Brown's mission grew from strength to strength, and because of its link with the new administration it earned a new social prestige.

9

CHIEF MATUNGI
The Loss of Identity
Congo

Editor's Notes: Colin Turnbull, a distinguished British anthropologist, spent many years doing field work in Africa. While in the Congo, he devoted days to interviewing a local ex-tribal chief who had been deposed by Belgian colonialists. Matungi's devastating personal account reveals the step-by-step process of destruction of local cultures and the installation of colonial rule. Turnbull (1924–1994) served as head of the Department of African Ethnology at the American Museum of Natural History in New York City.

You white people had not come to live here when I was a child, and your teachers did not set up their schools until they needed to make use of us. Then I was a man. So I was thought of, conceived and born in the manner of my ancestors, and I became a man in the manner of my ancestors. My mother had never eaten strange foods, nor been forced to do strange work, so her belly was clean and her milk was clean and I was clean.

My father was a good man. He was young when Bulamatadi (H. M. Stanley) came through our country three times, making war on everyone, but he fought back. He fought just as he fought the BaNgwana who stole our people and sold them to the Arabs, and just as he would have fought anyone who threatened his family. He was not like Effundi Mustafa, that old hypocrite who smiles in your face and poisons the food he offers you with evil thoughts. Effundi Mustafa says he sat on Bulamatadi's knee, and it is probably true, for he was a child then. But my father would have killed me before he would have allowed me to be so defiled. Because of these feelings, and because of all the fighting, he had to run away with many others to the country of the BaLese, and there, for want of BaBira girls, he married my mother. But this is not a bad thing for a chief's son to do. It helps to make friends with those who live around us . . . except with the BaNgwana. They do not know what friendship is, and their mouths lie even before they speak; we would never marry with them.

Not long after I finished drinking my mother's milk my father returned here. His own father had been killed by Bulamatadi. He had heard that the white men were all in a camp and were ill for shortage of food. He thought he would bring some bananas and make peace, for the camp was on the edge of his old plantation. But he and all the others with him were killed as they approached. It was like this wherever Bulamatadi went . . . he would have killed all of us, just as he killed his own men or left them to die. This is the man on whose knees Effundi Mustafa sat.

When the other white men came later we were afraid, because we thought that they too had come to kill us. For a long time they left us alone. They built their villages and we used to give them food. They called the chiefs together and said they came in friendship and wanted to help us, and particularly they wanted to stop us from fighting among ourselves. This was a good thing, because for too long we had been fighting. That was the fault of the BaNgwana, because the BaNgwana used their magic to turn men's minds and make them traitors, so that they told where our camps were and how we could be surprised and captured. In those days we could trust nobody except our own family, and sometimes even they were bewitched.

I was chief in my father's place then, and even though I remembered what had happened to my father I offered to help the white man. They accepted my help, and for many months they ate my food. Then more and more white men came, and their villages grew. They brought some of their own food with them, yet they needed more of ours than we could spare. They did not do their own work but they asked us to supply men and women to do their work for them. I refused, because our people had work enough to do to keep their own fields cultivated and their own roofs thatched without working for foreigners. The white men said that in that case we would have to supply them with more food. They did not ask, they demanded, as though it was their land. I told them that it was my land, and my father's, and his father's before him, and that if they wanted to stay as my guests they were welcome to use the land to make their own plantations—there was room enough for all—but they would have to do their cutting and planting themselves. They said they had come to help us, but all they did was to send out men with guns whenever any of us reported any fighting among our neighbors. It was a good thing to stop the fighting, and we had all agreed. But when their men with guns started forcing us to work it was a bad thing. I took my family and my village and we all moved away deep into the forest and lived like savages until we could build another plantation.

The BaNgwana were the only people who helped the white man then, and they sold themselves just as they had sold us before. And it was the BaNgwana who told the white man exactly where we were living in the forest so even there we were not free from their guns. If we had had guns we would have driven them out, because they had not come to help us as they had said, they had come to make us slaves on our own land. But we had no guns.

After some years the white men were so many that they were able to send parties of soldiers into the forest. Their soldiers were not white, they were black like us, but they came from tribes to the north who were our enemies, so they were not on our side. We were forced to move back to where the white men were building the big road that now runs from Kisanganyi (Stanleyville). It took many years to build, and they demanded that we supply men—so many from each village—as well as food for all their soldiers, who stood with their guns in case we tried to escape. The white men did not always carry guns themselves, often they carried whips and they beat us like animals.

I remembered my father, and I said I would not let my people work for them. Because of the guns that had brought my people back to the roadside I said that we would supply whatever food we could spare, and for a time the white men accepted that. But they were not pleased. Then they came around and told us we had to plant cotton and other things we did not want to plant. They said they would pay us but I explained that if we planted cotton we would have to grow less food. They said we could buy food with the money we got for the cotton and I told them this was like the play of children, because we could easily grow our own food without money, and have enough left over to give them.

It was then that they told me that I was not a man, that I was evil, that I did not want to help my people, that I only wanted to make trouble. Therefore, they said, I was no longer chief. Masoudi was to be chief in my place. Masoudi was a weak young man who had been to one of the first schools set up by the white men, near their village of Matadi. He was like Effundi Mustafa. He had come from a BaBira family, but had followed the BaNgwana and sold himself to the white man. He had no heart, had no spirit. He was as you see him now, an empty shell filled with the words and thoughts of foreigners. He was not one of us. I told the white men that Masoudi could never be chief, because of this reason. He was a Christian as well, and that meant he could not lead the people as the representative of their ancestors, and he could not initiate men into manhood. Nobody would follow him.

The white men simply said that the people might not follow him; but they would obey him because if they didn't the police would be sent in with their guns. In any case, they said, tribal initiation was thoroughly evil and a wasteful thing. Didn't we realize that all the time the boys were doing nothing in the initiation camp, for month after month, they could be working on the plantations or on the road gangs? I tried to explain that initiation was necessary for us, for only by initiation can we fit ourselves to join the ancestors when we die.

The uninitiated have no right to respect in this life or after, and without initiation man would become an animal, living for himself alone, with no consideration for his family or his tribe.

I remember that was the first and last real argument I had with the white men. I tried hard to explain the way matters were with us, because I knew they were doing a terrible and wrong thing. But they would not listen. They were as children or as fools who can talk but can not reason, who can see but can not understand. Talk with such people is empty. Their heads were filled with strange notions. They said that we were to supply men to work alongside the BaNdaka, even with the Zande savages from the north . . . they only had enough sense to realize that nobody would work with the BaNgwana. They said we were all one people, even though we all speak different tongues. They said we were all friends, even though we are enemies. They said we were all under one God, by which they meant their God, and his son, the King Leopold. Here maybe they were right, for their God seems more powerful than ours, and more terrible and bloody.

[It was here that Matungi paused to ask me questions that were difficult to answer. How could our God be a God of peace and love when his symbol is a heart torn out and shown mutilated with thorns and dripping with blood; when we like to remember him as a tortured figure savagely nailed on a cross; when he insisted on our magically eating his flesh and drinking his blood every week; and when he gave us guns? And how could he be a good God when he allowed his people to fight among each other and kill each other all the time? It was all very well to fight people of a different god, like the BaNgwana, or the Azande or even the BaNdaka, though they were closer, but for a people to fight among each other, among one's own kindred, and then boast about it, this was to Matungi as incomprehensible as it was evil.]

The chief of the white men came to our village himself and called all the people together. He told them that I was no longer chief, that Masoudi was. People were astounded, because to them this was a heresy, and they expected the white man to be struck dead. But I stepped forward and said that the white man's head was turned by the sun and he did not understand that Masoudi could never be chief. However, Masoudi was like white men, so let him call himself chief, and let him take on all the foolishness of trying to deal with them. I told my people that I wanted nothing to do with the white man, and I did not want to be responsible to the ancestors for polluting the soil of our fathers by following the white man's ways. I gladly gave up being a chief in the eyes of the white man, but to them, my people, I would remain as had always been.

This pleased the village, and I think it, even pleased Masoudi, who also knew that he could never really be chief. But the white men caught me and told one of their soldiers, an Azande, to beat me. For this I have never forgiven them. They could have beaten me themselves, for they had proved themselves stronger with their guns, and it would have been no disgrace. But to have me beaten by one of those savages from the north is a shame I shall never forget. Even our enemies we treat like men, not like children. For a long time this made me burn inside with a fire, eating at my stomach, eating my strength and my sense. But I became wiser, and now that I know the white man better I do not feel hot; because he will kill himself as surely as he kills others. In trying to destroy the pride of others he loses his own, and becomes a worm. Look at them now. They are truly a people who fight themselves. They pretend they fight us, but they eat out of their own hearts and their own souls, and they are empty flesh. When they are gone there will be nobody to weep, only rejoicing. They lie so much to others, they cheat and they steal from each other and they sleep with each others' wives. They may be more powerful than we but we are greater, because we are men, not animals.

After Masoudi became chief I had nothing to do with the white men for some time. I thought that if I left them alone they would leave me and my people alone, and for a while it was so. Masoudi saw to it that cotton was planted, and that there were extra plantains to feed the road gangs, and he told some men to work on the roads. They asked me if they should do these things, and I told them that these things were nothing to do with me—they were white men's matters and Masoudi was the white man's chief. If they did not obey, then the white man would simply send in his foreign soldiers with whips and guns and lock them up in cages, like animals.

Even then I did not realize just how evil the white man was. I thought he was merely stealing our land, and sometimes our lives. This is to be expected when one tribe is stronger than another and when it needs more room for its people. But they were not content with this—they wanted to steal our souls as well.

It is our custom to come to the head of the family whenever there is any dispute we can not settle, and if the head of the family can not deal with it, he takes it to the chief. If the chief can not settle it, he takes it to the paramount chief. We do this because we believe it is better for disputes to be settled as simply as possible, and by the people themselves. It would be easy for the chief to settle all disputes simply by commanding, but this would merely stop the fight, it would not cure the wound. So we discuss our grievances, and all members of the family take a part because blame is seldom on one side alone. In this way many disputes were brought to me because I was the senior member of our village, Masoudi was not. I come from the oldest branch of the family. Men who were having trouble with their wives would bring their cases to me; women whose husbands failed to give them children or who beat them too often also came. Complaints about the BaNgwana and their bad magic always came straight to me, because I knew how to deal with those savages, for I have magic of my own.

But Masoudi did not like this, and he complained to the white man. The white man came and told me I was to hear no more cases, for I was no longer chief. Masoudi was to hear them, and record them in a special book, or send the disputants to the tribunal at Matadi if the case was serious. The white man said that if he ever heard that I was trying cases again, he would have me locked up in one of his boxes. He had been building these boxes at Matadi, and now he had a whole building full of them. Many men went in and never came out. There is a big graveyard right beside it, even today, and men are buried there without any consideration for the ancestors, and their souls are lost.

I paid little attention to the white man's warnings, because my people still would not go to Masoudi. I talked to Masoudi and told him that I would not interfere with his work, but that he was not to interfere with mine. If anyone brought a case to him he could enter it in his book and send it to the tribunal, but that he was not to let his eyes see what I was doing. He understood, and so I continued to be what I was, the real chief.

I had one other big fight with the white man though, and it was this fight that convinced me he was evil. Through Masoudi he managed to get all he wanted in the way of cotton, plantains and road workers. In time he came to collect taxes from all of us, out of the money he paid us for the cotton and plantains. The rest of the money he took back by fining us for various things, but none of this worried us very much. It was what we expected from a conquering people. But then the white man began to say that we were not to have more than one wife, and that we were to stop exchanging gifts of wealth at times of marriage. In this way he made many men and women lose their self-respect. What pride can a woman have if her husband does not think highly enough of her to give her parents a gift of many goats as a token of his esteem and trust? And what safety and happiness can the parents feel if they can not say, "Our son-in-law has given us so many goats he must intend to treat our daughter well and to care for her, for no man could afford to lose so much wealth?"

But even worse than this, the white man began to try to prevent our holding our initiation ceremonies, celebrating the manhood of our youth. They said that if we wanted to educate the boys we should send them to a mission school where they would learn to recite from a book. They said that our initiation schools were savage, and a waste of time. For all those months the boys and their fathers were secluded they could not work in the fields, and so fell behind in their work demanded of them by law. And during all this time even the women fell off in their work because they were busy drinking and dancing. In addition the white man added their lie that these schools were for no other purpose than to stir up discontent. If it were not so, why did we not allow the white man in to watch and supervise?

I told the white man that we did not let him watch because he would defile our youth with his filth; that his eyes were evil, and he could only bring evil to our souls; that his body was unclean and he would desecrate the holy ground of the ancestors; that his mind was twisted and he would only see and tell untruths; that his heart was stone and he would not understand and respect and so he could only bring unhappiness to us and to our ancestors. If it were otherwise, as it was with you, we would let him see—provided he purified his body and mind and heart in the way we do. But it could not be otherwise with him, for white men are what they are, animals. I told him that neither I nor my people would ever fail in our duties to the ancestors, and initiation is the highest duty, for only by initiation can we fit ourselves to join the ancestors when we die.

He did not like my words, but he listened. He was angry, but he saw that I and my people would never give way. He told me that people like myself should be locked away in a box forever, that we were concerned only for ourselves, that we did not wish the good of our people. I walked away and left him talking to himself.

Every three years I called out the dancers and we held initiations in all the villages around us, for even though I am chief only of this village, I am the initiation leader of many villages. And every three years the white men went around trying to persuade mothers not to let their sons enter. But I told the mothers that this was because the white men did not want the children to become men, that they wanted them to live and die as children, unfit to join the ancestors, because in this way white men would gradually win all the land, and we would just die out, with a home neither in this life nor in the afterlife. And so the women always entered their children, and the children became men, and we still survive and we are still worthy of our ancestors, still worthy to live on the ground they won for us. And one day it will be ours again, completely.

Only once did I get into real trouble—and that was over a young boy whose father was a Christian, and who had sent the boy to a mission school. He was the only Christian of his kind in Ndola, though there were a number of others of different kinds in the same village. They never talked to each other and they had different ceremonies and different priests. They said bad things about each other all the time. The young boy, Ibrahimo, was much more friendly with his own people than he was with the Christians, unlike his father. He wanted to join his friends in the initiation, and become a man with them, because he knew that otherwise he would be alone, like his father, not belonging anywhere. Being a Christian did not seem to make him part of the white man's world, anyway. So I tried to persuade Ibrahimo to come with me, and I tried to persuade his father. His mother also tried to persuade her husband, but our efforts were empty. The boy was collected in a car and taken away, far to the other side of Matadi, to a mission hospital. There he was circumcised, and the white man said that was as good as our circumcision, so we should treat him like a man. But now Ibrahimo can never become a man—he has had manhood taken away from him by the white man, and he has had his soul taken away from him. Perhaps when he dies he will go to the white man's world, but that can not be a good thing; and as long as he lives here he will belong nowhere.

Because of all I did and because of a curse I put on Ibrahimo's father to make him give way to his wife and child, I myself was sent to the tribunal at Matadi, and once again they threatened to put me in a box. But the ancestors were with me, and I was merely fined and told to go. I paid the fine with goats and chickens I stole from Masoudi, because it was really his doing, and I put a curse on Ibrahimo's father that people should always steal from him, just as he had stolen the very life from his son.

I have tried hard to understand the white man and his ways, but I can only see harm. What happiness have they brought us? They have given us a road we did not need, a road that brings more and more foreigners and enemies into our midst, causing trouble, making our women unclean, forcing us to a way of life that is not ours, planting crops we do not want, doing slave's work. At least the BaNgwana left us our beliefs, but the white man even wants to steal these from us. He sends us missions to destroy our belief and to teach our children to recite fine-sounding words; but they are words we believe in anyway, most of them. And we live according to our beliefs, which is more than the white man does. And the missions teach the children to have no respect for their parents. Is that a good thing? And they take them away from their parents, and then the other white men take them away to foreign lands. They say these lands are not foreign, because they are next to ours—but they must be foreign, because their beliefs are different. The circumcised can not live with the uncircumcised. Let the uncircumcised live by themselves, for them that is the right thing to do, and we have no quarrel with them for that—it is merely not our way. But let us live our way, because for us that is right.

The white man talks of law where we talk of the way of our ancestors; he talks of what is right or wrong where we talk of what is good or bad. I have looked at their way and do not like it, and I do not believe it is good for our people. It is better to do something because one believes in the ancestors than because one is afraid of being beaten or put in a box. And it is better to believe that something is good because goodness comes from it, than merely to say, "It is so because we have written it so in our book." Perhaps the white man believes in his own way; if so, let him keep it, and let us keep ours, and let us both be men, not animals.

In the initiation schools, we teach our boys about the ancestors that gave them birth, and they are born again by the ancestors, as men. We teach them how they must behave as men in order to live in a way pleasing to the ancestors, so that when they die they will live in peace. And that is why they find it easy to live the way they should—no man wants to die to be left alone, unwanted in either world, as Ibrahimo will die.

The white man says we teach our children to hate the white man in our initiation schools. We do not. We merely teach them to believe, and to be men. We are not like the Kitawala (a secret society of recent origin, primarily anti-white), for the Kitawala only exists to teach hatred of the white man, it teaches how to kill those who have tried to destroy our souls. It is not a good thing, but the white man brought it on himself. In the old days there was the Anyota (the leopard-man society, a traditional secret society) and other beliefs like it, which killed in times of trouble. But it only killed one or two, and only until such time as the deaths made people realize that they were going against the ancestors. When they realized this, and behaved as they should, the trouble ended and the killings ended. But the white man said the Anyota was evil, and the white man killed all the members it could find. And so the white man brought about a trouble that could only be ended, in some people's minds, by killing the white man himself. Our people do not believe like this, but we can understand it.

A man should behave the way he believes. To make someone else behave in a different way by pointing a gun at him, or by threatening him with a beating or with the box is evil, because it makes him less of a man, it makes him go against his beliefs; it makes him dishonest. Yet the white man says this is right. The white man has made it almost impossible for us to keep our beliefs, he makes us do bad things every day; he forces us to offend our ancestors. I do it myself, because I am afraid of the box. It is easier to plant the white man's cotton, to work for him on the roads, to treat him as though he were master of our souls as well as of our bodies. I hope the ancestors will understand and forgive.

I have tried to keep my dignity. I have tried to remain a man in the eyes of my father whatever I may have done with my body, I have never betrayed my beliefs with my mind. But for my children it is different. They do not know good and bad as I know it; the white man fills their heads with different ideas and they doubt. I circumcise my sons, but I can not circumcise their minds and their hearts. I can make their bodies acceptable, but they have to make their souls fit for the afterlife.

I have seen too much uncleanliness to have escaped its touch myself. But I have tried. And until I die, which can not be long, I shall keep trying, for myself and my people. After I am dead there will be no one left, unless somewhere I have planted a seed that has yet to grow and provide nourishment for those who live on. If I have done this, then maybe I too shall be thought fit to be given life at the side of my fathers.

MISSIONARIES AND EMPIRE

When the white man first came here, he had the Bible and we had the land. Then the white man said to us, "Come, let us kneel and pray together." So we knelt and closed our eyes and prayed, and when we opened our eyes again, lo!—we had the Bible and he had the land.

Archbishop Desmond Tutu, repeating the parable that had passed among his
   Xhosa people.

10

CHIEF KABONGO

The Coming of the Pink Cheeks
Kenya

Editor's Notes: Chief Kabongo (who lived from the 1870s to 1950s) of the Kikuyu tribe in Kenya describes the step-by-step undermining of tribal society by the aggressive British colonists and missionaries. The main source of conflict was land which native people regarded as sacred and belonging to the whole tribe. On the other hand, colonists assumed that land belonged to the King of England and was to be bought or seized by individual owners. This undermining of the tribe's sole means of livelihood had devastating results and caused starvation as well as environmental degradation. The hut tax and the imposition of tribal chiefs appointed from outside, instead of by local tribal councils, further devastated traditional societies.

Richard St. Barbe Baker (1889–1982) was an important English forester, environmentalist, and author of many books. In Kenya he founded Men of the Trees, an organization supporting reforestation which he then took to other places in the world. In 1955 he published Kabongo, *which he described as, "the simple story of a Kikuyu from birth to within a few hours of his death, as told by himself."*

The Europeans were called Muthungu (Pink Cheeks); and St. Barbe Baker was proud to be known as Muthungu wa Miti (Pink Cheek of the Trees).

One evening my father called me to him and told me the stories he had heard of the baba neoipe, the White Fathers, men from a far land across the seas, who had come to parts of our country some time before. I too had heard of these but never had I seen one. There were strange tales of new ways of communication by marks made on a kind of white leaf. There were tales of a new

From *Kabongo: The Story of a Kikuyu Chief*, by Richard St. Barbe Baker. Oxford: George Ronald Publisher, 1955, pp. 93–126, selections. Reprinted by permission of the publisher.

god and a new magic for making sick men well. A friend of my very youngest brother had been to a place where these people were and had seen them and spoken to them and was going back to learn how to make these marks. He told how these men had pink cheeks and eyes like the sky and how they wore hair on their chins. Always too they wore long clothes so that their limbs were hidden. They were kind men, he said, and one could speak our tongue. They gave food to all who went to hear their tales and many would go for that alone. . . .

It was from this time that changes came to our people. Other strangers came from afar, bringing many new ways and things.

They brought red beads and coils of iron and brass wire which our women liked and bales of cotton cloth to wear. They had sticks which sent out fire and could kill a long way off. They were always on safari, going from place to place and we thought they were lonely and we were sorry for them, for it seemed to us that they had no home.

At first, my father was troubled in his thoughts and wondered if these were the people who were meant in the prophecy of the great medicine-man, Mogo wa Kebiro, who a very long time ago had dreamt that strangers would come into the land who would do terrible things to our people, having sticks which made fire and an Iron Snake which no spears or arrows could kill. He had warned our people to be polite to these strangers, but not invite them into our homes. We must not fight them, for we could not kill the Iron Snake and they would answer with sticks which threw fire. . . .

The first time I met one of these strangers was at a meeting of our Council. He was already there when I came. He was seated on a curious seat of wood and cloth, with places to rest his arms and back. He looked ill to me, for his face was pale, with yellow hair on it. I could not see his body, for it was hid by clothes and his feet were tied up tight in leather. On his head was something like a basket upside down, only much thicker. Fire came out of a small black stick in his mouth.

Beside him on the ground sat a Kikuyu, who spoke with this Pink Cheek in his own tongue and told him all that was said by the Elders and who told the Elders what the Pink Cheek had said. Two strangers, men from the coast country, sat behind with many boxes beside them and straps for carrying them lying at their feet. . . .

He was speaking when I came and at some length. When he stopped, the interpreter took it up.

"The Muthungu wants to grow a new kind of food," he said, "and for this he needs land. In return for land to plant he will show you his new way of growing and will give you a new kind of Muro, which will dig the earth in half as much time as the old."

"How much land does he want?" asked the leading Elder.

'He wants enough land for his hut and for his shamba [farm].' He will walk with you and show it and put a stick where he wants,' replied the man.

The Elders drew together to discuss. The Pink Cheek sat in his seat.

The Elder who had sold his land to my father, he who was the son of Ndemo, spoke.

"I have much land," he said, "and my sons are few. Until my grandsons marry there is land that I do not need. Let the Pink Cheek stranger have some of that land on which to grow his new food. For we must remember the words of the seers and be kind to these men who may bring us good."

The elders agreed and asked the interpreter to explain. He turned to the Pink Cheek and spoke.

The Pink Cheek smiled, nodded and made a sign to the strangers who carried his boxes. From one they took a roll of cloth and laid it at his feet.

"This is a gift the Muthungu would ask you to accept," the interpreter told them.

At a sign from the leading Elder, some of the others too came forward and, at the Pink Cheek's feet, they laid eggs and two live fowls which they were offering to him. The leading Elder bade him welcome and said that the Elders wished him all prosperity. With a grand sweeping gesture of his arm, the elder made him free of all our country, a customary way of expressing hospitality.

When, as the sun grew hot, and after many signs of friendship, the Pink Cheek went away with his men, we sat in consultation over the event. Some were pleased and expected much from this newcomer, while others were fearful. I myself could not feel good or bad. Perhaps there would be both. The Pink Cheek man had not the fierce look of a warrior.

I felt we could only wait and see.

We waited for two moons and then he came back. This time there came others with him, two Pink Cheeks and many men from the coast who spoke Kiswahili which our Pink Cheek began to speak also. One of the others spoke it a great deal; he it was who gave orders to the men. Under his direction they settled themselves in an old clearing three spears' throw from our shamba. They put up a hut for the Pink Cheeks made of poles and cloth and they burned big fires. Very quickly they began to work. As I weeded in my shamba, I could hear the noise of their hatchets and the crash of the trees they were felling. They were felling big trees and after some days when they had all they wanted, they began to build huts. The huts they built were not like ours. They were square and divided into several parts and they had doors that were only for light and not for entering. They built many of these huts and we wondered what they were for. Round the clearing they put a wall of wood. Then they began to make bigger clearings, and they dug the ground with a knife on a wheel which was pulled by an ox. This they called a plough. It was very quick to dig.

When the growing season came and the harvest, we said that Ngai must be pleased with these people, for their crops were good, very good, and the grain they grew was big.

They brought new cattle with them of a big kind, and chickens larger than I had ever seen, whose eggs were the size of two of ours. They brought good magic for illness as well and it seemed that they were all medicine men. When their own men were ill they gave them this magic and soon they were well again. Our own people began to go them for this, taking them offerings of honey and antelope, which they liked very much.

They seemed to be settled and prospering. When they wanted to make more clearings they would ask us to help and our young men would go and work. For this work they would pay them as in their country is the custom, instead of all helping each other.

At first they would pay them with new grains or eggs that would grow into big chickens; but one day they were given round pieces of metal. At first they could not understand. But one of the men from the coast told them that this metal, which they called a coin or money, would in the towns buy them wonderful things, such as wheels that men walked on and that went very fast. Strange tales these men told, and it was not long before these things began to come to the market and these metal coins became a usual way of buying and selling. . . .

For some years my eldest son had been going to a school kept by some Pink Cheeks only two hours' journey away. These were not the White Fathers, to whom my brother had gone, but were quite different. They wore clothes like the Pink Cheeks who farmed, and many of them were women. They had a medicine house where there were many ill people; there were good medicine-men and good things were done and sick people were made well. Every day my son would go before the sun was high and would come back before the sun set. Then he would eat and fall asleep, too tired to sit around the fire and be told the stories and history of our people or hear of the work that had been done or learn the customs and ways of our people and their laws and conduct. . . .

It was in these days that a Pink Cheek man came one day to our Council. He came from far, from where many of these people lived in houses made of stone and where they held their own Council.

He sat in our midst and he told us of the King of the Pink Cheeks, who was a great king and lived in a land over the seas.

"This great King is now your King," he said. "And this land is all his land, though he has said you may live on it as you are his people and he is as your father and you are as his sons."

This was strange news. For this land was ours. We had bought our land with cattle in the presence of the Elders and had taken the oath and it was our own. We had no king, we elected our Councils and they made our laws. A strange king could not be our king and our land was our own. We had had no battle, no one had fought us to take away our land as, in the past, had sometimes been. This land we had had from our fathers and our fathers' fathers, who had bought it. How then could it belong to this king?

With patience, our leading Elder tried to tell this to the Pink Cheek and he listened. But at the end he said, "This we know. But in spite of this, what I have told you is a fact. You have now a King—a good and great King who loves his people and you are among his people. In the town called Nairobi is a Council or Government that acts for the King. And his laws are your laws. . . . "

For many moons this thing was much talked of by us. Then, when no more Pink Cheeks came and things went on as they had always been, we spoke no more.

Sometimes we heard of strange happenings, or even saw them ourselves, but for the most part life was still as it had always been. The Iron Snake, which I had never seen, had come and had carried men on it, not of our people; then a big path was made through the country half a day from our land. It was wide enough for three elephants to walk abreast. And stones were laid on it and beaten flat, so that grain could have been threshed there.

As the years passed and more and more strange things happened, it seemed to me that this path or road was a symbol of all changes. It was along this road now that came news from other parts; and along it came the new box-on-wheels that made men travel many days journey in one day and that brought things for the market that the women wanted to have, clothes or beads to wear and pots for cooking. Along this road the young men went when they left to work with the Pink Cheeks and along it too they went when that day came that they traveled to fight in the war over the sea that the Pink Cheeks made against each other.

By the time that my father, Kimani, died and his spirit joined those of our ancestors, our own land was poor too. For even though many of our family had gone away to work for the Pink Cheeks, our numbers had increased and there was now no room for the land to rest and it was tired. The food it grew was poor and there was not enough grown on it for all to eat. Those of our family who worked for the Pink Cheeks sent us food and coins that we could buy food with, for else we could not live.

Little by little, too, the rains fell less. When I was a boy I remember the rains came in plenty twice every year, the little rains and the big rains, and on the hottest days there would be heavy dews, for the trees kept the land cool.

Now it was different; now the little rains had gone and the big rains had become little rains. The big rivers had become little ones and dried up in the hottest time, and I saw this was not good.

Now that my father, Kimani, was dead, I had been chosen Muramati of our *mbari*. I was also now a Ceremonial Elder, a member of the Sacrificial Council. . . .

. . . a young man, son of one of my brothers, who was a schoolteacher [said,] "I have read in books that it is the trees that make the rains come. Now that the trees are cut down there is no rain. In the Sacred Grove on the hills there is rain. . . . "

As there was now so little land and we were so many, the boys as they became men would go away, some to work on farms for the Pink Cheeks, some to a new kind of school-farm for men, where they learned the new customs and also some curious ways; for these grown men were made to play games like little boys, running after balls which they threw. This they did instead of good work.

Munene, one of my younger brothers, had been one of these. He had been away a long time, and when he came back he wore clothes like a Pink Cheek and he came with one of them, in a box-on-wheels, which is called motor-car, along the new road.

The Pink Cheek called a Council together and when all, both Elders and the young men, were assembled and sat round, he spoke. He spoke of Munene; he told us of his learning and of his knowledge of the customs of the Pink Cheeks and of his cleverness at organizing.

"Because of this," he said, "and because he is a wise man, the Government, the Council of Muthungu that meets in Nairobi, have honored him and, in honoring him, are honoring you all."

He paused and looked around at us. Beside him Munene stood smiling.

"He has been appointed Chief of this district and he will be your mouth and our mouth. He will tell us the things that you want to say and he will tell you the things that we want to say to you. He has learned our language and our laws and he will help you to understand and keep them."

We Elders looked at each other. Was this the end of everything that we had known and worked for? What magic had this son of my father made that he who was not yet an Elder should be made leader over us all who were so much older and wiser in the ways of our people? It was as if a thunderbolt had fallen among us.

The Pink Cheeks went on,

"Your new Chief will collect the tax on huts, and choose the places for the new schools that you will build everywhere, so that your children may be taught to read and write. He will raise the money for that from you all. I have spoken. . . . "

When the Pink Cheek had gone there was much talk. We asked Munene to tell us how this had come about and why he was set above the Elders in this way.

"It is because they do not understand our laws and Councils," he told us. "Because I speak their language and because when I went away in their wars I had many medals."

The medals we knew about, for we had seen them. Many had them.

We spoke then of the tax on huts. It was heavy, for some men had many huts. Those men who had gone to work on the farms of the Pink Cheeks sent us money, but this we needed to buy food. More men, therefore, must go.

Munene gave us some good advice. He told that men were wanted in Nairobi to build the new houses made of stone, both for the Pink Cheeks to live in and where they sat to make business and trading. Our men could go there and earn coins and then they could come back when they had plenty.

This was good, for in this way we would pay our tax and no man would be taken by the Pink Cheeks for not paying. So our young men went away down the new road, we were left to grow what food we could, and all was as usual. . . .

It was while these men were still away to make money for our hut tax that ten of our people came back from the farms where they worked. They were not needed, they said, there was no work for them there. With many others, they had been sent back without money and without food, because there were bad people who troubled the land.

This was the beginning. Along the new road had come big boxes-on-wheels that they called lorries [trucks], in which they had carted logs from the forest. Now these came filled with people. Many had no homes, for their land had gone to the Pink Cheeks. Some had no homes because their land had gone to be mined for gold. We could not let them starve, so we took them on our land.

It was the end of the dry season and there was little food left in the storehouses. Our *mbari* had now grown big, and all these newcomers on our land must eat too. Altogether there were 1,200 people on the 200 acres of land my grandfather's father had bought. There was not enough room to grow all the food.

In the dry season many goats and cattle had died for want of water. The harvest had been thin and there was little left, and there was no money to buy food; the last had gone for our hut tax. I heard the crying of children and I saw the women weaken in their work. The old men would sit near their huts, too feeble to walk. . . .

The Council met again under the Mugomo tree. There were few, for the new laws of the Pink Cheeks had forbidden big meetings. I looked round at my friends and was sad. Their faces were anxious and their skin was loose on their bones. Even Muonji, who always used to joke, had no smile. For each one had been hungry for many days, and each one told the same story. Everywhere there was a shortage of food, for there was no land and all the time people were being sent back from distant parts. There was uneasiness and some of our tribesmen were troubling our people too much because they wanted to drive the Pink Cheeks from our country. This the Elders told in Council and were uneasy, for we wanted no war with the Pink Cheeks; we only wanted land to grow food.

"We must ask the Council of the Pink Cheeks to lend us some of the land we had lent to them," said one who came from a place where there was land held by the government for future farms and not yet in use.

All agreed that this would be good and for Munene, who as Chief was our spokesman, we made a message to give to the Governor. What we told to Munene he made marks with and, when we had finished, he spoke it to us again and it was good.

Munene took our message and he took also a gift of honey and eggs and went away down the long road and left us to wait.

We waited many days, with hope. It was a whole moon before Munene came back. He came to us slowly and sadly, and we knew from his way that the news was bad.

"They will not give the land," he said. "They say they have no more land for us. . . . "

So I am sitting before my hut and I wait. For soon the time will come for me to creep away into the forest to die. Day by day my people grow thinner and weaker and the children are hungry; and who am I, an old man, to eat the food that would come to them?

As I sit I ponder often on the ancient prophesy of Mogo wa Kebiro. Has the Pink Cheek brought good to my people? Are the new ways he has shown us better than our own ways?

Something has taken away the meaning of our lives; it has taken the full days, the good work in the sunshine, the dancing and the song; it has taken away laughter and the joy of living; the kinship and the love within a family; above all, it has taken from us the wise way of our living in which our lives from birth to death were dedicated to Ngai, supreme of all, and which, with our system of age groups and our Councils, insured for all our people a life of responsibility and goodness. Something has taken away our belief in our Ngai and in the goodness of men. And there is not enough land on which to feed. . . .

The young men are learning new ways, the children make marks which they call writing, but they forget their own language and customs, they know not the laws of their people, and they do not pray to Ngai. They ride fast in motor-cars, they work firesticks that kill, they make music from a box. But they have no land and no food and they have lost laughter.

11

JOMO KENYATTA

THE GENTLEMEN OF THE JUNGLE
Kenya

Editor's Notes: Kenya became a British colony in 1895. In his 1938 anthropological work, Jomo Kenyatta includes this folk tale which he says illustrates the relationship between the Gikuyu and the Europeans. It describes, in satirical form, the gradual process by which the English absorbed most of the land in Kenya, the process which took place during the life of Chief Kabongo.

Kenyatta, known as the founding father of Kenya, served as its first president from 1964 until 1978. He studied anthropology in England with a brief stint at a Moscow University. Upon his return to Kenya, he became a political activist and served in various leadership roles in political organizations devoted to the expulsion of the British.

Once upon a time an elephant made a friendship with a man. One day a heavy thunderstorm broke out, the elephant went to his friend, who had a little hut at the edge of the forest, and said to him: "My dear good man, will you please let me put my trunk inside your hut to keep it out of this torrential rain?"

The man, seeing what situation his friend was in, replied: "My dear good elephant, my hut is very small, but there is room for your trunk and myself. Please put your trunk in gently."

The elephant thanked his friend, saying: "You have done me a good deed and one day I shall return your kindness."

But what followed? As soon as the elephant put his trunk inside the hut, slowly he pushed his head inside, and finally flung the man out in the rain, and then lay down comfortably inside his friend's hut, saying: "My dear good

---

Jomo Kenyatta, *Facing Mount Kenya* (New York: Vintage Books, 1965), 47–51.

friend, your skin is harder than mine, and as there is not enough room for both of us, you can afford to remain in the rain while I am protecting my delicate skin from the hailstorm."

The man, seeing what his friend had done to him, started to grumble; the animals in the nearby forest heard the noise and came to see what was the matter. All stood around listening to the heated argument between the man and his friend the elephant. In this turmoil the lion came along roaring, and said in a loud voice: "Don't you all know that I am the King of the Jungle! How dare anyone disturb the peace of my kingdom?"

On hearing this the elephant, who was one of the high ministers in the jungle kingdom, replied in a soothing voice, and said: "My lord, there is no disturbance of the peace in your kingdom. I have only been having a little discussion with my friend here as to the possession of this little hut which your lordship sees me occupying."

The lion, who wanted to have "peace and tranquility" in his kingdom, replied in a noble voice, saying: "I command my ministers to appoint a Commission of Enquiry to go thoroughly into this matter and report accordingly." He then turned to the man and said: "You have done well by establishing friendship with my people, especially with the elephant, who is one of my honourable ministers of state. Do not grumble any more, your hut is not lost to you. Wait until the sitting of my Imperial Commission, and there you will be given plenty of opportunity to state your case. I am sure that you will be pleased with the findings of the Commission."

The man was very pleased by these sweet words from the King of the Jungle, and innocently waited for his opportunity, in the belief that naturally the hut would be returned to him.

The elephant, obeying the sound of this master, got busy with other ministers to appoint the Commission of Enquiry. The following elders of the jungle were appointed to sit in the Commission: (1) Mr. Rhinoceros; (2) Mr. Buffalo; (3) Mr. Alligator; (4) The Rt. Hon. Mr. Fox to act as chairman; and (5) Mr. Leopard to act as Secretary to the Commission.

On seeing the personnel, the man protested and asked if it was not necessary to include in this Commission a member from his side. But he was told that it was impossible, since no one from his side was well enough educated to understand the intricacy of jungle law. Further, that there was nothing to fear, for the members of the Commission were all men of repute for their impartiality in justice, and as they were gentlemen chosen by God to look after the interests of races less adequately endowed with teeth and claws, he might rest assured that they would investigate the matter with the greatest care and report impartially. The Commission sat to take the evidence.

The Rt. Hon. Mr. Elephant was first called. He came along with a superior air, brushing his tusks with a sapling which Mrs. Elephant had provided, and in an authoritative voice said: "Gentlemen of the Jungle, there is no need for me to waste your valuable time in relating a story which I am sure you all know.

I have always regarded it as my duty to protect the interests of my friends, and this appears to have caused the misunderstanding between myself and my friend here. He invited me to save his hut from being blown away by a hurricane. As the hurricane had gained access owing to the unoccupied space in the hut, I considered it necessary, in my friend's own interests, to turn the undeveloped space to a more economic use by sitting in it myself; a duty which any of you would undoubtedly have performed with equal readiness in similar circumstances."

After hearing the Rt. Hon. Mr. Elephant's conclusive evidence, the Commission called Mr. Hyena and other elders of the jungle, who all supported what Mr. Elephant had said. They then called the man, who began to give his own account of the dispute. But the Commission cut him short, saying: "My good man, please confine yourself to relevant issues. We have already heard the circumstances from various unbiased sources; all we wish you to tell us is whether the undeveloped space in your hut was occupied by anyone else before Mr. Elephant assumed his position?"

The man began to say: "No, but—"

But at this point the Commission declared that they had heard sufficient evidence from both sides and retired to consider their decision. After enjoying a delicious meal at the expense of the Rt. Hon. Mr. Elephant, they reached their verdict, called the man, and declared as follows: "In our opinion this dispute has arisen through a regrettable misunderstanding due to the backwardness of your ideas. We consider that Mr. Elephant has fulfilled his sacred duty of protecting your interests. As it is clearly for your good that the space should be put to its most economic use, and as you yourself have not yet reached the stage of expansion which would enable you to fill it, we consider it necessary to arrange a compromise to suit both parties. Mr. Elephant shall continue his occupation of your hut, but we give you permission to look for a site when you can build another hut more suited to your needs, and we will see that you are well protected."

The man, having no alternative, and fearing that his refusal might expose him to the teeth and claws of members of the Commission, did as they suggested. But no sooner had he built another hut than Mr. Rhinoceros charged in with his horn lowered and ordered the man to quit. A Royal Commission was again appointed to look into the matter, and the same finding was given. This procedure was repeated until Mr. Buffalo, Mr. Leopard, Mr. Hyena and the rest were all accommodated with new huts. Then the man decided that he must adopt an effective method of protection, since Commissions of Enquiry did not seem to be of any use to him. He sat down and said: *Wg'enda thi ndagaga* motegi,' which literally means 'there is nothing that treads on the earth that cannot be trapped,' or in other words, you can fool people for a time, but not for ever.

Early one morning, when the huts already occupied by the jungle lords were all beginning to decay and fall to pieces, he went out and built a bigger and better hut a little distance away. No sooner had Mr. Rhinoceros seen it than he came rushing in, only to find that Mr. Elephant was already inside, sound asleep. Mr. Leopard next came in at the window, Mr. Lion, Mr. Fox and Mr. Buffalo entered the doors, while Mr. Hyena howled for a place in the shade and Mr. Alligator basked on the roof.

Presently they all began disputing about their rights of penetration, and from disputing they came to fighting, and while they were all embroiled together the man set the hut on fire and burnt it to the ground, jungle lords and all. Then he went home, saying: "Peace is costly, but it's worth the expense," and lived happily ever after.

12

WILLIAM CONTON
COMING HOME
Gambia

Editor's Notes: The first excerpt from William Conton's semi-autobiographical novel describes his astonishment at encountering for the first time a British laborer upon his arrival in Liverpool from Africa. The second excerpt deals with the description of changes at home upon Conton's return after five years of education in England. By this time, the process of colonization was well on its way to destroying the ancient, closely-knit tribal customs and bringing in so-called modernization characterized by materialism and loss of individual initiative.

Conton (1925–2003) was born in Gambia, West Africa. He was educated in schools in West Africa, as well as at Durham University in England from which he received a bachelor's degree. He spent his career in education in Sierra Leone and later at the United Nations Educational, Scientific, and Cultural Organization (UNESCO).

Liverpool next day was gray, cold, wet and foggy; and the promised land looked most unpromising from the deck of the ship. Once ashore, however, the towering buildings, massed traffic, and attractive shops kept us staring and gaping while waiting for our trains to various parts of the country. The sight of white people *en masse* was itself something which required some getting used to; but the thing that took us really aback was our first sight of a white man sweeping a gutter. He was a short, seedy-looking, rather dirty man, with heavy working boots and stained, well-worn clothes, but unmistakably a white man nevertheless; and actually standing right down in the gutter sweeping it, collecting the rubbish on a shovel and tipping it into a wheelbarrow. We stood

From *The African*, by William Conton (Boston: Little, Brown, 1960): pp. 53–55, 114–119, 120–124.

in utter disbelief, at some little distance from him, expecting him at any moment either to vanish like a gremlin down the nearest drain, or else to turn dark brown. I suppose if you had asked us beforehand who swept gutters in England, we should have replied, after a moment or two's reflection, that we supposed some of the English drains, at least, must have the honor of being swept by white men; for even all the stowaways and workless migrants from Africa and the West Indies could not provide enough labor for so many menial tasks. But no one had prepared us beforehand by any such question; and the sight of that man almost felled us.

"Thank God for bringing me here," breathed Appiah reverently, the first among us to recover his breath. "I always suspected there was some good reason for my coming to Britain."

And I think that summed up how most of us felt. We did not lose respect for the white man—very far from it. What we did lose, however (and long overdue was the loss), was an illusion created by the role the white man plays in Africa: that he is a kind of demigod whose hands must never get dirty, who must not be allowed to carry anything heavier than a portfolio or wield any implement heavier than a pen. Without realizing it, we had come to think of the white man only in the role of missionary, civil servant, or senior business executive, one who was always behind the desk, never in front of it. We saw him as one who always gave orders, never took them, who could have any job he liked for the asking. So to realize that that man was perfectly happy working in that gutter (snatches of his melancholy whistling reached us faintly where we stood) was a most salutary experience. It was now possible for us to like the white man. For before you can like (as distinct from merely admiring or emulating), you must feel kinship, a shared humanity, the possibility of common experiences and destinies. As we resumed our walk past the sweeper, he looked up and grinned cheerfully at us, leaning for a moment on his brush. We waved and grinned back; and in that mute exchange of greetings there was erased in a moment the memory of the behavior of the stewards on board. The latter had acted as if the gods had decreed that the black man should minister and the white man be ministered unto, and that they were stewards and we passengers only by special dispensation. Our friend the road-sweeper, on the other hand, was so far from harboring any such notions that he had found time to give us, in his own way, a welcome to Liverpool.

We were soon to find, as countless thousands of colonial students in the United Kingdom must have found, that the Britisher at home is an altogether different creature, and a much more lovable one, than the Britisher overseas. . . .

Thus, five years after I had first left it, I returned to my country, a little sadder and a little wiser. And it was to a very different country that the M. V. *Adonkia* was carrying me that July. I first noticed the change in the attitude of the ship's crew. The shipping company had at last come to realize that it would lose more now by alienating the African first-class passenger than by alienating his white counterpart. The balance of power in Africa was swinging irresistibly across the color bar, and a lot of ideas required adjusting in consequence. It was clearly a bitter pill for most of those stewards to swallow. I was amused to notice that now African passengers were receiving ungrudging and even ingratiating service on board. Moreover (an even greater transformation, in a sense) African stewards had been engaged, and were accepted perfectly naturally by their white colleagues and by white passengers alike.

The contemplation of these changes whetted even further my curiosity to get home and observe at first hand what had taken place in West Africa during those five years to overcome such deep-seated prejudices and habits. I was soon to see that developments were in motion on that continent as complex and profound as any which had overtaken a race of human beings anywhere at any time.

I landed at home to find that, during my absence, my country too had been swallowing pills—a large and indigestible dose of the materialism of "Western civilization." I came back to a stimulated land, pepped up into frantic, exhausting activity. It was not merely physical appearances that had altered so completely, the buildings, harbors, roads, bridges and so on, although the change here was marvelous enough. Much more fascinating to me were the changes in the people and, I soon found, much more disturbing too. New motives for action, new attitudes toward others, were as apparent in them as in the shipping company's crews. There were new lusts too, which I did not remember being so blatantly indulged formerly—the lust for quick power, for quick riches; the unconcern as to what methods were employed in the process; the readiness to use, and even deliberately to foster, age-old intertribal animosities. These had now been given a terribly sharp edge, driven with the force and on the scale possible in a community which had been suddenly presented with the whole gamut of Western institutions. It was not that the African was just a nice chap, innocent and simple, who had been corrupted overnight by too intimate an association with an evil acquaintance. Rather was it that, by setting out on a deliberate policy of abandoning almost abruptly a way of life which our forebears had pursued contentedly for many centuries, and adopting that of a distant northern people, we had reached a point where we were finding it increasingly difficult to keep a foothold on anything. We were in danger of losing our sense of direction, of purpose, of faith in ourselves.

I found myself drawn helplessly (and, I may add, without any feeling of regret) into the same aimless, puzzled, befogged existence. Short-term, materialistic objectives which in a clearer atmosphere I should have recognized as quite inadequate seemed all that was worth living for. Collecting as many degrees as possible; seeing in supporting a political party or leader merely the chance to draw in time a minister's salary of three thousand per annum; progressing as rapidly as possible up the ladder of car ownership which stretched from the Ford Popular to the Cadillac—all around me these were the things that now mattered, and I slipped easily into the same frame of mind. There had been a great increase in wealth, most of it obtained through unlicensed diamond mining (which every single Songhaian worth his salt had by now convinced himself was illegal without being immoral). Through this activity fortunes substantial by any standards and fabulous by ours could be picked up in a matter of weeks. Some of the consequences were laughable—there were diamond miners whose new American cars served them not only as vehicles, but also as living room, dining room, and bedroom. There were others who put brand-new carpets in their houses and then respectfully walked round them every time they wished to cross the room. Change was still being asked for and given when church collections were taken up, as it always had been. But this was now often done as a gesture which helped to draw attention to the color of the banknote the worshiper put in the plate, instead of, as before, out of genuine necessity. On my first visit to Lokko after my return, I met a young man of about my own age whom I remembered as a carefree urchin. He had not had a single day of schooling; nor, when I left the village, had he a single pair of trousers to his name. Now he was supervising the putting of finishing touches on the largest house in Lokko—his own property, with two stories, and a gleaming aluminum roof, complete with built-in water tank. He did not trouble to disguise the source of his new-found wealth; and in fact a visit which it was known he had paid, without evident reason, to Europe via the Lebanon would have given everyone the clue if he had. The only point for speculation about that journey was which particular method had been used on this occasion to prevent discovery of the stones by the increasingly sharp-eyed customs officials at Sagresa Airport. Musa himself was reticent on this score, but his sister boasted loudly that the diamonds had left the country stitched between the soles of his shoes.

"Drivers only see the smoke from other people's cars," she would reply to anyone who suggested that her brother had done something wrong, "not from their own." And who was I to deny the truth of this modern version of the "beam in thine own eye" retort?

Small wonder then that my homecoming was not, either for me or for my family, the business of noble sentiments and high hopes which my departure had been. We were all glad to be reunited of course. But after the embracing, the libations and thank-offerings, and the traditional dances and formal parties were over, it seemed as if everyone were relieved to be able to get back to the more urgent business of making a living in a world incomparably faster, and more ruthlessly competitive, than that I had left. Only in the American mission compound did I find that the atmosphere of sanity and calm still survived—and the irony of this was faintly bitter.

I know now, of course, that it was not merely lust for filthy lucre that was making us forget ideals of service and the need for admitting higher responsibilities. The struggle to earn a livelihood in Songhai had now become much harder for those into whose hands the new wealth had not fallen. The price of staple foods had soared as their production had declined because of the exodus from farming to mining; and rice was being imported from as far away as Italy. I know that my father and mother were facing very acute difficulties at home; and though they never complained to me, every penny I was able to give them I knew was put to good use. But my giving was sometimes grudging, to my own surprise. In Europe, there are official and state-administered welfare services. In Negro Africa, as I had told the Morrises, the structure of poor relief, old-age pensions, sickness and unemployment benefits had always been equally well-devised and equally adequate for its purposes—although it was entirely private and "voluntary." Your "brother" was anyone who originated from the same village or town, and to refuse to help him in time of need was unthinkable. But all this was changing fast now. The sense of family inter-dependence, cement of our society, seemed to be going out of the country with the diamonds; and the European's exaggerated individualism, his constant exalting of the single human being, at the polls, in the classroom, and in the sight of God, was sweeping in. Social cohesion was being pawned for the material well-being of the individual, and our mental hospitals were beginning to fill up as a result. Birthrights were being sold daily in our markets for a mess of pottage.

I cannot describe myself as being so much disillusioned as unhinged. I was rudderless, at the mercy of every wind, without purpose or stability. . . .

13

CHIEF AWOLOWO

CLASH BETWEEN OLD AND NEW Nigeria

Editor's Notes: A unique feature of this excerpt is the extended account of what Nigerian tribal life was like prior to the coming of the white men. Their arrival generated fear and uncertainty as British rule supplanted local tribal rule and belief in one God was proclaimed against belief in many. Also unusual is the high praise accorded the missionaries as upright, dedicated, and altruistic who were bent on practicing what their Bible taught.

Chief Awolowo (1909–1987) was born in western Nigeria, earned a law degree from the University of London and became a well-known leader in national Nigerian politics. This excerpt is taken from his autobiography in which he recalls his bewilderment, as a 12-year-old boy, at the clash of his tribal society with that of the encroaching white man.

The society into which I was born was an agrarian and peaceful society. There was peace because under the *Pax Britannica* there was a total ban on intertribal as well as intratribal war, and civil disturbances of any kind and degree were severely suppressed and ruthlessly punished. There was peace because there was unquestioning obedience to constituted authority. There was peace because the people lived very close to nature, and she in her turn was kind and extremely generous to them. And there was peace because the family life was corporate, integrated and well regulated. The order of precedence in the family and in the community as a whole was essentially in accordance with age. The little ones were given every legitimate indulgence. The parents, grand-parents, and, more often than not, the

From *AWO: The Autobiography of Chief Obafemi Awolowo*. Published by the Syndics of the Cambridge University Press © Cambridge University Press, 1960, pp. 6–13. Reprinted with the permission of Cambridge University Press.

great grandparents, were all there—living in one and the same compound, sometimes under one and the same roof—to pet them. Discipline, when occasion called for its application, was severe and spartan. The sturdy members of the family were also there to cater for the aged parents or grand-parents as the case might be. The land was fertile, and the rains fell in their due season. At that time there was more than enough land for everybody. Land was and still is owned not by the individual but by the family. This is the custom in Ijebu as well as in other parts of Yorubaland [Western Nigeria].

Every member of the family is entitled to cultivate any portion of his family land either on the paternal or maternal side. Because of the fertility and suffi-ciency of farmland, only a minimum amount of effort was required to satisfy the sparse wants of the individual. Until western civilization began to make its inroad into the lives of the people, it did not require too much exertion to provide food, shelter and clothing. Food was obtained with the minimum of effort from the farms. Shelter was easily provided by erecting mud walls and covering them with thatch or certain kinds of leaves for a roof. Friends and rel-atives usually helped one another in building one another's houses in turn. It was one of the obligatory duties of a son-in-law to help build the house of his father-in-law, and annually to help repair the roof thereof. The amount of clothing required was limited to the demands of a peasant farming life and of the annual festivities. There were many annual festivals, all of which were and still are held during the period of harvest. There was plenty of leisure.

Notwithstanding its ostensible mirth, peace and tranquility, the society into which I was born was one which was riddled with fear, uncertainty and sup-pression. There was the fear of the white man who was the supreme lord of any area placed under his jurisdiction. His word was law, and his actions could never be called in question by any member of the community. Those Africans who dared to criticise the white man lived in Lagos, and they went by the un-Biblical English names of Williams, Macauley, etc. There were one or two westernised and politically conscious individuals in Ijebu Remo who played the role of champion and defender of the people's rights. But apart from being somewhat oppressive themselves, they were not quite so effective. The barriers between the people and the white official were language, and the lat-ter's undisguised aloofness. The sources of the people's fear of him were his strange colour, his uncanny power to shoot people down at long range, and his obvious unimpeachable authority. There was the fear of the white man's carriers and messengers who were a law unto themselves.

There was the fear of the local chieftains who were more or less the agents of the British Government, and who, as a result, acquired new status, prestige and power. The form and the system of government in Ijebu Remo, before the advent of British rule, were respectively monarchical and gerontarchal. At the head of each town in Ijebu Remo, as in other parts of Yorubaland, there was a king. Under British rule all the Yoruba kings were designated Obas, since there could only be one reigning monarch at one and the same time in the Empire. The fact remains, however, that the English equivalent for "Oba" is "King." Apart from the Oba, there are Chiefs in each town. It is the prerogative of the Oba, in consultation with his Chiefs, to confer a chieftaincy title on any citizen who in his judgement possesses the necessary qualities. The candidate for a chieftaincy title must be an outstanding person in the community, possessing good character and integrity, and fairly well-to-do. It is a maxim among the Ijebus that "A rascal or a poverty-stricken person is not qualified for a chieftaincy title." He must also have a reputation for tact and wise counsel. He must be of a very ripe age. The appointment of educated, enlightened, well-to-do or prominent young persons as Chiefs is a modern innovation, and it is an eloquent proof of the importance attached to western education and culture in present-day Yoruba society.

The affairs of each town were administered by the Oba and his Council of Chiefs, subject to such checks and balances as were provided by the reactions of the populace to any given measure. In the days before British rule, an unpopular Council would not remain long in office. In Ijebu, the younger elements under the Balogun would attack the houses of the guilty Chiefs and completely destroy them. If the Oba was the guilty party, he would be advised by the Chiefs to retire, and this might take one of two forms: suicide or voluntary exile.

Under British rule, these methods were no longer applicable, and as there were no popularly elected Councils at the time, the Oba and Chiefs, instead of regarding themselves as being responsible to their people as before, considered themselves responsible to the white man who in the view of the people was unapproachable as well as unassailable and invincible. In due course, therefore, the word of the Oba and his Chiefs also became something of a law. If they chose to be tyrannical there was nothing that anyone could do about it, unless there was an educated or semi-educated person around to advise on and help in writing a petition to the white man. But it required a good deal of guts to write petitions criticising the Oba and his Chiefs. It was regarded by many white men, then in the Administrative Service, as gross impudence bordering on sedition to write critical letters, petitions, or remonstrances about an Oba. During the first five years of this century, two educated citizens of Ijebu Remo who summoned up enough courage to call attention in a petition to what they regarded as glaring cases of injustice and misrule on the part of one of the Remo Obas, were arrested, tried summarily, and sent to gaol for some months for their impertinence.

There was the fear of innumerable gods, and of the medicine-men who claimed and were credited with all manner of supernatural and magical powers. Every natural phenomenon, like drought, unusual flood, or thunder, was attributable to the anger of one of the gods. Every serious ailment or disease or organic disorder like severe headache, ulcer, tuberculosis, elephantiasis, barrenness, or mental malady, never happened to man save through the agency of an irate god or a malevolent and offended medicine-man. Whenever someone had fallen on bad times, or was seriously ill, it had always been because he had offended one or more of the gods or medicine-men in some inexplicable manner. The well-known remedy in any one of these cases was the offering of sacrifices as prescribed by the medicine-man who was the earthly accredited intermediary between a given god and mortal beings, supported by the taking by the patient of an indiscriminate quantity of various assortments of herbal preparations and medicinal powder.

The newly converted Christians were in a quandary. They believed in one God as against a multiplicity of gods; they believed that all the graven images or idols which they previously worshipped were nothing but the blind, deaf and dumb things that they really are; they believed in Jesus Christ as a Saviour and Redeemer and as an Intercessor between them and God; they believed also in hell with its brimstone and unquenchable fire; and in short they believed in the Apostle's Creed, and in as much of the teachings of Christ as were imparted to them. But in spite of their belief, they suffered from serious ailments and diseases whose causes were unknown to them, in the same way as the pagans. At best, they ascribed the cause in each instance to the work of Satan, whose agents, according to them, the medicine-men were. They believed in the efficacy of certain herbs in the cure of ailments and diseases, but their belief in this connection had not always been justified by results. They believed in the potency of prayer.

In a society where most people did not have anything at all like a bath more than half-a-dozen times in a year, the Christians were in a class by themselves. They cultivated the habit of having a really good bath, and of putting on their best apparel, at least every Sunday. Christian men and women had to cooperate in maintaining the church and the Mission House in a state of perfect cleanliness. This in its turn had some influence on the way the Christians looked after their own houses. As time went on, the Christians looked cleaner because they lived more hygienic lives, and in consequence many of them and their children became immune from some diseases like yaws. In this, they saw some evidence of the triumph of their faith. But as they still suffered from other diseases in the same manner as the pagans; as there were no hospitals and trained doctors around; and as the medicine-men continued blatantly and garrulously to claim to possess the power of dealing with such diseases, the occasions when the faith of a new Christian convert was shaken were much more numerous than now.

They were, however, immensely sustained in their faith by the activities of the missionaries of those days. These Christian missionaries were intrepid pioneers, and conscientious and selfless evangelists of a great doctrine. They reflected the spirit and teachings of Christ as much as any human being could, in their day-to-day contact with their new flock. They lived more or less with the people, and conducted constant visitations. They cared for the flock in sickness, helped them in times of trouble, and, through the instrumentality of the administrative authorities, protected them against attacks or unnecessary buffetings and threats from the pagan elements. In spite of the prevailing fears, therefore, I was made to realise quite early in life that Christianity was, of a surety, superior in many respects to paganism. . . .

Until I visited Abeokuta [a Western Nigerian city] in 1921, I had thought that the white man was a superman. To me, his colour symbolised delicacy innocence and purity, because it resembled very much the colour of Ikenne children [Western Nigerian] at birth. Why he remained white and we grew black beat my little imagination. I don't think I saw more than half-a-dozen white men before I went to Abeokuta. There was a Rev. G. Henry Lester—a Wesleyan minister of religion. I saw him fairly often—on Empire Days and when, during my pupillage at the Wesleyan School, Ikenne, he came there for inspection. There was a Rev. L. C. Mead—another Wesleyan minister. I saw him only once, but I vividly remember him. He came in the company of the Rev. Lester to inspect our school.

On a number of occasions, I saw white officials who passed through Ikenne at different times. The first white official I saw was carried in a hammock by two hefty Nigerians. His luggage was carried by a number of Nigerian carriers. He was ministered unto by a number of messengers and police constables. We were told that a white man used to sleep in the hammock in the course of the journey. But the one I saw did have an open book on his chest whilst he was being carried through Ikenne. Presumably he had been reading the book before he reached our town. Almost all the little urchins in the town flocked around to have a glimpse of him. What a mighty man I thought he was, so specially favoured by God to have a white skin and to occupy such a position of exalted superiority. The second one I saw spent about two days in Ikenne. His tent was pitched in the market place. The children—particularly school children—were there to have a look at him and his carriers, messengers, police constables and interpreter. A few days before his arrival, the Oba of Ikenne had caused a public proclamation to be made for firewood, yams, chickens, water and other necessaries to be provided in plenty in the market place for the use of the Ajele (Administrative Officer). Certain specified age-groups were saddled with the responsibility. But apart from the Oba and his chiefs (aged people all of them) who must visit the Ajele to pay their respects, no other adult or able-bodied person—man or woman—would dare to come too near to the Ajele, especially when his carriers and messengers were about to depart, or when they were actually on their journey. It was the practice for the messengers and carriers to impress anyone forcibly into the service of the Ajele as a relief for themselves. Those who had the misfortune of falling into their hands had been forced to carry the Ajele's luggage until the messengers and carriers could get hold of other persons as substitutes, or until they were about to reach their destination. The forced carriers were entitled to neither money nor thanks for their labour.

14

KOFI AWOONOR
THE SCHOOL INSPECTOR
Ghana

Editor's Notes: This excerpt from Kofi Awoonor's "allegorical tale of Africa" describes the arrival of a 22-year-old British inspector to evaluate the class of an unprepared teacher. The students are encountering the white man's curriculum as well as, for some students, the first white man up close in the form of the inspector.

Awoonor, poet, author, and educator, was born in 1935 and educated in Ghana and London. His career has included faculty appointments at universities in the United States and Ghana. Since his imprisonment for 10 months by the military government in 1975, he has become politically active. In the 1990s, he was Ghana's ambassador to the United Nations.

Deme Primary School in 1936 was not a very peculiar school. It was built by the Roman Catholic missionaries who came long after their rivals in Christ the Methodists had built their church on a small hill. Then came the Presbyterians. These churches flourished together in the word of God, nourishing their priests on the crops of the farms and fish from the Aka River.

The school was not separated from the church. The instructions included writing, reading and arithmetic—the three Rs. The most important subject however was catechism. Instructions in these subjects were brisk and accompanied by the rod. They were conducted by cheerless old men who were scarcely literate, but who understood and had received the calling.

"Class stand!"

"Good morning, sir."

"Good morning, children."

"Sit down."

"Kofi Alakpa."

"Present, sir."

"Yao Avugla."

"Present, sir."

"Florence Dodzavudzi."

"Absent."

"Why? I am sure her mother has brought forth another baby."

"Who said that?"

"Tsitsa it is me."

"I've taught you not to say, It is me. Give him a knock on the head, the boy nearest him. Fine."

"What should you say?"

"It is I."

"Good, next time don't forget, you silly goat, hopeless cow."

"Class stand, sit, stand, sit."

After the drill intended to keep the children awake the teacher cleared his throat.

"Now, catechism!"

This was a favorite subject. Those from Christian homes liked it. It was those children whose parents were pagans and heathens who didn't feel comfortable with the subject.

"Who made you? You."

Silence.

He doesn't know it. Keep standing.

"Next!"

"God made me."

"Why did God make you? Next!"

"He made me so that I do His will here and go to serve Him in heaven."

"What are the sacraments? Next!"

"Baptism, Confession, Communion, eh, eh, eh."

He doesn't know it. "Keep standing."

"What are the holy sacraments? Next. Next. Next."

"All right. All those who failed to answer questions, fallout."

Then a bundle of well-cut canes would be brought out by the class prefect. And the laggards would have six lashes on their backs.

The bell would ring for recreation. This was the time all the children waited for. Those who had coppers would rush to the women who sold beans, gari [cassava], rice and stew. And many other delicious foods. Those who didn't have coppers would go begging with cupped hands.

Give me some or your mother will have a baby with crooked hands. Then they would collect rice, beans, palaver sauce, abolo [bread] in their cupped hands and retire behind the big nim tree on the compound and eat.

These were the children who were not properly trained at home. Those who had received good training at home but didn't get morning coppers came to school with either roasted corn or gari and a cube of sugar in their pockets. When the bell rang for recreation, they retired behind the school latrine and scooped corn or gari into their mouths. When they finished their meals they rushed to the women sellers for water to drink. Sometimes they were given. Sometimes they were not given.

The following year, the school got permission to establish a senior school. This was after the Inspector had visited the school, inspected the new classrooms built the previous year. It was completed because the children worked extra hard cutting bricks, fetching water, collecting and selling firewood, thatch, and mats to pay the bricklayers and to purchase roofing sheets from the local U.A.C. store by the market.

Mr. Smith, the School Inspector, visited the school a term after the senior school had opened. He went to Cambridge University where he got a fourth in history, ancient history. He was young, twenty-two, and energetic. His prospects in the colonial education service were bright. This was his second year in Africa. He lived in Keta, in a big bungalow by the sea with four servants—a cook, a steward boy, a driver, and a night watchman whom he always suspected of being a thief. He wrote home regularly to his mother in a village in Suffolk. He wrote home about the beauty of the country, of the natives, how eager they were to have education, well, some of them. But he could not stand the infernal night drumming that they carried on. He was learning about the customs of the tribes, particularly that of the area in which he was called upon to work. They worship thunder! They have native schools, seminaries one may call them, where they produce young cult priests every year. He had seen their processions in town, a weird affair in which young initiates danced the whole day to the point of physical exhaustion.

To him, the concept of the white man's burden was vague, undefined. He saw it in terms of a well-paid job, a good house, and a vision of arriving at the top—if the Empire was still there. Of course nothing can happen to the good old Empire. He wrote regularly to Susan. They met in Cambridge. He hadn't had the courage to propose to her yet. But it would come.

When Mr. Smith stepped out of his official Vanguard at Deme one morning, Mr. Agbodzan, the head teacher of the Roman Catholic School, was ordering the removal of all canes from the classrooms. He had not been to a Teacher Training College. But he had got to the top through sheer will power and hard work. His favorite maxim was, "Brighten the corner where you are." Brighten the corner where you are, my boys.

When the Teacher Training College at Hohoe was opened he was too old to pass the entrance examination. But he held the External Certificate. Almost every year Mr. Agbodzan vanished to Accra to sit for London Matriculation. After the eighth attempt, the children had made up the story that he was told by the examination people in the capital not to come again. If he did they would write a letter to his Education Circuit head. So he stopped going to sit for the London Matriculation in unheard-of subjects like algebra, geometry, trigonometry, and some said Latin was included.

He was an interpreter at church on Sundays, especially on great feast days, like the feast of the patron saints Peter and Paul. His white drill suit would be well starched and ironed, his hair cut, and he would wear a black tie which he bought at a Conference of Headmasters at St. Augustine's College in Cape Coast many years ago. He would anticipate every move of Father James, and move silently to join him at the foot of the altar to listen and interpret the word of God.

He was a respected member of the community. People brought cases to him to judge because he possessed both the wisdom of his fathers and the white man's wisdom.

Tall, well-built, bald, he was a disciplinarian who ruled his household with an iron fist. Woe betide any boy who was brought up before him for a major breach of a serious school regulation. He ruled the school with a fervent lay preacher voice, and a bundle of twelve well-cut canes behind his cupboard in his office.

Mr. Agbodzan walked up nervously and offered his hand to Mr. Smith, the Inspector of Schools, Keta District. Mr. Smith ignored the offered hand. He could not afford the luxury of personal intimacies. These fellows must be put in their places.

"Good morning, Mr. Smith, I hope you had a good ride. Our roads are bad, sir."

"Good morning. Can I see the school logbook?"

"Yes, certainly, Mr. Smith. In my office, sir!"

The Headmaster strode ahead perspiring. Mr. Smith, a short man, walked with the cocky dignity of the representative of the King and the Empire in the field of education.

The logbook was dully inspected, and Mr. Smith wrote in it with red ink.

"Can I see a class in session, Mr. Headmaster?"

"Yes, certainly, Mr. Smith. Class Five, sir."

"Can I go into class Four?"

The Headmaster was not prepared for this. He had had class Five prepared for inspection because Mr. Kwawu, the class Five teacher, was a reliable old teacher who knew how to teach and who understood discipline. Mr. Adama, the new teacher in class Four, was merely a boy, a product of the new Training College, inexperienced. More sweat poured down his face.

"Class stand! Class, this is the Inspector of Schools, Mr. Smith."

"Good morning, master, good morning, sir!" chanted the children.

"Will you continue the lesson, Mr. Adama? Inspector would like to observe the class in session."

This was Mr. Adama's first year as a teacher. He had been taken unawares. How could the Headmaster do this to him? Adama twitched his mouth, brought out a large red handkerchief and wiped his face.

"Before you continue, may I see the class register? Yes, sir."

Mr. Smith looked into the register perfunctorily and signed the day's page in red ink.

"You can continue the class."

"Yes, sir."

"Class stand, sit, stand, sit."

After the drill, Mr. Adama cleared his throat, his heart in his mouth.

"What insect carries malaria fever?"

Several of the children who would normally have put up their hands did not because they were afraid. One tiny boy in the front row whose nose was always running put up his hand timidly, and a small voice a little louder than a whisper said, "Tsetse fly."

"Wrong, next!"

"Mosquito."

"Yes, which mosquito?"

"Anopheles."

"Good. Now. Who discovered disease germs? You, Kofi Alakpa."

"George Stevenson."

"Wrong, next!"

"Florence Nightingale."

"Wrong, next!" Mr. Adama was becoming desperate. He was drenched in sweat. His handkerchief hung limply from his shirt pocket where he had nervously stuffed it.

"Next!"

"Louis Pasteur."

A little smile played on Mr. Smith's face. He paced the classroom slowly in between the desks and eyed the children with the mischievous twinkle of a censorious uncle.

"Class stand! Sit, stand! Sit."

The inspection was over. Mr. Smith wrote in Mr. Adama's teaching notebook in red ink. As he stepped out, the class like one man stood.

He stepped out into the morning sun, and lit a cigarette. Mr. Agbodzan followed him to his car. The School Inspector sat at the back and said, "Good morning."

"Good morning, sir, safe safe journey, sir."

The school breathed again. Mr. Agbodzan was annoyed. He was very angry.

"And I am older than him, am I his co-equal?" he muttered, addressing no one in particular. "What is this? Eh? He will write his report and it will severely go against the school. And me."

That day Deme Roman Catholic School went into mourning. Teachers caned whole classes on the slightest provocation and pretext. Old offenses were dug up and the appropriate lashes administered promptly. Those who had missed church service about three weeks previously and had even forgotten about it were put on the backs of stalwart boys from the villages, and whipped like dogs. No one in class Four got away that day. It was a weary day of loud noises of lashes, of screams, tears and no joy. A few of the little ones pissed in their clothes, and they had to find rags to wipe the urine from the floor. As they searched for rags they rubbed their buttocks with their left hand and strove to wipe tears away with their right hand. It was a weary day.

Mr. Agbodzan, the Headmaster, was very angry. He called a hasty staff meeting in his office.

"Gentlemen," he said, concentrating his gaze on Mr. Adama, "you are all capable of guessing Mr. Smith's report. It is bound to be adverse. And the responsibility of answering before the General Manager falls squarely—he loved the expression "falls squarely"—on my shoulders. Yes, on my shoulders. He paused with the emphasis on the words staring venomously at Mr. Adama."

"What shall we do? Yes, gentlemen. What shall we do?" His voice collapsed in a near whisper, a sudden giving up, a submission overcame him. He turned round, pulled his chair and sat down. The staff sat glum, silent, utterly lost.

The history of colonial education is one long war between the young and arrogant white school inspectors and the teachers. This was eventually brought to the mission that administered and ran a particular school. It was a sad dismal war in which the young pupils were caught, the veritable first victims of every first volley from the cannons of the pedagogues.

15

FRANCIS OBIKA
THE RETURN OF THE SOLDIER
Nigeria

Editor's Notes: Francis Obika was born at Ogidi in Nigeria and was trained as a pharmacist. After serving in the civil service for five years, he followed the profession of pharmacy. In this story, he describes what happens when native conscripts are demobilized and sent home from the wars. Having glimpsed the white man's world as colonial soldiers fighting for Britain, they abandon ancestral villages for the cities. Readers may recall words to a popular American song from World War I days:

> *"How ya gonna keep 'em,*
> *down on the farm,*
> *After they've seen Paree?"*

On the heels of War followed hardship. There were none to work in the farms any more. There were none to clear the roads again. The walls fell and remained fallen. The houses leaked but remained unrepaired. The thatches rotted on the roofs but there was none to renew them. There were no young men to lead the maidens to dances any more. Decay set in in every aspect of life.

Wives were paid allotments for their husbands on active service. They used the money to pay for the food and other services which they could no longer provide for themselves. Some soldiers sent money to their relatives to keep for them till they returned. When the money had grown big, evil thoughts entered the minds of those relatives. They wished the soldiers might die on the battlefields so that they could use the money for themselves. Some even

Francis Obika, "The Return of the Soldier," in *African Voices: An Anthology of Native Writing*, ed. Peggy Rutherfoord (New York: Vanguard Press, 1960 [© 1958]): pp. 163–164.

went to native doctors to make charms which could cause the death of a soldier on a battlefield.

Some soldiers did die on battlefields. That was not remarkable, for why else did they go to war but to feed the cannons? Some marched from one battlefield to another with charmed lives. Some were taken prisoners in enemy countries. Some deserted their units and embraced new countries. Some even managed to return to Ojindu after their desertion. Some won distinctions on one battle-field after another. Some were maimed and carried back to Ojindu. Some suffered shell shock and became insane. Those who persevered to the end did not return until the two atom bombs had demolished Hiroshima and Nagasaki.

Then the great homeward march began. They came by giant steamers over endless seas. It took many months, many weeks and many days. The great reunion was marked by happy celebrations. The fatted calf was killed and its blood sprinkled on the shrine of the ancestors. There was so much to tell by those who returned. Those who had imagination painted the pictures with art until those who had not exposed the crude truth. Then the wonder did not last nine days.

Not all the home-comings were happy. There were some tragedies. Some ran amok when they came home to find their trusts betrayed. Some found their wives with children they did not help to bear. Other armies had stayed at Ojindu while they were away. Mankind being the same all the world over, the flesh had overcome the spirit. Some returned to find all kith and kin extinct. There was sorrow and there was joy. Life had to be built afresh. They had received the war gratuity promised by the Government. At first it seemed a good lump of money. But soon they found it could not do everything.

The war veteran looked on the soil. It had grown poor through years of ceaseless cultivation. He thought of the life he had led in the army. Apart from the actual fighting there was plenty to eat. He thought of the countries he had visited. He thought of the new life in foreign lands. Why should be spend his life toiling to no profit? His soul rebelled. He had seen the happier side of life. He wanted to have a share of the good things of life. He turned from the soil, donned the khaki uniform again and went to the cities. From office to office he presented himself. The ex-serviceman became the problem of the day. The Government had promised them employment. Let the Government redeem its promise. The politicians caught the cry of ex-serviceman. The press printed banner headlines in support of the ex-serviceman. There was not enough employment to go round. An opportunity was created for rogues to get rich. Jobbery became the order of the day. Whatever was left of the war gratuity was handed over to the men in the key places in order to get a job no matter what sort. In some cases money could not avail simply because there were no more jobs. In desperation the veteran turned his attention to other sources. But he was determined not to go back to the land.

At first one man went to the cities. Then followed another; and then there was a rush. The temporary rejuvenation of social life in Ojindu created by the arrival of her youths from the wars was gone. This time it was worse because the youths married the maidens and all went away. The hopes of re-establishment of the old order were fast receding. There would never be any more folk dances. Maidens with quivering breasts ripe like mangoes would no more step to the rhythm of the music played on flutes, drums and gongs. The folk tales would no more be told beneath the stars at night, nor the carnivals be held under the moon. What a civilization! What a vengeance!

16

EDWARD ATIYAH
COMING OF THE AIRPLANE
Sudan

Editor's Notes: This selection describes the impact of European technology on the people of the Sudan, as told by an Arab observer. He depicts the dazzling moment in the lives of the Sudanese when the first airplane arrived and then their reaction to motion pictures.

Edward Atiyah (1903–1964), the author of several books, was born in Lebanon (then Syria), and educated in an English school in Egypt and then at Oxford University. Subsequently, he spent 20 years as a civil servant in Sudan's capital, Khartoum. After settling in Britain, he served as Secretary of the Arab League in London.

The mechanical inventions of the West were beginning to invade the Near East about that time. The telegraph and the railway had been there for some time. They were familiar to my generation, but not to the extent that breeds contempt. Now new wonders were appearing. The electric tram, electric light, motor-cars and gramophones. Miracle after miracle, and all invented by Europeans. When you first heard of these strange things you perhaps doubted, but then the miracles arrived and you saw and heard them. There were, too, rumours of stranger, more incredible miracles, of motor-cars that could fly, ships that went under the sea, and telegraphy without wire; and all, all invented by the extremely clever Europeans. Surely the cleverest people in the world, much cleverer than the Orientals who had never invented anything.

Among the factors that wrought for the apotheosis of the West in Eastern minds, the mechanical aspect of European civilization—inventions and scientific appliances—was beyond doubt the most potent. For there was not and

Edward Atiyah, *An Arab Tells His Story* (London: John Murray, 1946), pp. 29–31. Reprinted with permission from Joe Atiyah.

never had been anything corresponding to it in the East. Oriental genius had produced great religions, achieved great triumphs in art and literature, constructed colossal empires, but it had never tamed and canned the elements, packed scientific principles into little mechanical parcels. And it happened that while the intellect of awaking Europe was ferreting out and applying the secrets of nature, the East was passing through a phase of decline and somnolence. When therefore this flood of mechanical inventions burst in upon the Near East towards the end of the 19th and the beginning of the 20th century, Easterners were completely dazzled and fascinated by these undreamt-of wonders and the mysterious power that lay behind them.

I was eleven when I saw the first aeroplane. It was 1914 (just before the war) and we were living at Omdurman. Early in the winter rumours began to go round that a French aviator was coming to Khartoum. No aeroplane had yet visited the Sudan, and so everybody was tremendously excited about it, especially the natives, most of whom at first would not believe that there were such things as aeroplanes. Then the rumours became more and more definite; the name of the aviator was given, the route he was following, the approximate date of his arrival, the place of landing. It was becoming real, imminent. At last the day and the hour were announced; and the whole population of Khartoum, from the Governor-General, to street boys, assembled to see the miracle. The landing-place was in a stretch of sand some way outside the town, and we went there by cab. I was consumed with excitement. A good many of the natives were still skeptical, thought that there must be some trick afoot, some huge jest. Impossible that a man, a real man, should come in a machine flying like a bird. Impossible.

2 o'clock . . . 2:15 . . . 2:30 . . . Excitement, impatience, doubt. And then a low distant drone, and a black speck in the sky, there, coming from the north. A hush for a second . . . exclamations, jabberings, strained necks, stretched arms.

There he is, there he is! Yes . . . No . . . yes . . . no . . . yes, yes, yes. The noise is louder, the speck is bigger.

"What? that thing," said a doubting Sudanese standing next to us. "Why it is a vulture, and the noise is coming from the Power Station."

But soon all doubt, all argument ceased. The vulture was above our heads, huge as ten eagles, filling the air with its deafening drone, and as it circled down, a human arm stretched out of it and waved to the crowd. The miracle had come off. Several Sudanese falling on their knees with upstretched arms exclaimed: "There is no god but Allah; the Resurrection Day has come."

Before the machine reached the ground, the seething crowd, beyond itself with excitement, had broken through the police cordon, and rushed towards the landing spot. The Governor-General, who according to plan was to advance with becoming dignity towards the machine, and welcome the distinguished aviator, while the watching crowd watched from a respectful distance, had to forget his dignity and advance with hurried steps to be able to get there at all, while the crowd pushed and jostled in its mad eagerness to see this huge artificial bird, and especially the man in it. Was it really a man, this weird-looking creature with its leather head and huge protruding oval eyes, stepping down on to the ground? See, see, he's waving his arm again, he is shaking hands with the Governor-General. *Wallahi zol, zol sahib.* (By God it's a man, a real man!) But even after this, our old Sudanese woman-servant had still some lingering doubts. "Really, Ya Sitt," she asked my mother when we had gone back home, "is it a real man, a *zol* like us, who eats and drinks and gets married?"

The cinema in its early days produced some curious reactions in the more primitive parts of the Sudan. An English friend of mine took with him a film-projector and some films to an out-station in Kordofan. One day he gathered several hundred tribesmen, and treated them to a performance. They squatted out on the sand before the screen, and shouted in great excitement at every picture. One of the films was an animated-drawings story, in which a man attacks a dog with an axe and splits him into two, after which the severed hind part runs along its legs until it catches up the front part, and the dog is thus reintegrated.

"By the living God," said one of the spectators of this miracle, "if I hadn't seen it with my own eyes, I should never have believed it." This, of course, was an extreme case of unquestioning credulity in a primitive African. But even in Syria and Egypt, on sophisticated minds with a great civilization in their cultural background, these inventions made a profound impression.

Here was something uncanny, apparently supernatural, and it was entirely the product of Western minds. No conjurer producing rabbits from a hat could have more impressed an assembly of unsophisticated children. The children had yet to learn that the conjurer was no god, and that they too when they grew up, could, if they took the trouble, learn to produce rabbits from a hat. . . .

True, the older and more fanatical Moslems disapproved of these inventions. They looked upon them with aversion and suspicion, as the diabolical contrivances of the Kuffar (unbelievers), as something alien to Islam and the Koran, since they did not exist when the Prophet of God walked the earth. They scented in them half consciously the coming of a new world, mysterious, pregnant with alarming possibilities, hostile to them because incompatible with their old world, in which they and their ancestors have lived, secure in their faith, untroubled in their beliefs and prejudices. They saw this new world coming, and had the first premonition that their old world, which they had hitherto thought eternal, would soon begin to slip away from under their feet.

FIRST ENCOUNTERS TIMELINE

Africa

1450	Portuguese explorers sail down the coast of Africa
1500s	European countries establish trading posts along West African coast
1652	Dutch found a permanent settlement in South Africa
1600s	Slave trade expands to South and North America
1807	Britain bans the slave trade
1808	United States bans further importation of slaves
1850s	Decline of the slave trade
1874–1877	H. M. Stanley explores the Congo
1879	King Leopold II of Belgium commissions Stanley to obtain land rights in the Congo
1880	Leopold claims huge part of central Africa as Congo Free State
1885	Berlin Conference agrees on rules for establishing colonies in Africa
1880–1902	The scramble for Africa; only Liberia and Ethiopia remain independent
1903	British Consul Roger Casement investigates conditions in Congo Free State
1908	Congo Free State becomes Belgian Congo
1950s–1960s	African colonies become independent states

Part Two

FIRST ENCOUNTERS
IN NORTH AMERICA

INTRODUCTION

Between 10 to 50 thousand years ago, according to archeological evidence, small groups of people crossed a land bridge across from Asia on what is now the Bering Sea to settle in North America. Eventually some migrated to the southern hemisphere.

As a harbinger of what was to take place again nearly 500 years later, the first European contacts with the New World occurred in Newfoundland early in the eleventh century. These Viking visits were brief and sometimes bloody. No permanent settlements were established.

In 1492, Christopher Columbus, seeking a new route to Asia, landed on the Caribbean island of San Salvador. Other voyages followed and the Spanish spread throughout the Caribbean. In 1515, Vasco Núñez de Balboa took control of Panama which provided the gateway to the land of gold in the south.

The Spanish also moved into North America. In 1519, Hernán Cortés and 700 Conquistadors landed on the east coast of Mexico to start the long march to the Aztec capital, Tenochtitlan, modern-day Mexico City. By 1521, the Spanish had captured and destroyed the city; the survivors were forced to convert to Catholicism.

In 1565, the Spanish turned their attention northward to found St. Augustine in northern Florida. Although the Spanish established a few settlements further north in the Carolinas, their major effort was in the west. Numerous bands of soldiers and accompanying missionary priests were dispatched to conquer and establish self-sustaining missions. Here, newly captured Indians were forced to convert and live, work, and worship away from tribal influences. Soon Spain could boast that its domain stretched across the continent to the Pacific Ocean.

The northern European nations were slower to explore and colonize. In the sixteenth century they were preoccupied with the Reformation and European wars. By the seventeenth century, England, France, and the Netherlands were ready to explore and settle in the New World. In the first decade of the seventeenth century the English founded Jamestown, the French settled Quebec, and the Dutch settled New Netherland. For the next two centuries, the colonization of North America proceeded almost without pause as the Europeans pushed the indigenous peoples further and further west. The European powers now had new battlegrounds in which to fight each other; European wars often spilled over into the New World. They sought allies among the Indian tribes and these conflicts sometimes developed into full-scale wars. After one European war, New Netherland was traded to the English in exchange for other colonial possessions. After another, the French were forced to surrender Canada to the British. The huge territory of the Mississippi basin went back and forth between the Spanish and the French until it was bought by President Thomas Jefferson for the United States in 1803 from French Emperor Napoleon Bonaparte.

During this time, tens of thousands of Europeans came to the North America to seek a better life. Many sought freedom from oppressive European governments. But there were other obvious attractions: large expanses of fertile land, good climate for agriculture, water power, many coastal indentations for harbor use, and navigable rivers in key locations. No other region in the Western Hemisphere could match these conditions.

In the process of creating colonies, and then nations, in the New World the indigenous Indian societies were destroyed. Two powerful forces speeded the process of disintegration, the insatiable need of the Europeans for more land and the devastating diseases they brought with them.

Two diametrically opposed and irreconcilable views of land ownership served as constant fuel for the breakdown of European-Indian relations. For the Europeans, land was for private ownership and use, a commodity to be bought and sold. The Indians had no concept of the individual ownership of land, which could not be sold; it was for the benefit of all. The history of this period is marked by a full range of nefarious activities designed to take land from native people: by wars, raids, broken agreements and treaties, corruption, and alcohol. There were some positive attempts to retain land in Indian hands which sometimes worked for a period of time, but in the long run, nearly every arrangement collapsed. The end result was that the Indians were confined to reservations, often far from their ancestral homelands.

The second force contributing to European success in overwhelming Indian societies was the spread of diseases unknown in the Americas before the arrival of Europeans, and from which, the indigenous people had no immunity. Smallpox, influenza, measles, pneumonia, tuberculoses, diphtheria, and other diseases periodically reduced tribal villages to small numbers, sometimes to zero. These plagues played a major role in the European conquest of

North America. Early missionaries claimed that God had weakened the Indian by disease in order to plant Christianity in the New World.

The history of the absorption of the North American continent by the Europeans and their descendents, the Americans and Canadians, was, of course, written by the conquerors who believed their actions were fully justified by God and manifest destiny. But some native voices have survived, and they describe a very different version of the same sequence of events. This is the story presented in the selections given here. From the amazement with which the people greeted the arrival of the Europeans, through their sorrow at the loss of liberty and land, native voices tell their own history.

17

INDIAN CHIEFS
Arrival of the Dutch on Manhattan
New York

Editor's Notes: This account of a first encounter in 1609 on what is now Manhattan Island, New York, was recorded and then translated by a Moravian missionary, John Heckewelder in the 1770s. The events, preserved in oral history, were told to him by senior members of the Delaware and Mahican tribes living in northern New Jersey and on the Hudson River. The account is an example of the extreme confusion caused by the belief that the new visitors were supreme beings or gods. It also describes the attempts by the visitors to ingratiate themselves by giving gifts of tools and other artifacts as a subtle first step towards pushing the Indians further and further west.

A long time ago, when there was no such thing known to the Indians as people with a *white* skin, (their expression), some Indians who had been out a-fishing, and where the sea widens, espied at a great distance something remarkably large swimming, or floating on the water, and such as they had never seen before. They immediately returning to the shore apprised their countrymen of what they had seen, and pressed them to go out with them and discover what it might be. These together hurried out, and saw to their great surprise the phenomenon, but could not agree what it might be; some concluding it either to be an uncommon large fish, or other animal, while others were of opinion it must be some very large house. It was at length agreed among those who were spectators, that as this phenomenon moved towards the land, whether or not it was an animal, or anything that had life in it, it would be well to inform all the Indians on the inhabited islands of what they had seen, and put them on

---

John Heckewelder, "Meeting the Dutch at Manhattan," in *The World Turned Upside Down: Indian Voices from Early America*, ed. Colin G. Calloway (Boston: St. Martin's Press, 1994), pp. 35–38.

their guard. Accordingly, they sent runners and watermen off to carry the news to their scattered chiefs, that these might send off in every direction for the warriors to come in. These arriving in numbers, and themselves viewing the strange appearance, and that it was actually moving towards them (the entrance of the river or bay), concluded it to be a large canoe or house, in which the great Mannitto (great or Supreme Being) *himself* was, and that he probably was coming to visit them. By this time the chiefs of the different tribes were assembled on York Island, and were counselling (or deliberating) on the manner they should receive their Mannitto on his arrival. Every step had been taken to be well provided with a plenty of meat for a sacrifice; the women were required to prepare the best of victuals; idols or images were examined and put in order; and a grand dance was supposed not only to be an agreeable entertainment for the Mannitto, but might, with the addition of a sacrifice, contribute towards appeasing him, in case he was angry with them. The conjurors were also set to work, to determine what the meaning of this phenomenon was, and what the result would be. Both to these, and to the chiefs and wise men of the nation, men, women, and children were looking up for advice and protection. Between hope and fear, and in confusion, a dance commenced. While in this situation fresh runners arrive declaring it a house of various colours, and crowded with living creatures. It now appears to be certain that it is the great Mannitto bringing them some kind of game, such as they had not before; but other runners soon after arriving, declare it a large house of various colours, full of people, yet of quite a different colour than they (the Indians) are of; that they were also dressed in a different manner from them, and that one in particular appeared altogether red, which must be the *Mannitto* himself. They are soon hailed from the vessel, though in a language they do not understand; yet they shout (or yell) in their way. Many are for running off to the woods, but are pressed by others to stay, in order not to give offence to their visitors, who could find them out, and might destroy them. The house (or large canoe, as some will have it) stops, and a smaller canoe comes ashore with the red man and some others in it; some stay by this canoe to guard it. The chiefs and wise men (or councillors) had composed a large circle, unto which the red-clothed man with two others approach. He salutes them with friendly countenance, and they return the salute after their manner. They are lost in admiration, both as to the colour of the skin (or these whites) as also to their manner of dress, yet most as to the habit of him who wore the red clothes, which shone with something they could not account for. He *must* be the great Mannitto (Supreme Being) they think, but why should he have a *white skin*? A large hockhack [Their word for gourd, bottle, decanter] is brought forward by one of the (supposed) Mannitto's servants, and from this a substance is poured out into a small cup (or glass) and handed to the Mannitto. The (expected) Mannitto drinks; has the glass filled again, and hands it to the chief next to him to drink. The chief receives the glass, but only smelleth at it, and passes it on to the next chief, who does the same. The glass thus passes through the circle without the contents being tasted by any one; and is upon the point of being returned again to the red-clothed man, when one of their number, a spirited man and great warrior jumps up—harangues the assembly on the impropriety of returning the glass with the contents in it; that the same was handed them by the Mannitto in order that they should drink it, as he himself had done before them; that this would please him; but to return what he had given to them might provoke him, and be the cause of their being destroyed by him. And that, since he believed it for the good of the nation that the contents offered them *should* be drank, and as no one was willing to drink it *he would*, let the consequence be what it would; and that it was better for one man to die, than a whole nation to be destroyed. He then took the glass and bidding the assembly a farewell, *drank it off*. Every eye was fixed on their resolute companion to see what an effect this would have upon him, and he soon beginning to stagger about, and at last dropping to the ground, they bemoan him. He falls into a sleep, and they view him as expiring. He awakes again, jumps up, and declares that he never felt himself before so happy as after he had drank the cup. Wishes for more. His wish is granted; and the whole assembly soon join him, and become intoxicated. [The Delawares call this place (New-York Island) *Mannahattanink* or *Mannahachtanink* to this day. They have frequently told me that it derived its name from this general *intoxication*, and that the word comprehended the same as to say, the *island or place of general intoxication*. The Mahicanni (otherwise called Mohiggans by the English, and Mahicanders by the Low Dutch) call this place by the same name as the Delawares do; yet think it is owing or given in consequence of a kind of wood which grew there, and of which the Indians used to make their bows and arrows. This wood the latter (Mohiccani) call "*gawaak*." The universal name the Monseys have for New York, is *Laaphawachking*, which is interpreted, *the place of stringing beads (wampum)*. They say this name was given in consequence of beads being here distributed among them by the Europeans; and that after the European vessel had returned, wherever one looked, one would see the Indians employed in stringing the beads or wampum the whites had given them.]

After this general intoxication had ceased (during which time the whites had confined themselves to their vessel), the man with the red clothes returned again to them, and distributed presents among them, to wit, beads, axes, hoes, stockings, &c. They say that they had become familiar to each other, and were made to understand by signs; that they now would return home, but would visit them next year again, when they would bring them more presents, and stay with them awhile; but that, as they could not live without eating, they should then want a little land of them to sow some seeds in order to raise herbs to put in their broth. That the vessel arrived the season following, and they were much rejoiced at seeing each other; but that the whites laughed at them (the Indians,) seeing they knew not the use of the axes, hoes, &c., they had given them, they having had these hanging to their breasts as ornaments; and the stockings they had made use of as tobacco pouches. The whites now put handles (or helves) in the former, and cut trees down before their eyes, and dug the ground, and showed them the use of the stockings. Here (say they) a general laughter ensued among them (the Indians), that they had remained for so long a time ignorant of the use of so valuable implements; and had borne with the weight of such heavy metal hanging to their necks for such a length of time. They took every white man they saw for a Mannitto, yet inferior and attendant to the *supreme Mannitto*, to wit, to the one which wore the red and laced clothes. Familiarity daily increasing between them and the whites, the latter now proposed to stay with them, asking them only for so much land as the hide of a bullock would cover (or encompass), which hide was brought forward and spread on the ground before them. That they readily granted this request; whereupon the whites took a knife, and beginning at one place on this hide, cut it up into a rope not thicker than the finger of a little child, so that by the time this hide was cut up there was a great heap. That this rope was drawn out to a great distance, and then brought round again, so that both ends might meet. That they carefully avoided its breaking, and that upon the whole it encompassed a large piece of ground. That they (the Indians) were surprised at the superior wit of the whites, but did not wish to contend with them about a little land, as they had enough. That they and the whites lived for a long time contentedly together, although these asked from time to time more land of them; and proceeding higher up the Mahicanittuk (Hudson river), they believed they would soon want all their country, and which at this time was already the case.

AN ENGLISH MASSACRE

[In 1637] led by several veterans of the Thirty Years' War in Europe, the Puritans fell upon a Pequot fortress on the Mystic River. After setting the Indians' wigwams ablaze, the soldiers proceeded to shoot and hack to pieces anyone who attempted to escape the inferno. By the end of the day, approximately four hundred Pequot men, women, and children were dead. "It was a fearful sight to see them thus frying in the fire and the streams of blood quenching the same," [Governor] Bradford wrote, "and horrible was the stink and scent thereof; but the victory seemed a sweet sacrifice, and they gave the praise thereof to God." Bradford saw the devastation as the work of the Lord. The Narragansetts, however, saw nothing divine in the slaughter.

Nathaniel Philbrick, *Mayflower*, New York: Viking Adult, 2006, p. 178.

18

MICMAC INDIAN SPOKESMAN

RIDICULING THE FRENCH
Canada

Editor's Notes: In Colonial times, there was a widespread assumption among the French settlers of eastern Canada, in fact among all settlers, that the Indians' ways of living were far inferior to their own. This assumption is challenged by a Micmac tribal elder whose speech to a group of French settlers in 1677 was translated by Father Chréstien Le Clerq, a Franciscan Recollet missionary to the Micmacs of the Gaspé Peninsula. The elder's comparison of cultures is a powerful reminder that the loser's point-of-view provides a unique opportunity to examine the winner's culture.

I am greatly astonished that the French have so little cleverness, as they seem to exhibit in the matter of which thou hast just told me on their behalf, in the effort to persuade us to convert our poles, our barks, and our wigwams into those houses of stone and of wood which are tall and lofty, according to their account, as these trees. Very well! But why now . . . do men of five to six feet in height need houses which are sixty to eighty? For, in fact, as thou knowest very well thyself, Patriarch—do we not find in our own all the conveniences and the advantages that you have with yours, such as reposing, drinking, sleeping, eating, and amusing ourselves with our friends when we wish? This is not all . . . my brother, hast thou as much ingenuity and cleverness as the Indians, who carry their houses and their wigwams with them so that they may lodge wheresoever they please, independently of any seignior whatsoever? Thou art not as bold nor as stout as we, because when thou goest on a voyage thou canst not carry upon thy shoulders thy buildings and thy edifices. Therefore it

Chréstien Le Clerq, "A Micmac Responds to the French," in *The World Turned Upside Down: Indian Voices from Early America*, ed. Colin G. Calloway (Boston: St. Martin's Press, 1994), pp. 50–52.

is necessary that thou preparest as many lodgings as thou makest changes of residence, or else thou lodgest in a hired house which does not belong to thee. As for us, we find ourselves secure from all these inconveniences, and we can always say, more truly than thou, that we are at home everywhere, because we set up our wigwams with ease wheresoever we go, and without asking permission of anybody. Thou reproachest us, very inappropriately, that our country is a little hell in contrast with France, which thou comparest to a terrestrial paradise, inasmuch as it yields thee, so thou sayest, every kind of provision in abundance. Thou sayest of us also that we are the most miserable and most unhappy of all men, living without religion, without manners, without honour, without social order, and, in a word, without any rules, like the beasts in our woods and our forests, lacking bread, wine, and a thousand other comforts which thou hast in superfluity in Europe. Well, my brother, if thou dost not yet know the real feelings which our Indians have towards thy country and towards all thy nation, it is proper that I inform thee at once. I beg thee now to believe that, all miserable as we seem in thine eyes, we consider ourselves nevertheless much happier than thou in this, that we are very content with the little that we have; and believe also once for all, I pray, that thou deceivest thyself greatly if thou thinkest to persuade us that thy country is better than ours. For if France, as thou sayest, is a little terrestrial paradise, art thou sensible to leave it? And why abandon wives, children, relatives, and friends? Why risk thy life and thy property every year, and why venture thyself with such risk, in any season whatsoever, to the storms and tempests of the sea in order to come to a strange and barbarous country which thou considerest the poorest and least fortunate of the world? Besides, since we are wholly convinced of the contrary, we scarcely take the trouble to go to France, because we fear, with good reason, lest we find little satisfaction there, seeing, in our own experience, that those who are natives thereof leave it every year in order to enrich themselves on our shores. We believe, further, that you are also incomparably poorer than we, and that you are only simple journeymen, valets, servants, and slaves, all masters and grand captains though you may appear, seeing that you glory in our old rags and in our miserable suits of beaver which can no longer be of use to us, and that you find among us, in the fishery for cod which you make in these parts, the wherewithal to comfort your misery and the poverty which oppresses you. As to us, we find all our riches and all our conveniences among ourselves, without trouble and without exposing our lives to the dangers in which you find yourselves constantly through your long voyages. And, whilst feeling compassion for you in the sweetness of our repose, we wonder at the anxieties and cares which you give yourselves night and day in order to load your ship. We see also that all your people live, as a rule, only upon cod which you catch among us. It is everlastingly nothing but cod—cod in the morning, cod at midday, cod at evening, and always cod—until things come to such a pass that if you wish some good morsels, it is at our expense; and you are obliged to have recourse to the Indians, whom you despise so much, and to beg them to go a-hunting that you may be regaled. Now tell me this one little thing, if thou hast any sense: Which of these two is the wisest and happiest—he who labours without ceasing and only obtains, and that with great trouble, enough to live on, or he who rests in comfort and finds all that he needs in the pleasure of hunting and fishing? It is true . . . that we have not always had the use of bread and of wine which your France produces; but, in fact, before the arrival of the French in these parts, did not the Gaspesians live much longer than now? And if we have not any longer among us any of those old men of a hundred and thirty to forty years, it is because we are gradually adopting your manner of living, for experience is making it very plain that those of us live longest who, despising your bread, your wine, and your brandy, are content with their natural food of beaver, of moose, of waterfowl, and fish, in accord with the custom of our ancestors and of all the Gaspesian nation. Learn now, my brother, once for all, because I must open to thee my heart: there is no Indian who does not consider himself infinitely more happy and more powerful than the French.

19

BASIL H. JOHNSTON
THE PROPHECY
Canada

Editor's Notes: This satire, though ostensibly written as a prediction of the coming of the white man, is actually a first impression of his arrival told with light-hearted ridicule. Basil Johnston, a member of the Ojibwa Indian tribe of southern Canada, was born in 1929. In 1954 he graduated from Loyola College in Montreal and subsequently pursued an academic and literary career.

"Tonight I'm going to tell you a very different kind of story. . . . It's not really a story because it has not yet taken place; but it will take place just as the events in the past have occurred." Daebaudjimoot paused to fill his pipe. "And even though what I'm about to tell you has not yet come to pass, it is as true as if it has already happened because the auttissookaunuk [muse] told me in a dream."

They, the men, women, and children from the neighbouring lodges who had come, waited for Daebaudjimoot to begin. The adults had long ceased to believe the tribal storyteller. Still they came, as they had done so for years, to relive the delight and faith of childhood which moved some of the old to say, "he makes me feel like a child again sitting at my grandparents' feet." But unlike the children present who believed Daebaudjimoot, the adults spoke slightingly of the storyteller but not without affection. "W'zaumaudjimoh (he exaggerates)," they said of him. But there was not a man, woman, or child in the village who was not enriched in some way, either in mind or happier in spirit, once having heard Daebaudjimoot.

Daniel Moses and Terry Goldie, eds., *An Anthology of Canadian Native Literature in English*, 3rd ed. (New York: Oxford University Press, 2005), pp. 97–99. Beverley Slopen Literary Agency. Reprinted by permission of the author.

"Tonight I'm going to tell you about white people." There was a moment of silence, astounded silence, and then an outburst of laughter as the audience perceived the incongruity of the notion. An albino caribou; an albino beaver, yes! but albino people? Who ever heard of White People? Even Daebaudjimoot had to laugh. The laughter gradually subsided.

"Are they like the maemaegawaehnsuk (little people like leprechauns, elves)?" a man asked, inciting another wave of laughter.

"Are they like the Weendigoes?" an old woman enquired, igniting more guffaws. The old laughed at such notions; the young laughed to hear the adults giggle, roar, snigger and to see them twist their mouths and cheeks into a hundred shapes. At the same time the young wondered what beings in addition to the Weendigoes, maemaegawaehnsuk, pauheehnsuk, zauwobeekumook, and Pauguk lurked in the forests and roamed about at night.

"What do these White People look like?" another old lady asked when she dried her eyes.

"The men and women that I speak of are all white, face, bodies, arms, hands, and legs, pale as the rabbits of winter. And . . . they are hairy . . . hair growing on their arms, legs, chests, backs, and arm-pits . . . and some men grow hair upon their faces around their mouths, drooping down from their chins, like moose beards." Daebaudjimoot had to interrupt his narrative again for the nervous titters and embarrassed cackles that set off another uproar. The children chuckled and chortled as they imagined their playmates, maybe brothers and sisters, goateed like moose.

Daebaudjimoot continued, "different too is the colour of their hair; some yellow as goldenrod; a few red as cranberries, and others black as our hair. In old age the white people's hair turns white; on some men the hair falls off entirely so that their heads are as smooth and shiny as are pumpkins.

"Their eyes too are unlike ours; round . . . quite round . . . like the eyes of raccoons . . . and blue like the colour of blueberries."

There was more laughter but by now the men, women, and children were nursing aching bellies and paining sides.

"And their dress too is as quaint as their appearance. For one thing, they cover their bodies completely, day and night, summer and winter; only their faces being visible. On their heads are head-winders that they wear indoors and out-of-doors, in sunshine and in rain. The men and boys wear a peculiar garment which is a loin cloth and leggings made of one piece to cover their hams but the garment is so tight that the men walk like mud-hens. Each time that they go to toilet even to drain their bladders they must unfurl these rump binders down to their ankles. The women's garments are not much better than those of their men. The women wear a robe that covers them from their wrists and neck down to the very ankles. Underneath these loose bad-hangers the women wear tit flatteners and belly compressors. Their moccasins are made of a very hard substance, almost like wood, and cover their legs up to their very knee caps. It is only at night that the White People remove some of these garments."

"Are they ashamed of their hair? of their organs?" an old woman quipped, rousing tired laughter.

Daebaudjimoot resumed his narrative. Hours later he predicted, "When they come, they will come from the east across a great body of salt water; and they will arrive on board great wooden canoes five times the length of one of our own canoes. At either end of these long canoes are tall timbers. From the limbs of these timbers are suspended blankets for catching the wind to drive the canoes without the aid of paddles."

"Are they ash or maple? Fresh wood or dead? They go against the wind?" voices asked and made remarks ridiculing the idea of an oversized canoe with trees at either end.

"You laugh because you cannot picture men and women with white skins or hair upon their faces; and you think it funny that a canoe would be moved by the wind across great open seas. But it won't be funny to our grandchildren and their great-grandchildren.

"In the beginning the first few to arrive will appear to be weak by virtue of their numbers, and they will look as if they are no more than harmless passers-by on their way to visit another people in another land who need a little rest and direction before resuming their journey. But in reality they will be spies for those in quest for lands. After them will come countless others like flocks of geese in their migratory flights. Flock after flock they will arrive. There will be no turning them back.

"Some of our grandchildren will stand up to these strangers but when they do, it will have been too late and their bows and arrows, war-clubs, and medicines will be as nothing against the weapons of these white people whose warriors will be armed with sticks that burst like thunder-claps. A warrior has to do no more than point a fire stick at another warrior and that man will fall dead the instant the bolt strikes him.

"It is with weapons such as these that the white people will drive our people from their homes and hunting grounds to desolate territories where game can scarce find food for their own needs and where corn can bare take root. The white people will take possession of all the rest and they will build immense villages upon them. Over the years the white people will prosper, and though the Anishinaubaeg may forsake their own traditions to adopt the ways of the white people, it will do them little good. It will not be until our grandchildren and their grandchildren return to the ways of their ancestors that they will regain strength of spirit and heart.

"There! I have told you my dream in its entirety. I have nothing more to say."

"Daebaudjimoot! Are these white people manitous or are they beings like us?"

"I don't know."

As the men, women, and children went out, a young man who had lingered behind remarked: "It's good to listen to you, but I don't believe you."

OLD TASSEL SPEAKS

Old Tassel of the Cherokee tribe met at Long Island of Holston [Tennessee], July 1777, with U.S. Commissioners to negotiate a treaty. His band listened intently.

Much has been said of the want of what you term "Civilization" among the Indians. Many proposals have been made to us to adopt your laws, your religion, your manners, and your customs. We do not see the propriety of such a reformation. We should be better pleased with beholding the good effects of these doctrines in your own practices than with hearing you talk about them, or of reading your newspapers on such subjects. You say, "Why do not the Indians till the ground and live as we do?" May we not ask with equal propriety, "Why do not the white people hunt and live as we do?"

Virginia Irving Armstrong, ed., *I Have Spoken*, Chicago: Sage Books, 1971, p. 30.

20

JANITIN
JANITIN IS NAMED JESUS
California

Editor's Notes: Dominican priests in the southwestern states measured their success by the number of Indians they baptized and the number put to work at their mission.

In the late 1880s, a member of the Kamia tribe named Janitin revealed to an interviewer the details of his capture as a young man by Dominican fathers. He was then forcibly baptized and made to work at the Mission San Miguel near what is now San Diego. Although some Spanish priests were noted for their kindness and support of Native Americans, this incident illustrates the ugly side of confrontation as cultures collide.

I and two of my relatives went down from the Sierra of Neji to the beach of el Rosarito, to catch clams for eating and to carry to the sierra as we were accustomed to do all the years; we did no harm to anyone on the road, and on the beach we thought of nothing more than catching and drying clams in order to carry them to our village.

While we were doing this, we saw two men on horseback coming rapidly towards us; my relatives were immediately afraid and they fled with all speed, hiding themselves in a very dense willow grove which then existed in the canyon of the Rancho del Rosarito.

As soon as I saw myself alone, I also became afraid of those men and ran to the forest in order to join my companions, but already it was too late, because in a moment they overtook me and lassoed and dragged me for a long distance, wounding me much with the branches over which they dragged me, pulling me

From "Testimonia de Janatin," BANC MSS M-M 295, "Apuntes Historicos de la Baja California," The Bancroft Library, University of California, Berkeley. Reprinted by permission.

lassoed as I was with their horses running; after this they roped me with my arms behind and carried me off to the Mission of San Miguel, making me travel almost at a run in order to keep up with their horses, and when I stopped a little to catch my wind, they lashed me with the *lariats* that they carried, making me understand by signs that I should hurry; after much traveling in this manner, they diminished the pace and lashed me in order that I would always travel at the pace of the horses.

When we arrived at the mission, they locked me in a room for a week; the father [a Dominican priest] made me go to his habitation and he talked to me by means of an interpreter, telling me that he would make me a Christian, and he told me many things that I did not understand, and Cunnur, the interpreter, told me that I should do as the father told me, because now I was not going to be set free, and it would go very bad with me if I did not consent in it. They gave me *atole de mayz* [corn gruel] to eat which I did not like because I was not accustomed to that food; but there was nothing else to eat.

One day they threw water on my head and gave me salt to eat, and with this the interpreter told me that now I was Christian and that I was called Jesus: I knew nothing of this, and I tolerated it all because in the end I was a poor Indian and did not have recourse but to conform myself and tolerate the things they did with me.

The following day after my baptism, they took me to work with the other Indians, and they put me to cleaning a *milpa* [cornfield] of maize; since I did not know how to manage the hoe that they gave me, after hoeing a little, I cut my foot and could not continue working with it, but I was put to pulling out the weeds by hand, and in this manner I did not finish the task that they gave me. In the afternoon they lashed me for not finishing the job, and the following day the same thing happened as on the previous day. Every day they lashed me unjustly because I did not finish what I did not know how to do, and thus I existed for many days until I found a way to escape; but I was tracked and they caught me like a fox; there they seized me by lasso as on the first occasion, and they carried me off to the mission torturing me on the road. After we arrived, the father passed along the corridor of the house, and he ordered that they fasten me to the stake and castigate me; they lashed me until I lost consciousness, and I did not regain consciousness for many hours afterwards. For several days I could not raise myself from the floor where they had laid me, and I still have on my shoulders the marks of the lashes which they gave me then.

21

CHIEF JOSEPH
ADDRESS IN WASHINGTON, D.C.
Oregon

Editor's Notes: Chief Joseph, leader of a band of Nez Percés Indians in Oregon, had always advocated peace with the white man. But he was unwilling to sign any treaty giving up his people's land and refused to move to a reservation. Conflict was inevitable. In 1877, the Nez Percés were forced from the land by General Oliver Howard, and, after a heroic struggle, exiled to Kansas. There Joseph continued his efforts to win permission to return to the land of his fathers.

In 1879, he was allowed to come to Washington to meet President Rutherford B. Hayes and other officials to plead his case. He also gave a speech, the first part of which is given here, to an audience which included members of congress, diplomats, and members of the cabinet. In an attempt to explain why war had recently broken out, he goes back to the first appearance of the white man and the early peaceful relations. Then he reviewed the history of treaties between the Nez Percés and the government, focusing on the Indians' perceptions of the increasingly ominous land-grabbing tactics of the Europeans. The speech was printed in the North American Review *and was widely admired. In spite of his eloquence, bravery, and fame, he was not able to win a return to the ancestral lands for his people, only to another part of the northwest. He is said to have died of a broken heart.*

My friends, I have been asked to show you my heart. I am glad to have a chance to do so. I want the white people to understand my people. Some of you think an Indian is like a wild animal. This is a great mistake. I will tell you all about our people, and then you can judge whether an Indian is a man or not. I believe much

From "An Indian's View of Indian Affairs," by Chief Joseph, *North American Review*, vol. 128, no. 269 (April 1879): 415–420.

Portrait of Chief Hinmaton Yalakit (Thunder Rolling in the Heights) also called Chief Joseph in Native dress in 1877. (*Source*: Photograph by Frank Jay Haynes, Bismark, North Dakota. National Anthropological Archives, Smithsonian Institution, SPC BAE 4605 01605207.)

trouble and blood would be saved if we opened our hearts more. I will tell you in my way how the Indian see things. The white man has more words to tell you how they look to him, but it does not require many words to speak the truth. What I have to say will come from my heart, and I will speak with a straight tongue. Ah-cum-kin-i-ma-me-hut (the Great Spirit) is looking at me, and will hear me.

My name is In-mut-too-yah-lat-lat (Thunder traveling over the Mountains). I am chief of the Wal-lam-wat-kin band of Chute-pa-lu, or Nez Percés (nose-pierced Indians). I was born in eastern Oregon, thirty-eight winters ago. My father was chief before me. When a young man, he was called Joseph by Mr. Spaulding, a missionary. He died a few years ago. There was no stain on his hands of the blood of a white man. He left a good name on the earth. He advised me well for my people.

Our fathers gave us many laws, which they had learned from their fathers. These laws were good. They told us to treat all men as they treated us; that we should never be the first to break a bargain; that it was a disgrace to tell a lie; that we should speak only the truth; that it was a shame for one man to take from another his wife, or his property without paying for. We were taught to believe that the Great Spirit sees and hears everything, and that he never forgets; that hereafter he will give every man a spirit-home according to his deserts: if he has been a good man, he will have a good home; if he has been a bad man, he will have a bad home. This I believe, and all my people believe the same.

We did not know there were other people besides the Indian until about one hundred winters ago, when some men with white faces came to our country. They brought many things with them to trade for furs and skins. They brought tobacco, which was new to us. They brought guns with flint stones on them, which frightened our women and children. Our people could not talk with these white-faced men, but they used signs which all people understand. These men were Frenchmen, and they called our people "Nez Percés," because they wore rings in their noses for ornaments. Although very few of our people wear them now, we are still called by the same name. These French trappers said a great many things to our fathers, which have been planted in our hearts. Some were good for us, but some were bad. Our people were divided in opinion about these men. Some thought they taught more bad then good. An Indian respects a brave man, but he despises a coward. He loves a straight tongue, but he hates a forked tongue. The French trappers told us some truths and some lies.

The first white men of your people who came to our country were named Lewis and Clarke. They also brought many things that our people had never seen. They talked straight, and our people gave them a great feast, as a proof that their hearts were friendly. These men were very kind. They made presents to our chiefs and our people made presents to them. We had a great many horses, of which we gave them what they needed, and they gave us guns and tobacco in return. All the Nez Percés made friends with Lewis and Clarke, and agreed to let them pass through their country, and never to make war on white men. This promise the Nez Percés have never broken. No white man can accuse them of bad faith, and speak with a straight tongue. It has always been the pride of the Nez Percés that they were the friends of the white men. When my father was a young man there came to our country a white man (Rev. Mr. Spaulding) who talked spirit law. He won the affections of our people because he spoke good things to them. At first he did not say anything about white men wanting to settle on our lands. Nothing was said about that until about twenty winters ago, when a number of white people came into our country and built houses and made farms. At first our people made no complaint. They thought there was room enough for all to live in peace, and they were learning many things from the white men that seemed to be good. But we soon found that the white men were growing rich very fast, and were greedy to possess everything the Indian had. My father was the first to see through the schemes of the white men, and he warned his tribe to be careful about trading with them. He had suspicion of men who seemed so anxious to make money. I was a boy then, but I remember well my father's caution. He had sharper eyes than the rest of our people.

Next there came a white officer (Governor Stevens), who invited all the Nez Percés to a treaty council. After the council was opened he made known his heart. He said there were a great many white people in the country, and many more would come; that he wanted the land marked out so that the Indians and white men could be separated. If they were to live in peace it was necessary, he said, that the Indians should have a country set apart for them, and in that country they must stay. My father, who represented his band, refused to have anything to do with the council, because he wished to be a free man. He claimed that no man owned any part of the earth, and a man could not sell what he did not own.

Mr. Spaulding took hold of my father's arm and said, "Come and sign the treaty." My father pushed him away, and said: "Why do you ask me to sign away my country? It is your business to talk to us about spirit matters, and not to talk to us about parting with our land." Governor Stevens urged my father to sign his treaty, but he refused. "I will not sign your paper," he said; "you go where you please, so do I; you are not a child. I am no child; I can think for myself. No man can think for me. I have no other home than this. I will not give it up to any man. My people would have no home. Take away your paper. I will not touch it with my hand."

My father left the council. Some of the chiefs of the other bands of the Nez Percés signed the treaty, and then Governor Stevens gave them presents of blankets. My father cautioned his people to take no presents, for "after a while," he said, "they will claim that you have accepted pay for your country." Since that time four bands of the Nez Percés have received annuities from the United States. My father was invited to many councils, and they tried hard to make him sign the treaty, but he was firm as the rock, and would not sign away his home. His refusal caused a difference among the Nez Percés.

Eight years later (1863) was the next treaty council. A chief called Lawyer, because he was a great talker, took the lead in this council, and sold nearly all the Nez Percés' country. My father was not there. He said to me: "When you go into council with the white man, always remember your country. Do not give it away. The white man will cheat you out of your home. I have taken no pay from the United States. I have never sold our land." In this treaty Lawyer acted without authority from our band. He had no right to sell the Wallowa (*winding water*) country. That had always belonged to my father's own people, and the other bands had never disputed our right to it. No other Indians ever claimed Wallowa.

In order to have all people understand how much land we owned, my father planted poles around it and said: "Inside is the home of my people—the white man may take the land outside. Inside this boundary all our people were born. It circles around the graves of our fathers, and we will never give up these graves to any man."

The United States claimed they had bought all the Nez Percés' country outside of Lapwai Reservation, from Lawyer and other chiefs, but we continued to live in this land in peace until eight years ago, when white men began to come inside the bounds my father had set. We warned them against this great wrong, but they would not leave our land, and some bad blood was raised. The white men represented that we were going upon the warpath. They reported many things that were false.

The United States Government again asked for a treaty council. My father had become blind and feeble. He could no longer speak for his people. It was then that I took my father's place as chief. In this council I made my first speech to white men. I said to the agent who held the council:

"I did not want to come to this council, but I came hoping that we could save blood. The white man has no right to come here and take our country. We have never accepted any presents from the Government. Neither Lawyer nor any other chief had authority to sell this land. It has always belonged to my people. It came unclouded to them from our fathers, and we will defend this land as long as a drop of Indian blood warms the hearts of our men."

The agent said he had orders, from the Great White Chief at Washington, for us to go upon the Lapwai Reservation, and that if we obeyed he would help us in many ways. "You *must* move to the agency," he said. I answered him: "I will not. I do not need your help; we have plenty and we are contented and happy if the white man will let us alone. The reservation is too small for so many people with all their stock. You can keep your presents; we can go to your towns and pay for all we need; we have plenty of horses and cattle to sell, and we won't have any help from you; we are free now; we can go where we please. Our fathers were born here. Here they lived, here they died, here are their graves. We will never leave them." The agent went away, and we had peace for a little while.

Soon after this my father sent for me. I saw he was dying. I took his hand in mine. He said: "My son, my body is returning to my mother earth, and my spirit is going very soon to see the Great Spirit Chief. When I am gone, think of your country. You are the chief of these people. They look to you to guide them. Always remember that your father never sold his country. You must stop your ears whenever you are asked to sign a treaty selling your home. A few years more, and white men will be all around you. They have their eyes on this land. My son, never forget my dying words. This country holds your father's body. Never sell the bones of your father and your mother." I pressed my father's hand and told him I would protect his grave with my life. My father smiled and passed away to the spirit-land.

I buried him in that beautiful valley of winding waters. I love that land more than all the rest of the world. A man who would not love his father's grave is worse than a wild animal.

For a short time we lived quietly. But this could not last. White men had found gold in the mountains around the land of winding water. They stole a great many horses from us, and we could not get them back because we were Indians. The white men told lies for each other. They drove off a great many of our cattle. Some white men branded our young cattle so they could claim them. We had no friend who would plead our cause before the law councils. It seemed to me that some of the white men in Wallowa were doing these things on purpose to get up a war. They knew that we were not strong enough to fight them. I labored hard to avoid trouble and bloodshed. We gave up some of our country to the white men, thinking that then we could have peace. We were mistaken. The white man would not let us alone. We could have avenged our wrongs many times, but we did not. Whenever the Government has asked us to help them against other Indians, we have never refused. When the white men were few and we were strong, we could have killed them all off, but the Nez Percés wished to live at peace.

If we have not done so, we have not been to blame. I believe that the old treaty has never been correctly reported. If we ever owned the land we own it still, for we never sold it. In the treaty councils the commissioners have claimed that our country had been sold to the Government. Suppose a white man should come to me and say, "Joseph, I like your horses, and I want to buy them." I say to him, "No, my horses suit me, I will not sell them." Then he goes to my neighbor, and says to him: "Joseph has some good horses. I want to buy them, but he refuses to sell." My neighbor answers, "Pay me the money, and I will sell you Joseph's horses." The white man returns to me, and says, "Joseph, I have bought your horses, and you must let me have them." If we sold our lands to the Government, this is the way they were bought.

On account of the treaty made by the other bands of the Nez Percés, the white men claimed my lands. We were troubled greatly by white men crowding over the line. Some of these were good men, and we lived on peaceful terms with them, but they were not all good.

Nearly every year the agent came over from Lapwai and ordered us on to the reservation. We always replied that we were satisfied to live in Wallowa. We were careful to refuse the presents or annuities which he offered.

Through all the years since the white men came to Wallowa we have been threatened and taunted by them and the treaty Nez Percés. They have given us no rest. We have had a few good friends among white men, and they have always advised by people to bear these taunts without fighting. Our young men were quick-tempered, and I have had great trouble in keeping them from doing rash things. I have carried a heavy load on my back ever since I was a boy. I learned then that we were but few, while the white men were many, and we could not hold our own with them. We were like deer. They were like grizzly bears. We had a small country. Their country was large. We were contented to let things remain as the Great Spirit Chief made them. They were not; and would change the rivers and mountains if they did not suit them.

Year after year we have been threatened, but no war was made upon my people until General Howard came to our country two years ago and told us that he was the white war-chief of all that country. He said: "I have a great many soldiers at my back. I am going to bring them here, and than I will talk to you again. I will not let white men laugh at me the next time I come. The country belongs to the Government, and I intend to make you go upon the reservation."

22

GEORGE BENT

THE INVISIBLE KILLER

U.S. Midwest

Editor's Notes: Some historians have estimated that during the 500 year period between the arrival of Christopher Columbus and the start of the twentieth century, upwards of 85 percent of the indigenous population died from diseases contracted by exposure to the newcomers. Without immunity and beyond the efforts of local medicine men, millions died from such formerly unknown diseases as influenza, scarlet fever, small pox, cholera, measles, and tuberculosis. History records that much missionary activity was devoted to the provision of medical assistance, to little avail. George Bent, the half-white, half-Cheyenne son of a trader describes here the devastating effects of the cholera scourge of 1849 which took place when he was six years old.

Then in 49, the emigrants brought the cholera up the Platte Valley, and from the emigrant trains it spread to the Indian camps. "Cramps" the Indians called it, and they died of it by the hundreds. On the Platte, whole camps could be seen deserted with the tepees full of dead bodies, men, women and children. The Sioux and Cheyennes, who were nearest to the road [wagon train], were the hardest hit, and from the Sioux the epidemic spread northward clear to the Blackfeet, while from the Cheyennes and Arapahos it struck down into the Kiowa and Comanche country and created havoc among their camps.

Our tribe suffered very heavy loss; half of the tribe died, some old people say a war party of about one hundred Cheyennes had been down the Platte, hunting for the Pawnees, and on their way home they stopped in an emigrant camp and saw white men dying of cholera in the wagons. When the Cheyennes saw these sick white men, they rushed out of the camp and started for home on the run, scattering as they went; but the terrible disease had them already in its grip, and many of the party died before reaching home, one of my Indian uncles and his wife dying among the first.

The men in the war party belonged to different camps, and when they joined these camps, they brought the cholera with them and it was soon raging in all the villages. The people were soon in a panic. The big camps broke up into little bands and family groups, and each little party fled from the rest. . . .

[My] grandmother (White Thunder's widow) and [my] stepmother, Yellow Woman, took the children that summer out among the Cheyennes, and they went to the Canadian, I think, where the Kiowas and Comanches were to make medicine. During the medicine dance an Osage visitor fell down in the crowd with cholera cramps. The Indians broke camp at once and fled in every direction, the Cheyennes north toward the Arkansas. They fled all night and halted on the Cimarron.

Here a brave man whose name I have forgotten—a famous warrior— mounted his war horse with his arms and rode through the camp shouting, "If I could see this thing [the cholera], if I knew where it was, I would go there and kill it!" He was taken with the cramps as he rode, slumped over on his horse, rode slowly back to his lodge, and fell to the ground.

The people then broke camp in wild fright and fled north through the big sand hills all that night. [My] grandmother died that night among the sand hills. [My] stepmother had [us] children on a poledrag. She left the Indians on the Arkansas and went up to Bent's Fort [his father's trading post].

23

CHARLES EASTMAN

Their Wondrous Works and Ways
Minnesota

Editor's Notes: Charles Eastman, a member of the Santee Sioux Indian tribe of Minnesota, was taken, as a child, to Canada to escape the U.S. military massacre of his tribe in 1862. He did not see a white man until he was 16. Later he took advantage of Dartmouth College's hospitality to Indian applicants and graduated, before moving on to Boston University for a medical degree. Later he wrote widely read books on Sioux life and Indian culture.

This excerpt from his autobiography tells of his listening in amazement to his uncle's first-hand account of contacts with the whites whose achievements were alleged to be supernatural. A somewhat unusual feature of the account is the inclusion of some positive, as well as the usual alleged negative aspects of the white culture.

I had heard marvelous things of this people. In some things we despised them; in others we regarded them as wakan (mysterious), a race whose power bordered upon the supernatural. I learned that they had made a "fireboat." I could not understand how they could unite two elements which cannot exist together. I thought the water would put out the fire, and the fire would consume the boat if it had the shadow of a chance. This was to me a preposterous thing! But when I was told that the Big Knives had created a "fire-boat-walks-on-mountains" (a locomotive) it was too much to believe. . . .

I had seen guns and various other things brought to us by the French Canadians, so that I had already some notion of the supernatural gifts of the white man; but I had never before heard such tales as I listened to that morning. It was said that they had bridged the Missouri and Mississippi rivers, and that they made immense

From *Indian Boyhood*, by Charles Eastman (New York: McClure, Philips & Co., 1902), pp. 280–284.

Charles Alexander Eastman in Native American dress, a 1931 photographic postcard image. (*Source*: Photograph by Frank Bennett Fiske [Library of Congress Prints and Photographs Division/LC-USZ62-42187].)

houses of stone and brick, piled on top of one another until they were as high as high hills. My brain was puzzled with these things for many a day. Finally I asked my uncle why the Great Mystery gave such power to the *Washichu* (the rich)— sometimes we called them by this name—and not to us Dakotas [Sioux].

"For the same reason," he answered, "that he gave to Duta the skill to make fine bows and arrows, and to Wachesne no skill to make anything." "And why do the Big Knives increase so much more in numbers than the Dakotas?"

"It has been said, and I think it must be true, that they have larger families than we do. I went into the house of an *Eashicha* (a German), and I counted no less than nine children. The eldest of them could not have been over fifteen. When my grandfather first visited them, down at the mouth of the Mississippi, they were comparatively few; later my father visited their Great Father at Washington, and they had already spread over the whole country.

"Certainly they are a heartless nation. They have made some of their people servants—yes, slaves! We have never believed in keeping slaves, but it seems that these *Washichu* do! It is our belief that they painted their servants black a long time ago, to tell them from the rest, and now the slaves have children born to them of the same color!

"The greatest object of their lives seems to be to acquire possessions—to be rich. They desire to possess the whole world. For thirty years they were trying to entice us to sell them our land. Finally the outbreak [Minnesota, 1862] gave them all, and we have been driven away from our beautiful country.

"They are a wonderful people. They have divided the day into hours, like the moons of the year. In fact, they measure everything. Not one of them would let so much as a turnip go from his field unless he received full value for it. I understand that their great men make a feast and invite many, but when the feast is over the guests are required to pay for what they have eaten before leaving the house. I myself saw at White Cliff (the name given to St. Paul, Minnesota) a man who kept a brass drum and a bell to call people to his table; but when he got them in he would make them pay for the food!

"I am also informed," said my uncle, "but this I hardly believe, that their Great Chief (President) compels every man to pay him for the land he lives upon and all his personal goods—even for his own existence—every year!" (This was his idea of taxation.)

"I am sure we could not live under such a law ..."

"In war they have leaders and war-chiefs of different grades. The common warriors are driven forward like a herd of antelopes to face the foe. It is on account of this manner of fighting—from compulsion and not from personal bravery—that we count no *coup* on them. A lone warrior can do much harm to a large army of them in a bad country."

It was this talk with my uncle that gave me my first clear idea of the white man.

HYPOCRISY

A Delaware chief spoke to David Heckewelder about the Gnadenhutten Massacre, 1782, when ninety Christian Indians were slain by 200 whites, led by Colonel David Williamson, because two reneged Indians had done injury to a white man many miles away.

"And yet these white men would be always telling us of their great Book which God had given them. They would persuade us that every man was bad who did not believe in it. They told us a great many things which they said was written in the Book; and wanted us to believe it. We would likely have done so, if we had seen them practice what they pretended to believe—and acted according to the good words which they told us. But no! While they hold the big Book in one hand, in the other they held murderous weapons—guns and swords— wherewith to kill us poor Indians. Ah! And they did too. They killed those who believed in the Book as well as those who did not. They made no distinctions."

Virginia Irving Armstrong, ed., *I Have Spoken*, Chicago: Sage Books, 1971, p. 33.

24

BLANCHE J. CRISS

THE ARRIVAL OF BIBLES IN NORTHWEST ALASKA

Alaska

Editor's Notes: This brief testimony about the arrival of missionaries in Northwest Alaska in her great-grandparents' day is unique in two ways. It represents one of the few testimonies of its kind in print from this part of the country, and it gives the people carrying Bibles credit for overcoming evil spirits and for providing a link with the modern world. For this the writer is profoundly thankful. Blanche Jones Criss, a member of the Iñupiat tribe, was born in 1947 and was brought up in Kotzebue, Alaska.

In the early twentieth century, missionaries introduced Western religion of the Native Iñupiaq Eskimos of Northwest Alaska, which changed Native Iñupiaq beliefs from traditional shamanism to Christianity.

My great-grandparents were the first generation introduced to the Quakers, who were the founders of the Friends Church in Northwest Alaska.

As a small child, I listened to my great-grandparents tell stories of how thankful they were that these "people who look different" came. My great-grandparents told of spirits whispering in the air at dusk and of how they had to dance until these shamanistic spirits went away. When these people carrying Bibles came, my great-grandparents were happy because they made these evil spirits go away.

My mother, as a member of another generation belonging to this new religion, took to the missionaries' ways with great faith by following her leaders. In yet another generation, I found myself in the middle of a vigorous transition period for religion in my hometown of Kotzebue.

From *Authentic Alaska: Voices of Its Native Writers*, by Susan B. Andrews and John Creed, published by the University of Nebraska Press, pp. 116–118. Reprinted by permission.

For example, during this time, we as members of this religion were not allowed many of the fun things that others did, such as going to local dances, including the local Eskimo dance festivities. We could not go to the movies, either. We also weren't allowed to listen to pop music in our home in Kotzebue, and, among other things, we could not play cards or read comic books. . . .

Yet, despite the problems and family disruptions the new religion caused, I still applaud these people with Bibles who paved their way into Northwest Alaska. Through strict discipline, they showed the Native Iñupiat Christian ways and taught them the English language. These things have linked the Iñupiat to the Western world.

After a century of regrouping and reorganizing, I have a sense that the next generation will have stronger faith and values to pass on to their children. With the Friends Church members' blessings, perhaps succeeding generations will participate in Eskimo dance festivities. A unique part of history has taken place within my lifetime. For that I am proud.

25

JEANNETTE ARMSTRONG

LITERARY DISEMPOWERMENT

Canada

Editor's Notes: In this paper prepared for the Saskatchewan (Canada) Writers Guild 1990 Annual Conference, Jeannette Armstrong, member of the Okanagen tribe, addresses two audiences, Native American writers and writers from the dominating culture. At the time of the first encounters, the foreign peoples were welcomed as guests, but their numbers grew until they achieved complete control and suppressed their one-time hosts. This paper is a powerful indictment of 498 years of domination by outsiders, and a plea for Native writers to rewrite the history of colonization.

Armstrong was born in 1948 on an Indian reservation in British Columbia, received a fine arts degree from the University of Victoria, and was appointed Director of the International School of Writing in Princeton, British Columbia. She is a writer, educator, and activist for indigenous rights and has received many honors and awards.

In order to address the specifics of Native people's writing and empowerment, I must first present my view on the disempowerment of first North American Nations.

Without recounting various historical versions of how it happened, I would like to refer only to what happened here.

Indigenous peoples in North America were rendered powerless and subjugated to totalitarian domination by foreign peoples, after they were welcomed as guests and their numbers were allowed to grow to the point of domination through aggression.

Jeannette Armstrong, "The Disempowerment of First North America Native Peoples and Empowerment through Their Writings," *Gatherings*, Vol. 1 (1990), Theytus Books Ltd. Reprinted with permission of Jeannette Armstrong and Theytus Books Ltd.

Once total subjective control was achieved over my peoples through various coercive measures and the direct removal of political, social, and religious freedoms accomplished, the colonization process began.

In North America this has been to systemically enforce manifest destiny or the so-called "White Man's burden" to civilize. In the 498 years of contact in The Americas, the thrust of this bloody sword has been to hack out the spirit of all the beautiful cultures encountered, leaving in its wake a death toll unrivalled in recorded history. This is what happened and what continues to happen.

There is no word other than totalitarianism which adequately describes the methods used to achieve the condition of my people today. Our people were not given choices. Our children, for generations, were seized from our communities and homes and placed in indoctrination camps until our language, our religion, our customs, our values, and our societal structures almost disappeared. This was the residential school experience.

Arising out of the siege conditions of this nightmare time, what is commonly referred to as the "social problems" of Native peoples emerged. Homes and communities, without children, had nothing to work for, or live for. Children returned to communities and families as adults, without the necessary skills for parenting, for Native life style, or self-sufficiency on their land base, deteriorated into despair. With the loss of cohesive cultural relevance with their own peoples and a distorted view of the non-Native culture from the clergy who ran the residential schools, an almost total disorientation and loss of identity occurred. The disintegration of family and community and nation was inevitable, originating with the individual's internalized pain. Increasing death statistics from suicide, violence, alcohol and drug abuse, and other poverty-centered physical diseases, can leave no doubt about the question of totalitarianism and genocide.

You writers from the dominating culture have the freedom of imagination. You keep reminding us of this. Is there anyone here who dares to imagine what those children suffered at the hands of their so-called "guardians" in those schools. You are writers, imagine it on yourselves and your children. Imagine you and your children and imagine how they would be treated by those who abhorred and detested you, all, as savages without any rights.

Imagine at what cost to you psychologically, to acquiesce and attempt to speak, dress, eat, and worship, like your oppressors, simply out of a need to be treated humanly. Imagine attempting to assimilate so that your children will not suffer what you have, and imagine finding that assimilationist measures are not meant to include you but to destroy all remnants of your culture. Imagine finding that even when you emulate every cultural process from customs to values you are still excluded, despised, and ridiculed because you are Native.

Imagine finding out that the dominating culture will not tolerate any real cultural participation and that cultural supremacy forms the basis of the government process and that systemic racism is a tool to maintain their kind of totalitarianism. And all the while, imagine that this is presented under the guise of "equal rights" and under the banner of banishing bigotry on an individual basis through law.

Imagine yourselves in this condition and imagine the writers of that dominating culture berating you for speaking out about appropriation of cultural voice and using the words "freedom of speech" to condone further systemic violence, in the form of entertainment literature about your culture and your values and all the while, yourself being disempowered and rendered voiceless through such "freedoms."

Imagine how you as writers from the dominant society might turn over some of the rocks in your own garden for examination. Imagine in your literature courageously questioning and examining the values that allow the dehumanizing of peoples through domination and the dispassionate nature of the racism inherent in perpetuating such practices. Imagine writing in honesty, free of the romantic bias about the courageous "pioneering spirit" of colonialist practice and imperialist process. Imagine interpreting for us your own people's thinking toward us, instead of interpreting for us, our thinking, our lives, and our stories. We wish to know, and you need to understand, why it is that you want to own our stories, our art, our beautiful crafts, our ceremonies, but you do not appreciate or wish to recognize that these things of beauty arise out of the beauty of our people.

Imagine these realities on yourselves in honesty and let me know how you imagine that you might approach empowerment of yourselves in such a situation. Better yet, do not dare speak to me of "Freedom of Voice", "Equal Rights", "Democracy", or "Human Rights" until this totalitarianistic approach has been changed by yourselves as writers and shapers of philosophical direction. Imagine a world where domination is not possible because all cultures are valued.

To the Native writers here, my words are meant as empowerment to you. In my quest for empowerment of my people through writing, there are two things of which I must steadfastly remind myself.

The first is that the reality I see is the reality for the majority of Native people and that although severe and sometimes irreparable damage has been wrought, healing can take place through cultural affirmation. I have found immense strength and beauty in my people.

The dispelling of lies and the telling of what really happened until everyone, including our own people understands that this condition did not happen through choice or some cultural defect on our part, is important. Equally important is the affirmation of the true beauty of our people whose fundamental co-operative values resonated pacifism and predisposed our cultures as vulnerable to the reprehensible value systems which promote domination and aggression.

The second thing I must remind myself of is that the dominating culture's reality is that it seeks to affirm itself continuously and must be taught that numbers are not the basis of democracy, people are, each one being important.

It must be pushed, in Canada, to understand and accept that this country is multi-racial and multi-cultural now, and the meaning of that. I must remind myself constantly of the complacency that makes these conditions possible, and that if I am to bridge into that complacency that I will be met with hostility from the majority, but, that those whose thoughts I have provoked may become our greatest allies in speaking to their own. It is this promotion of an ideal which will produce the courage to shake off centuries of imperialist thought and make possible the relearning of co-operation and sharing, in place of domination.

Our task as Native writers is twofold. To examine the past and culturally affirm toward a new vision for all our people in the future, arising out of the powerful and positive support structures that are inherent in the principles of co-operation.

We, as Native people, through continuously resisting cultural imperialism and seeking means toward teaching co-operative relationships, provide an integral mechanism for solutions currently needed in this country.

We must see ourselves as undefeatably pro-active in a positive sense and realize that negative activism actually serves the purpose of the cultural imperialism practised on our people. Lies need clarification, truth needs to be stated, and resistance to oppression needs to be stated, without furthering division and participation in the same racist measures. This is the challenge that we rise to. Do not make the commonly made error that it is a people that we abhor, be clear that it is systems and processors which we must attack. Be clear that change to those systems will be promoted by people who can perceive intelligent and non-threatening alternatives. Understand that these alternatives will be presented only through discourse and dialogue flowing outward from us, for now, because we are the stakeholders. We need the system to change. Those in the system can and will remain complacent until moved to think, and to understand how critical change is needed at this time for us all. Many already know and are willing to listen.

The responsibility of the Native writer is tremendous in light of these times in which world over, solutions are being sought to address the failed assimilationist measures originating out of conquest, oppression, and exploitation, whether under the socialist or capitalist banner. We as writers can show how support for Lithuanian independence and support for South African Black equality became farcical in the glare of the Constitutional position to First Nations here in Canada, who seek nothing more than co-operative sovereign relationships guaranteed in the principles of treaty making. No one will desire or choose to hear these truths unless they are voiced clearly to people who have no way to know that there are good alternatives and that instead of losing control we can all grow powerful together.

Finally, I believe in the basic goodness of the majority of people. I rely on the common human desire to be guilt free and fulfilled, to triumph, towards attainment of our full potential as wonderful, thinking beings at the forward edge of the Creator's expression of beauty.

I believe in the strength and rightness in the values of my people and know that those principles of peace and co-operation, in practice, are natural and survival-driven mechanisms which transcend violence and aggression. I see the destructive paths that have led us to this time in history, when all life on this planet is in peril, and know that there must be change. I believe that the principles of co-operation are a sacred trust and the plan and the intent of the Creator and therefore shall endure.

26

AZTEC WITNESSES
THE CONQUISTADORS ARRIVE
Mexico

Editor's Notes: In 1519, Hernán Cortés and 700 Spanish Conquistadors with 16 horses, muskets, and a few cannon, landed on the coast of Mexico. A year later, the Aztec capital, Tenochtitlan was besieged and destroyed. Later it was rebuilt as Mexico City. It has been said that of all the first encounters between native people and the white man in North America, this was the bloodiest. The Aztecs and their allies put up a sustained and determined resistance. The first encounter was a confused event because Aztec stories anticipated the return of a god who would reclaim his kingdom. This explains why, initially, the Aztecs welcomed Cortés and his men as gods, worthy of gifts to placate them. The historical accounts of the invasion of Mexico have been based almost entirely on the numerous letters and documents written by the Conquistadors. The following excerpts are taken from the rare and mostly overlooked accounts of the invasion through the eyes of the native population. Although the invaders had burned nearly all indigenous accounts of the conquest of Mexico, a remarkable Spanish missionary, Bernard de Sahagun, went to great lengths to gather surviving native writings. These were augmented by the testimony of living witnesses. De Sahagun transliterated the languages of the natives into the Latin alphabet, thus ensuring the preservation of these accounts for the historical record.

The first section relates the arrival of the Spanish on the coast and the reaction of Motecuhzoma (Montezuma). In spite of many gifts and expressions of welcome, he was imprisoned by the Spanish when they arrived at the capital. The Spanish seized the gold in the treasury and all of the king's personal treasure.

A MACEHUAL ARRIVES FROM THE GULF COAST

A few days later a macehual [common man] came to the city from Mictlan-cuauhtla. No one had sent him, none of the officials; he came of his own accord. He went directly to the palace of Motecuhzoma and said to him: "Our lord and king, forgive my boldness. I am from Mictlancuauhtla. When I went to the shores of the great sea, there was a mountain range or small mountain floating in the midst of the water, and moving here and there without touching the shore. My lord, we have never seen the like of this, although we guard the coast and are always on watch."

Motecuhzoma thanked him and said: "You may rest now."

The man who brought this news had no ears, for they had been cut off, and no toes, for they had also been cut off.

Motecuhzoma said to his *petlacalcatl* [head steward] "Take him to the prison, and guard him well." Then he called for a teuctlamacazqui [priest] and appointed him his grand emissary. He said to him: "Go to Cuetlaxtlan, and tell the official in charge of the village that it is true, strange things have appeared on the great sea. Tell him to investigate these things himself, so as to learn what they may signify. Tell him to do this as quickly as he can, and take the ambassador Cuitlalpitoc with you."

When they arrived in Cuetlaxtlan, the envoys spoke with the official in charge there, a man named Pinotl. He listened to them with great attention and then said: "My lords, rest here with me, and send your attendants out to the shore." The attendants went out and came back in great haste to report that it was true: they had seen two towers or small mountains floating on the waves of the sea. The grand emissary said to Pinotl: "I wish to see these things in person, in order to learn what they are, for I must testify to our lord as an eyewitness. I will be satisfied with this and will report to him exactly what I see." Therefore he went out to the shore with Cuitlalpitoc, and they saw what was floating there, beyond the edge of the water. They also saw that seven or eight of the strangers had left it in a small boat and were fishing with hooks and lines.

The grand emissary and Cuitlalpitoc climbed up into a broad-limbed tree. From there they saw how the strangers were catching fish and how, when they were done, they returned to the ship in their small boat. The grand emissary said: "Come, Cuitlalpitoc." They climbed down from the tree and went back to the village, where they took hasty leave of Pinotl. They returned as swiftly as possible to the great city of Tenochtitlan, to report to Motecuhzoma what they had observed.

When they reached the city, they went directly to the king's palace and spoke to him with all due reverence and humility: "Our lord and king, it is true that strange people have come to the shores of the great sea. They were fishing from a small boat, some with rods and others with a net. They fished until late and then they went back to their two great towers and climbed up into them. There were about fifteen of these people, some with blue jackets, others with red, others with black or green, and still others with jackets of a soiled color, very ugly, like our *ichtilmatli* [cloaks]. There were also a few without jackets. On their heads they wore red kerchiefs, or bonnets of a fine scarlet color, and some wore large round hats like small *comales* [flat dishes] which must have been sunshades They have very light skin, much lighter than ours. They all have long beards, and their hair comes only to their ears."

Motecuhzoma was downcast when he heard this report, and did not speak a word. . . .

Then Motecuhzoma gave the messengers his final orders. He said to them: "Go now, without delay. Do reverence to our lord the god.

Say to him: "Your deputy, Motecuhzoma, has sent us to you. Here are the presents with which he welcomes you home to Mexico."

THE MESSENGERS CONTACT THE SPANIARDS

When they arrived at the shore of the sea, they were taken in canoes to Xicalanco. They placed the baskets in the same canoes in which they rode, in order to keep them under their personal vigilance. From Xicalanco they followed the coast until they sighted the ships of the strangers.

When they came up to the ships, the strangers asked them: "Who are you? Where are you from?"

"We have come from the City of Mexico."

The strangers said: "You may have come from there, or you may not have. Perhaps you are only inventing it. Perhaps you are mocking us." But their hearts were convinced; they were satisfied in their hearts. They lowered a hook from the bow of the ship, and then a ladder, and the messengers came aboard.

One by one they did reverence to Cortés by touching the ground before him with their lips. They said to him: "If the god will deign to hear us, your deputy Motecuhzoma has sent us to render you homage. He has the City of Mexico in his care. He says: 'The god is weary.' "

Then they arrayed the Captain in the finery they had brought him as presents. With great care they fastened the turquoise mask in place, the mask of the god with its crossband of quetzal feathers. A golden earring hung down on either side of this mask. They dressed him in the decorated vest and the collar woven in the petatillo style—the collar of *chalchihuites* [jade], with a disk of gold in the center.

Next they fastened the mirror to his hips, dressed him in the cloak known as "the ringing bell" and adorned his feet with the greaves used by the Huastecas which were set with *chalchihuites* and hung with little gold bells. In his hand they placed the shield with its fringe and pendant of quetzal feathers, its ornaments of gold and mother-of-pearl. Finally they set before him the pair of black sandals. As for the other objects of divine finery, they only laid them out for him to see.

The Captain asked them: "And is this all? Is this your gift of welcome? Is this how you greet people?"

They replied: "This is all, our lord. This is what we have brought you."

CORTÉS FRIGHTENS THE MESSENGERS

Then the Captain gave orders, and the messengers were chained by the feet and by the neck. When this had been done, the great cannon was fired off. The messengers lost their senses and fainted away. They fell down side by side and lay where they had fallen. But the Spaniards quickly revived them: they lifted them up, gave them wine to drink and then offered them food.

The Captain said to them: "I have heard that the Mexicans are very great warriors, very brave and terrible. If a Mexican is fighting alone, he knows how to retreat, turn back, rush forward and conquer, even if his opponents are ten or even twenty. But my heart is not convinced. I want to see it for myself. I want to find out if you are truly that strong and brave."

Then he gave them swords, spears and leather shields. He said: "It will take place very early, at daybreak. We are going to fight each other in pairs, and in this way we will learn the truth. We will see who falls to the ground!"

They said to the Captain: "Our lord, we were not sent here for this by your deputy Motecuhzoma! We have come on an exclusive mission, to offer you rest and repose and to bring you presents. What the lord desires is not within our warrant. If we were to do this, it might anger Motecuhzoma, and he would surely put us to death."

The Captain replied: "No, it must take place. I want to see for myself, because even in Castile they say you are famous as brave warriors. Therefore, eat an early meal. I will eat too. Good cheer!"

With these words he sent them away from the ship. They were scarcely into their canoes when they began to paddle furiously. Some of them even paddled with their hands, so fierce was the anxiety burning in their souls. They said to each other: "My captains, paddle with all your might! Faster, faster! Nothing must happen to us here! Nothing must happen! . . . "

THE MESSENGERS' REPORT

. . . the messengers reported to the king. They told him how they had made the journey, and what they had seen, and what food the strangers ate. Motecuhzoma was astonished and terrified by their report, and the description of the strangers' food astonished him above all else.

He was also terrified to learn how the cannon roared, how its noise resounded, how it caused one to faint and grow deaf. The messengers told him: "A thing like a ball of stone comes out of its entrails: it comes out shooting sparks and raining fire. The smoke that comes out with it has a pestilent odor, like that of rotten mud. This odor penetrates even to the brain and causes the greatest discomfort. If the cannon is aimed against a mountain, the mountain splits and cracks open. If it is aimed against a tree, it shatters the tree into splinters. This is a most unnatural sight, as if the tree had exploded from within."

The messengers also said: "Their trappings and arms are all made of iron. They dress in iron and wear iron casques on their heads. Their swords are iron;

their bows are iron; their shields are iron; their spears are iron. Their deer carry them on their backs wherever they wish to go. These deer, our lord, are as tall as the roof of a house.

"The strangers' bodies are completely covered, so that only their faces can be seen. Their skin is white, as if it were made of lime. They have yellow hair, though some of them have black. Their beards are long and yellow, and their moustaches are also yellow. Their hair is curly, with very fine strands.

"As for their food, it is like human food. It is large and white, and not heavy. It is something like straw, but with the taste of a cornstalk, of the pith of a cornstalk. It is a little sweet, as if it were flavored with honey; it tastes of honey, it is sweet-tasting food.

"Their dogs are enormous, with flat ears and long, dangling tongues. The color of their eyes is a burning yellow; their eyes flash fire and shoot off sparks. Their bellies are hollow, their flanks long and narrow. They are tireless and very powerful. They bound here and there, panting, with their tongues hanging out. And they are spotted like an ocelot."

When Motecuhzoma heard this report, he was filled with terror. It was as if his heart had fainted, as if it had shriveled. It was as if he were conquered by despair . . .

The second section describes the massacre of the Aztecs by the Spanish at a great festival. This provoked resistance to the conquistadors who were forced to abandon the city. The Aztecs were then decimated by a terrible plague (probably smallpox, brought by the Spanish).

THE BEGINNING OF THE FIESTA

Early the next morning, the statue's face was uncovered by those who had been chosen for that ceremony. They gathered in front of the idol in single file and offered it gifts of food, such as round seedcakes or perhaps human flesh. But they did not carry it up to its temple on top of the pyramid.

All the young warriors were eager for the fiesta to begin. They had sworn to dance and sing with all their hearts, so that the Spaniards would marvel at the beauty of the rituals.

The procession began, and the celebrants filed into the temple patio to dance the Dance of the Serpent. When they were all together in the patio, the songs and the dance began. Those who had fasted for twenty days and those who had fasted for a year were in command of the others; they kept the dancers in file with their pine wands. (If anyone wished to urinate, he did not stop dancing, but simply opened his clothing at the hips and separated his clusters of heron feathers.)

The great captains, the bravest warriors, danced at the head of the files to guide the others. The youths followed at a slight distance. Some of the youths wore their hair gathered into large locks, a sign that they had never taken any captives. Others carried their headdresses on their shoulders; they had taken captives, but only with help.

Then came the recruits, who were called "the young warriors." They had each captured an enemy or two. The others called to them: "Come, comrades, show us how brave you are! Dance with all your hearts!"

THE SPANIARDS ATTACK THE CELEBRANTS

At this moment in the fiesta, when the dance was loveliest and when song was linked to song, the Spaniards were seized with an urge to kill the celebrants. They all ran forward, armed as if for battle. They closed the entrances and passageways, all the gates of the patio: the Eagle Gate in the lesser palace, the Gate of the Canestalk and the Gate of the Serpent of Mirrors. They posted guards so that no one could escape, and then rushed into the Sacred Patio to slaughter the celebrants. They came on foot, carrying their swords and their wooden or metal shields.

They ran in among the dancers, forcing their way to the place where the drums were played. They attacked the man who was drumming and cut off his arms. Then they cut off his head, and it rolled across the floor.

They attacked all the celebrants, stabbing them, spearing them, striking them with their swords. They attacked some of them from behind, and these fell instantly to the ground with their entrails hanging out. Others they beheaded: they cut off their heads, or split their heads to pieces.

They struck others in the shoulders, and their arms were torn from their bodies. They wounded some in the thigh and some in the calf. They slashed others in the abdomen, and their entrails all spilled to the ground. Some attempted to run away, but their intestines dragged as they ran; they seemed to tangle their feet in their own entrails. No matter how they tried to save themselves, they could find no escape.

Some attempted to force their way out, but the Spaniards murdered them at the gates. Others climbed the walls, but they could not save themselves. Those who ran into the communal houses were safe there for a while; so were those who lay down among the victims and pretended to be dead. But if they stood up again, the Spaniards saw them and killed them.

The blood of the warriors flowed like water and gathered into pools. The pools widened, and the stench of blood and entrails filled the air. The Spaniards ran into the communal houses to kill those who were hiding. They ran everywhere and searched everywhere; they invaded every room, hunting and killing.

But the Spanish returned and laid siege to the city. The last section describes some incidents in the long siege which lasted 80 days. Eventually the Aztecs had to surrender the city, thus bringing an end to the Aztec Empire.

FIFTEEN SPANIARDS ARE CAPTURED AND SACRIFICED

The warriors advanced to the sound of flutes. They shouted their war cries and beat their shields like drums. They pursued the Spaniards, harried and terrified them, and at last took fifteen of them prisoners. The rest of the Spaniards retreated to their ships and sailed out into the middle of the lake.

The prisoners were sacrificed in the place called Tlacochcalco [House of the Arsenal]. Their captors quickly plundered them, seizing their weapons, their cotton armor and everything else, until they stood naked. Then they were sacrificed to the god, while their comrades on the lake watched them being put to death.

Two of the barentines sailed to Xocotitlan again. They anchored there, and the Spaniards began attacking the houses along the shore. But when Tzilacatzin and other warriors saw what was happening, they ran to the defense and drove the invaders into the water.

On another occasion, the barkentines approached Coyonacazco to attack the houses. As the ships closed in, a few Spaniards jumped out, ready for battle. They were led by Castaneda and by Xicotencatl, who was wearing his headdress of quetzal feathers.

Then Castaneda shot the catapult. It struck one of the Aztecs in the forehead and he fell dead where he was standing. The warriors charged the Spaniards, driving them into the water, and then loosed a hail of stones from their slings. Castaneda would have been killed in this action if a barkentine had not taken him aboard and sailed away toward Xocotitlan.

Another barkentine was anchored near the turn in the wall, and still another near Teotlecco, where the road runs straight to Tepetzinco. They were stationed as guards in order to control the lake. They sailed away that night, but after a few days they came back again to their stations.

The Spaniards advanced from the direction of Cuahuecatitlan. Their allies from Tlaxcala, Acolhuacan and Chalco filled up the canal so that the army could pass. They threw in adobe bricks and all the woodwork of the nearby houses: the lintels, the doorjambs, the beams and pillars. They even threw canestalks and rushes into the water.

THE SPANIARDS ATTACK AGAIN

When the canal had been filled up, the Spaniard marched over it. They advanced cautiously, with their standard-bearer in the lead, and they beat their drums and played their chirimias [reed pipes] as they came. The Tlaxcaltecas and the other allies followed close behind. The Tlaxcaltecas held their heads high and pounded their breasts with their hands, hoping to frighten us with their arrogance and courage. They sang songs as they marched, but the Aztecs were also singing. It was as if both sides were challenging each other with their songs. They sang whatever they happened to remember and the music strengthened their hearts.

The Aztec warriors hid when the enemy reached solid ground. They crouched down to make themselves as small as possible and waited for the signal, the shout that told them it was the moment to stand up and attack. Suddenly they heard it: "Mexicanos, now is the time!"

The captain Hecatzin leaped up and raced toward the Spaniards, shouting: "Warriors of Tlateloco now is the time! Who are these barbarians? Let them come ahead!" He attacked one of the Spaniards and knocked him to the ground, but the Spaniard also managed to knock Hecatzin down. The captain got up and clubbed the Spaniard again, and other warriors rushed forward to drag him away.

Then all the Aztecs sprang up and charged into battle. The Spaniards were so astonished that they blundered here and there like drunkards; they ran through the streets with the warriors in pursuit. This was when the taking of captives began. A great many of the allies from Tlaxcala, Acolhuacan, Chalco and Xochimilco were overpowered by the Aztecs, and there was a great harvesting of prisoners, a great reaping of victims to be sacrificed.

The Spaniards and their allies waded into the lake because the road had become too slippery for them. The mud was so slick that they sprawled and floundered and could not stand up to fight. The Aztecs seized them as captives and dragged them across the mud.

The Spanish standard was taken and carried off during this encounter. The warriors from Tiatelolco captured it in the place known today as San Martin, but they were scornful of their prize and considered it of little importance.

Some of the Spaniards were able to escape with their lives. They retreated in the direction of Culhuacan, on the edge of the canal, and gathered there to recover their strength.

FIFTY-THREE SPANIARDS ARE SACRIFICED

The Aztecs took their prisoners to Yacacolco, hurrying them along the road under the strictest guard. Some of the captives were weeping, some were keening, and others were beating their palms against their mouths.

When they arrived in Yacacolco, they were lined up in long rows. One by one they were forced to climb to the temple platform, where they were sacrificed by the priests. The Spaniards went first, then their allies, and all were put to death. As soon as the sacrifices were finished, the Aztecs ranged the Spaniards' heads in rows on pikes. They also lined up their horses' heads. They placed the horses' heads at the bottom and the heads of the Spaniards above, and arranged them all so that the faces were toward the sun. However, they did not display any of the allies' heads. All told, fifty-three Spaniards and four horses were sacrificed there in Yacacolco.

The fighting continued in many different places. At one point, the allies from Xochimilco surrounded us in their canoes, and the toll of the dead and captured was heavy on both sides.

THE SUFFERINGS OF THE INHABITANTS

The Spanish blockade caused great anguish in the city. The people were tormented by hunger, and many starved to death. There was no fresh water to drink, only stagnant water and the brine of the lake, and many people died of dysentery.

The only food was lizards, swallows, corncobs and the salt grasses of the lake. The people also ate water lilies and the seeds of the colorin and chewed on deerhides and pieces of leather. They roasted and seared and scorched whatever they could find and then ate it. They ate the bitterest weeds and even dirt.

Nothing can compare with the horrors of that siege and the agonies of the starving. We were so weakened by hunger that, little by little, the enemy forced us to retreat. Little by little they forced us to the wall.

THE BATTLE IN THE MARKET PLACE

On one occasion, four Spanish cavalrymen entered the market place. They rode through it in a great circle, stabbing and killing many of our warriors and trampling everything under their horses' hooves. This was the first time the Spaniards had entered the market place, and our warriors were taken by surprise. But when the horsemen withdrew, the warriors recovered their wits and ran in pursuit.

It was at this same time that the Spaniards set fire to the temple and burned it to the ground. The flames and smoke leaped high into the air with a terrible roar. The people wept when they saw their temple on fire; they wept and cried out, fearing that afterward it would be plundered.

The battle lasted for many hours and extended to almost every corner of the market place. There was no action along the wall where the vendors sold lime, but the fighting raged among the flower stalls, and the stalls offering snails, and all the passageways between them.

GODS OR MEN?

Not all of the Indians took the Spaniards for gods, but all when confronted with their unexpected appearance asked themselves the question: "Are they gods or men?" All the societies we are concerned with have one thing in common: the invasion of their world by the unknown. All their documents, Aztec, Mayan, Inca, describe the strange attributes (beards, horses) and powers (writing, thunderbolts) of the Spaniards. The whole of Indian mythology implied the *possibility* that the white men might be gods and everywhere this was a source of doubt and anguish. The *answer* to the question "men or gods?" could be yes or no, depending on the particular circumstances of local history.

Nathan Wachtel, *The Vision of the Vanquished*, New York: Barnes and Noble, 1977, p. 24.

FIRST ENCOUNTERS TIMELINE

North America

1001	Vikings begin visits to Newfoundland
1492	Christopher Columbus lands on the island of San Salvador
1519	Hernán Cortés lands on coast of Mexico
1522	Fall of Aztec capital and destruction of Aztec Empire
1565	Spanish found St. Augustine in Florida
1607	English found Jamestown in Virginia
1608	French found Quebec
1609	Spanish found Santa Fé, capital of the southwest
1611	Dutch settle New Netherland (later New York)
1620	Pilgrims (English Separatists) found Plymouth Colony
1674	Dutch New Netherland becomes English New York
1763	French Quebec becomes British
1769	First Spanish mission in California founded near San Diego
1803	United States makes Louisiana Purchase from France
1879	Chief Joseph's speech in Washington, D.C.

Part Three

FIRST ENCOUNTERS IN SOUTH AMERICA

INTRODUCTION

In 1492, in addition to Christopher Columbus's famous exploit, another event took place in Spain which would have far-reaching historical consequences. In that year, Spain finally defeated the Moors, forcing them out of the Iberian Peninsula, thus terminating the 800 year war of liberation, the *Reconquista* (reconquest). Spain could begin to look outside to the new world which was then opening up, providing new opportunities for growth.

Within two decades, King Ferdinand and Queen Isabella of Spain had developed a bold, enterprising strategy that would capitalize on Columbus's discoveries. Spain would employ the energy and experience generated by the Reconquista in new directions, creating new colonies, converting the heathen to Christianity, by force if necessary, and bringing enormous wealth to the crown.

These goals would be achieved by the official commission of explorer-leaders and subsidizing their voyages across the Atlantic Ocean. They were called conquistadores (conquerors) and their bands were composed of men from all parts of Spanish society: nobles, soldiers, members of the working class, priests, and tradesmen, but also large numbers of illiterate, unemployed toughs with shady backgrounds, all drawn to the prospect of conquering, colonizing, and becoming rich. They had certain traits in common. Some were hardened by the endless wars against the Moors. All were steeped in the values of the Spanish Inquisition with its cruel use of torture and execution to force conversions.

The conquistadors' mission, supported by the Spanish royalty, was to venture to the New World to achieve three goals—conquer and colonize, convert the heathen to Christianity, by force if necessary, and send back to Spain quantities of gold and silver.

For the first 20 years or so, conquistadors confined their explorations to the islands of the Caribbean with mixed results. Then they began to hear rumors of a fabulously rich country somewhere to the southwest, across mountains and on a new ocean. Conquistador Vasco Núñez de Balboa and his men set out to traverse what is now the Isthmus of Panama. After an extended and difficult jungle trip, Balboa viewed the Pacific Ocean and claimed possession of that sea and the countries bordering it in the name of Spain. A remarkable feat was then accomplished. Four ships were disassembled on the Caribbean side and the parts dragged across the isthmus with enormous effort, to be reassembled on the Pacific side. The transportation needed to explore the countries of gold was now at hand.

Francisco Pizarro, the illiterate son of a Spanish colonel, made two exploratory voyages to the south and then persuaded the Spanish king to grant him permission to colonize the gold-rich empire of the Incas as governor. In 1532 Pizarro arrived at the heart of Inca territory and, with an absurdly small force of less than 200, defeated the Inca army of 80,000. The gold and treasure they found astounded the Spanish royalty. From then on, the conquistadors lost interest in the Caribbean and concentrated their efforts on what is now Peru. Throughout the first half of the sixteenth century, thousands of conquistadors left Spain for two new destinations, Peru to the south, and Mexico to the north, which had been taken from the Aztecs by another successful conquistador, Hernán Cortés.

The destruction of these large empires was accomplished through extreme brutality: repeated invasion, mass murder, execution of emperors, destruction of towns and public works, all helped by the spread of deadly European diseases.

For centuries, the only available accounts of the conquest of the New World were those written by the victors, but there were native voices recording the events at the time, or shortly thereafter, and these accounts have been rediscovered and studied in modern times. Four of these voices are presented here, narrating the encounters with the Europeans from the point of view of the defeated people.

The brutal conquest of the Inca Empire lasted until 1572 when the last Inca emperor was executed, leaving behind a ravaged and ruined countryside. The destruction was described by one of the most important Inca historians, Waman Puma, whose voice is heard at the end of this section.

27

GARCILASO DE LA VEGA

Execution of an Incan Emperor

Peru

Editor's Notes: Inca (King) Atahualpa's encounter with Francisco Pizarro took place after much careful preparation. He had heard of the brutality of Pizarro and his men, but he also believed, according to this writer, that the Spaniards were children of the Sun or divine. So he exchanged embassies with Pizarro, sent rich gifts and assurances of welcome, and agreed to a meeting. His troops numbered over 3,000 soldiers while Pizarro had just over 100. The meeting, in 1532, turned into a massacre. Thousands of soldiers and civilians were killed by a tiny invading army because the former were immobilized by fear that their opponents might be gods. Atahualpa was captured, and after paying an enormous ransom, was given a "show trial" and executed.

Garcilaso de la Vega (1539–1616) the author of this account, taken from his major historical work, Royal Commentaries, *was the son of an Incan princess and a Spanish captain, a first generation mestizo. He was educated in Peru but spent his adult life in Spain. He knew some of the people who participated in or witnessed the events he writes about and although he refers to the work of other historians, he corrected their facts and interpretations when he thought it necessary.*

When the emissaries arrived back among their own, they described the marvelous things they had seen in the Inca's palace, and the exquisite courtesy that had been shown them. Then they made equal division of the Inca's presents, with which everybody was delighted. But, like all good soldiers, they nevertheless did not neglect to prepare their weapons and their horses for the morrow, in order to be able to fight like Spaniards worthy of the name, despite the crushing superiority of Atahualpa's forces. When day dawned, they divided their cavalry, which only numbered sixty, into three groups of twenty men, commanded respectively by Ferdinand Pizarro, Ferdinand de Soto, and Sebastián de Belalcázar; then each one of these groups went and hid behind a wall, while waiting for the moment to swoop down on the Indians, thus increasing tenfold the effect of terror to which their appearance would give rise. The governor, Don Francisco Pizarro, took command of the infantry, which was composed of hardly more than one hundred men, and went to await King Atahualpa at one end of the main square.

Meanwhile, Atahualpa was advancing on a golden litter carried on the shoulders of his men, accompanied by his entire household and his court, and with a degree of magnificence that displayed as much pomp and majesty as it did military power. The litters were preceded by a multitude of servants, who cleared the ground, removing all stones and pebbles and even bits of straw, from the road over which the king was to travel. The military escort was composed of four squadrons, each one comprising eight thousand men. The first preceded the king, two more surrounded him, and the fourth closed the ranks, in the role of rear guard; all of these troops were commanded by General Rumiñaui. There was a distance of one league between the king's camp and the main square of the city, where the Spaniards were waiting for him; however, with all his pomp, it took him more than four hours to cover it. As we shall see later, it was not Atahualpa's intention to fight, but only to listen to the communications from the Pope and the Emperor that had been brought him by the Spaniards. The latter had been described to him as people who were so weak that they could not even climb a hill on their own feet: "That is why they have horses," people said, "some of them ride on their backs while others have to be pulled, hanging on to the horse's tail or to its girth; they are incapable of running as we do, nor can they carry anything heavy."

So all of this information, added to the fact that he considered the Spaniards to be divine beings, made Atahualpa quite unable to suspect the kind of reception that these people had been planning for him.

He entered the square with his three first squadrons, the fourth remaining outside. When he saw the handful of Spanish infantrymen awaiting him, in tightly serried ranks, as though filled with fear, the king said: "These people are messengers from God. See that no harm is done them, but, on the contrary, treat them respectfully and courteously."

Upon which, a Dominican friar approached the Inca, cross in hand, to speak to him in the name of the Emperor. This was Friar Vincente de Valverde.

Everything in the aspect of this man was calculated to excite the Inca's curiosity, for he had never seen anyone like him. He wore a beard, the tonsure, and the frock of his order; in one hand he held a wooden cross, and in the other, a book which, according to certain chroniclers was *The Summum*, by Sylvester, unless it was the breviary or the Bible.

"What is this Spaniard's estate?" asked the Inca. "Is he the superior, inferior, or equal of the others?"

One of the three dignitaries who had been attached to the Spaniards since their arrival in Cajamarca replied: "Inca, all I know is that he is a captain, a guide who speaks [by which he meant preacher], and a minister and messenger of the supreme God, Pachacamac [one of two supreme Inca deities], which makes him different from the others." . . .

King Atahualpa understood from the priest's peroration that the Pope had ordered, and that the Emperor [Charles V] desired him to give up his kingdoms willy-nilly: that he would be compelled to do so by fire, sword, and bloodshed; and that, like Pharaoh, he would be exterminated with all his army. From this he concluded that these guests whom he and his people called Viracochas [one of two supreme Inca deities], considering them as gods, had been transformed into mortal enemies of his people and of his line, since they had nothing but these cruel, pitiless things to say to him. And he felt so sad and so distressed that he could not refrain from uttering out loud the word "*Atac!*" which means, alas! Finally, rising above his sorrow, and restraining as best he could the passions that racked his soul, he, in turn, took the floor and spoke as follows:

Despite the fact that you have refused me all the other things I asked of your emissaries, it would at least have given me great pleasure if you had consented to speak to me through a more learned, more accurate, more experienced interpreter than the one you have; because you must know the incomparable value that words take on for anyone who wants to learn about the customs and the civil and political life of another people; indeed, you might be endowed with the greatest virtues, and it would be difficult for me to appreciate this through what I can see and understand, so long as you do not express yourselves. And how much more pressing still this necessity becomes when the encounter takes place between persons who come from regions that are so remote from one another as ours are. In reality, if such persons attempt to speak and negotiate through the intermediary of interpreters who know neither language, then they might as well choose a four-footed go-between, among their own cattle! I say this, man of God, because I surmise that your words are quite different from those spoken by this Indian; indeed the very reason for our meeting is evidence of this fact.

We are here to discuss peace, friendship, and permanent brotherhood, even an alliance between our two bloods, as was stated by your first emissaries when they came to call on me. And these words have a different sound from those your interpreter has just spoken; for he only speaks of war and death, of fire and sword, of banishment and destruction, of extinction of the royal blood of the Incas, of alienation of my kingdom, and, whether I will or no, of my vassalage to someone whom I do not even know. From all of this, I can only conclude two things: either your prince and you yourselves are but tyrants who go about ravaging and destroying everything they encounter in the world, appropriating by force kingdoms to which they have no right, killing, robbing, despoiling those who owe them nothing and have done them no harm; or else you are the ministers of God, whom we call Pachacamac, and He has designated you to punish and destroy us. If this be so, my vassals and I accept death and whatever else you may choose to do with us, not at all through fear inspired by your weapons or your threats, but in order that the last wishes of my father, Huaina Capac, may be fulfilled; for he commanded us, on his deathbed, to serve and honor the bearded men, like yourselves, who would come to this land after he had left it. For many years he had known that these men were cruising in their ships along the coast of our empire; and he told us that their laws and their customs, their science, and their bravery were greater than our own. This is why we called you Viracochas, meaning by this that you were the messengers of the great god Viracocha: his will and his indignation could not be other than just, and who could resist the power of his arms? But he is also full of pity and mercy, and therefore you, who are his messengers and ministers, you who are not human, but divine, you cannot allow a repetition of the crimes, the robberies, and all the other cruelty that was perpetrated in Tumbez and in the other regions you came through.

In addition to this, your herald spoke to me of five well-known men, whom I should know about. The first is the god three and one which make four [a garbled version of the Trinity], whom you call the creator of the universe; no doubt he is the same as the one we call Pachacamac and Viracocha. The second [Adam] is the one whom you say is the father of the human species, upon whom all other men have laid their sins. You call the third one Jesus Christ, who did not burden his fellow men with his sins, as all other men did, but who was killed. The fourth, you call the Pope, and the fifth, Charles.

Without taking the others into consideration, you call this latter the all-powerful sovereign of the universe and say that he is above everybody else. But then, if this Charles is the prince and lord of the entire world, how is it that the Pope should have had to grant him permission to make war upon me and usurp my kingdoms? And if this was necessary, this means that the Pope is a greater, more powerful lord than he is, and therefore the prince of the entire universe. I am surprised that I should have to pay tribute to Charles and not to the others; you give no reason for this, and I myself do not see any that would oblige me to do so. Because, if I were obliged, quite frankly, to pay service and tribute to someone, it seems to me that it would rather be to God who, as you say, created us all, and to that first man who was the father of all other men, and to Jesus Christ, who never burdened others with his sins, and, lastly, to the Pope, who can dispose of my person and of my kingdom, to assign them to others.

But if you say that I owe nothing to any one of these three, it seems to me that I owe even less to Charles, who was never lord of this land, and has never even seen it. And even if we were to admit that, having received the Pope's blessing, he really had some rights over me, would it not be just and fair that you should tell me this, before proclaiming threats of war, bloodshed, and death? I am neither so foolish nor so unreasonable as not to know how to obey him who exerts authority over me by rights, and justly and reasonably; but how am I to comply with the Pope's desires without knowing what they are?

Lastly, to come back to that eminent man, Jesus Christ, who refused to burden others with his sins, I should like to know how he died: was it from sickness, or at the hands of his enemies? And was he set among the gods before or after his death? I should like to know whether or not you consider as gods these five men whom you hold up to me, and whom you so venerate. For if this be the case, then you have more gods than we have, for we worship no god other than Pachacamac, who is our supreme God, after whom we worship the Sun, whose bride and sister is the Moon. . . .

In making his reply, the Inca reckoned with the awkwardness of the interpreter, Felipe. He pronounced his sentences slowly, breaking them up into short phrases, so as to give him ample time to understand. And, above all, instead of speaking the language of Cuzco, he chose that of Chinchasuyu, which the Indian understood much better. Despite these precautions, however, the king's thought was nevertheless quite imperfectly and barbarously translated, while the royal historians noted it faithfully on their *quipus* [knotted cords], in order that it might remain in their archives.

But the Spaniards, who had grown impatient during this long speech, suddenly sprang from their hiding places and attacked the Indians in order to rob them of their handsome gold jewels encrusted with precious stones which they were wearing for this solemn occasion. Other Spaniards climbed up a small tower, on top of which was an idol covered with gold and silver plate enhanced with precious stones. Soon there was immense confusion, the Spaniards struggling to take possession of these treasures, and the Indians to defend them. . . .

Shall we say, to summarize, that more than five thousand Indians were killed on that day, among whom were more than fifteen hundred old people, women, and children, who had come out of curiosity to be present at this unprecedented meeting. Some were suffocated in the crowd or trampled to death by the Spanish horses, while others—how many no one can say—died entombed under one of the walls of the square, which collapsed under the pressure of those who were trying to escape. And yet, as I said before, there were on hand more than thirty thousand armed Indian fighters, and the Spaniards only numbered one hundred and sixty! But all these Indians were haunted by the famous prediction of the Inca Viracocha, and they asked themselves if the moment had not arrived when, not only the Empire and its laws, but also their religion and its rites were about to disappear like so much smoke. For this reason, they neither dared to defend themselves, nor to offend the Spaniards whom they considered as gods and the messengers of Viracocha. Spanish historians themselves confirm the fact that Atahualpa forbade his troops to fight. . . .

The Spanish cavalrymen left their hiding places, hurling themselves like thunderbolts at the Indian squadrons, their lances in rest; and they transpierced as many as they could without encountering any resistance. Don Pizarro and his wildly impatient infantrymen had succeeded, meanwhile, in forcing their way to Atahualpa, because at the very idea of so rich a catch they already saw themselves the masters of all the treasures in Peru. The Indians crowded about the royal litter, ready to defend with their own bodies the Inca's sacred person. They were massacred one by one, however, without having made the slightest gesture of defense. Then Don Francisco, who had finally come up close to the king, seized the latter's clothing and, together, they were soon wrestling on the ground.

And thus it was that King Atahualpa became prisoner of the Spaniards, which fact, when the Indians realized it, made them flee in the greatest disorder. Being unable to leave by the only gate of the city, which was in the hands of the cavalry, they hurled themselves with such fury against one of the enclosing walls that they opened up a breach more than one hundred feet wide, through which they were able to escape to the plain. One author wrote that, on this occasion, by yielding to death-hunted men, this stone wall showed more tenderness and pity than the hearts of the Spaniards. Indeed, according to historians, the Spaniards were so angry when they saw the Indians escape, that they dashed across the plain in their pursuit and massacred a large number with their lances, until nightfall forced them to stop. They then pillaged the Inca's camp, where they amassed a considerable amount of booty. . . .

Meanwhile, the Inca Atahualpa, finding himself a prisoner, with his feet in irons, had offered to fill with gold the room he was kept in—which was a fine large room—in order to obtain his freedom.

"When he saw that the Spaniards shrugged their shoulders at this proposal, and turned their backs on him, as though they did not consider this possible," wrote Francisco Lopez de Gómara, "he touched the wall of his room, as high as he could raise his arms and, at this height, drew a red line that ran around the entire room.

"The gold and silver of my ransom will make a pile that high," he said, "on condition that you neither break nor smelt any of the objects that I shall have brought, until this limit will have been reached."

A date of payment was set, and once the deal was concluded, gold and silver began to flow into Cajamarca. But such immense quantities were needed that it seemed as though all Peru's resources would not be sufficient, and the time set came and went. Then the Spaniards began to grumble, saying that the Inca was poking fun at them, and that his envoys, instead of collecting gold and silver, were quite simply levying troops to come and free him. . . .

Atahualpa's trial was a solemn one and it lasted a long time. The court was presided over by Don Francisco Pizarro, with Don Diego de Almagro acting as assessor; Sancho de Cuéllar filled the role of clerk, another, that of prosecuting attorney, another, that of defense lawyer, to plead Atahualpa's case. Then there were two attorney generals, named by each one of the parties; two investigators, who collected the testimony and presented it to the court, and two barristers, who were simply there to give their opinions. Although I knew several of these men personally, I prefer not to name them. . . .

Ten witnesses were heard. Seven of them had been chosen among the servants of the Spaniards, and three from the outside, in order that they should not all be domestics. As Gómara writes, they said everything that the interpreter, Felipe, wanted to make them say. One of the non-domestic witnesses, named Quespe, who was captain of a company, and the last to be examined, replied each time with one single word, saying *i*, which means yes, or *manam*, which means no. And, in order that the judges might understand him and that the interpreter should not betray him, he raised and lowered his head two or three times when he said yes, and nodded it from left to right, in addition to a gesture with his right hand, when he wanted to say no; and the judges and ministers greatly admired the sagacity of this Indian.

But in spite of all that, they were not afraid to condemn to death so great and powerful a king as Atahualpa, and he was notified of his sentence, as we explained. Many of the Spaniards protested vehemently when they heard the sentence, not only among Pizarro's companions, but also among those of Almagro, because these latter were men with generous hearts, capable of feeling pity. . . .

In fact, things came to such a pass that they would have hurled themselves at one another and all been killed, if God had not stopped it by making others, who were less impassioned than they, intervene between the two groups, and thus succeed in appeasing the Inca's defenders, by telling them to consider the necessities that their own lives and the king's service rendered imperative; that it was not right for quarrels over infidels to divide Christians; and that, lastly, there were only fifty persons sharing their point of view, whereas more than three hundred upheld the point of view of the court; and that, if they should come to blows, they would have nothing to gain from it, but on the contrary, would only destroy themselves as well as such a rich kingdom as this one, which was theirs for all time, if they put its king to death.

These threats—or these good reasons—finally calmed Atahualpa's protectors, and they consented to his execution, which the others carried out.

Once the two kings, Huáscar Inca and Atahualpa, who were brothers as well as enemies, were dead, the Spaniards remained supreme masters of both Peruvian kingdoms, there being no one left to oppose or even contradict them, because all the Indians, whether they belonged to [the area of] Quito or to [the area of] Cuzco, had remained, after their kings were gone, like sheep without a shepherd.

A SPANISH JUSTIFICATION

Dr. Juan Ginés de Sepúlveda (1490–1573), a learned humanist and disciple of Aristotle, had never visited the New World, but he held firm opinions supported by his ponderous treatise arguing that it was just to war against and enslave the Indians. . . . Aristotle's proposition that some men are by nature slaves provided the foundation for Sepúlveda's argument. Just as children are naturally inferior to adults, women to men, and monkeys to human beings, so Indians, he said, were naturally inferior to Spaniards. "How can we doubt that these people—so uncivilized, so barbaric, contaminated with so many impieties and obscenities—have been justly conquered by such an excellent, pious, and most just king as was Ferdinand the Catholic and as is now Emperor Charles, and by such a most humane nation and excellent in every kind of virtue?"

Daniel J. Boorstin, *The Discoverers*, New York: Random House, 1983, p. 633.

28

TITU CUSI YUPANKI
NOT GODS BUT CONQUERERS
Peru

Editor's Notes: Manco was crowned emperor of the Incas in 1533, three years after the Spanish conquistador Francisco Pizarro had first entered Incan territory. At that time, believing that it would be in the best interests of his country to maintain peace with the newcomers, not yet seen as invaders, Manco pledged allegiance to the Spanish king. But inflamed by power and disdain for the native population, the conquistadors captured the emperor, placed him in irons, and subjected him to extreme forms of insult by raping Inca women before his eyes and urinating on his face.

Now, thoroughly disillusioned and infuriated by the behavior of the conquistadors, he secretly wrote to his generals and government officials explaining that he no longer considered the Spanish to be viracochas (small gods), but children of the devil.

In the first selection, below, he reveals his change of attitude. In the second selection, he instructs his army to secretly assemble and attack the invaders. At first, the ensuing battle was successful, but eventually the Spanish prevailed and Manco withdrew to another part of Peru to set up a new Inca kingdom.

Manco's son, Titu Cusi Yupanqui, who became emperor himself in 1560, could not write and knew no Spanish, but he dictated this history in the year before he was executed in 1571. It was then put into Spanish but languished in a library for 300 years before its rediscovery and publication.

When Gonzalo Pizarro (who was acting as the corregidor [governor] of Cuzco in the absence of the governor Francisco Pizarro), as well as Hernando Pizarro, Juan Pizarro, and many others were staying in the city, it happened that

Juan Pizarro, the brother of Hernando Pizarro, found out about how much silver my father had given to his brothers and called out in a fit of envy, "So, only my brothers get silver, but not I? By the devil, that is about to change! They'll have to give me gold and silver as well, the same as they gave to my brothers. If they don't, I'll teach them a lesson that they won't forget." With these threats, he gathered all the people and said, "Let's arrest him, let's arrest Manco Inca." When my father learned that in the city there was a conspiracy being planned against him, he ordered that all the chiefs of the land come together. Actually, many of them were already in Cuzco for the protection of his person. When he had them all gathered before him, he, after having consulted with the above-mentioned chief Vile Oma, gave them the following speech.

THE INCA'S SPEECH TO HIS CHIEFS ABOUT THE SIEGE OF CUZCO

"My much beloved sons and brothers, I never thought that I would find myself compelled to require of you what I am about to; for I thought and always took for granted that these bearded people whom you call Viracochas would never deceive or harm me, for I used to think and say that they had indeed come on orders of Viracocha. Now, however, I look back on my experiences with them and discover—as you have seen—how badly they have treated me and how poorly they have thanked me for all that I have done for them. They have disrespected me a thousand times; they have taken me prisoner and chained my hands and feet like you would a dog; and, not enough, after they have promised me that they would from now on respect our compact of mutual love and friendship, they are now engaged in a plot to capture and kill me. So now I will ask you, like one asks one's sons, to remember what you have so often urged me to do, which is precisely what I want to do now: you said that I should rise up against them and you asked why I tolerated them in my country. So far, I have been reluctant to do so because I deemed it impossible that the things would happen that I now see happening. But because this is the way it is and because they insist on vexing me, I find myself compelled to do them likewise. I will not tolerate any more of their chicaneries. On your lives, you have always shown me much love; and you did your best in fulfilling my wishes. Now, fulfill only this one and gather all that are here. Get ready to send your messengers all over the land, so that in twenty days' time all are united here in this city but without the knowledge of those bearded ones. Meanwhile, I will send messengers to Lima, to Quiso Yupanqui, my captain who governs that region, in order to inform him that on the day that we attack these Spaniards who are here, he is also to attack those Spaniards who are there. Thus, if he acts there at the same time as we act here, we will finish them off without any of them staying alive; and we will rid ourselves of this nightmare and will be happy thereafter." After he had finished explaining his plan to his captains about how to get their men ready for the impending battle with the Spaniards, they all replied in unison and with one voice that they were very glad, willing, and ready to carry out what my father had ordered them to do.

Thus, without further delay, they went to work as each sent envoys to the region that he controlled.

After these men had been sent out to the aforementioned regions and while the said Juan Pizarro roamed the land in a dangerous manner and with bad intentions, an Indian by the name of Antonico, who spoke the Spaniards' language, came to see my father and informed him that Juan Pizarro and the others wanted to arrest him the next day and even to kill him, unless he gave them much gold and silver. When my father heard what the said Indian (Antonico) told him, he believed him and made a pretext of going out to Callca to hunt. The Spaniards, who were clueless as to what my father was planning to do, had no objections and thought that they could carry out their evil design after his return, which they thought would be soon.

After my father had stayed in Callca for a few days and while the men whom he had sent for were gathering, he sent a dispatch from there via a courier to Quiso Yupanqui in Lima in order to inform him of the day and hour in which he was planning to attack the Spaniards, so that he, too, would attack them and that, thus, both attacks—Quiso Yupanqui's in Lima and my father's in Cuzco—would be carried out at the same time. As my father was busy with these things, the Spaniards sent him many letters in which they asked him to return home soon for, they said, they missed him very much. My father replied by saying that he was not finished hunting but that he would return as soon as he could. As the Spaniards realized that whenever they sent for him he did not want to return and that day after day he procrastinated more and sent ever less credible replies, they decided to go after him in order to bring him back by force or to kill him. They appointed some captains in Cuzco and while some of them went out to effect the said objective, the others stayed back in Cuzco ready to reinforce the first group if necessary. They arrived at the bridge over the Callca River, where they were engaged by some guards who were blocking their passage. The Spaniards began to fight my father's men but then returned to Cuzco, followed by many of my father's men, who were uttering many shrieks and loud shouts. On their retreat to Cuzco, the Spaniards were a bit shaken by the battle that had passed and the people who were pursuing them. When the Spaniards reached Carmenga, which oversees all of Cuzco, they called upon the help of their comrades, whose vigilance had not relented and who rushed to the support of those in distress. At the said town of Carmenga, they engaged in battle with the pursuers and many others who had come there in answer to my father's call. The outcome of the battle was that the Indians cornered the Spaniards in Cuzco without killing many of them. During the night, they kept them locked in and on edge with loud cries. However, they did not attack them because they were awaiting the many men who were supposed to arrive the next day and also because my father had ordered them not to attack. He had given that order not only because he wanted to take them more easily once the reinforcements had arrived but also because he wanted to negotiate with them.

THE SIEGE OF CUZCO

The following day, after they had withdrawn to Cuzco in this manner, they put up many well-equipped guards overnight at all the entrances. In the evening, a tumultuous crowd arrived near Cuzco. However, they did not attack the city because they thought that the night had advanced too far and that the great darkness would not permit them to overwhelm their enemies. Thus, they erected camps on all the elevated points and mountains that allowed them to overlook the city and placed a great number of guards and sentries all around the camps. In the morning of the following day, at nine o'clock, all the Spaniards were gathered information on Cuzco's central plaza (their precise number is unknown but it is said that they were numerous and that they had many blacks with them). Suddenly, a huge number of men appeared everywhere around Cuzco and closed in on the city—with much noise and music from their whistles, horns, and trumpets, as well as loud war cries. Their number was so great that the whole world appeared to darken; there must have been more than four hundred thousand advancing in the following order.

THE INDIANS' ADVANCE IN THE SIEGE

From Carmenga, which lies in the direction of the Chinchaysuyu, came Coriatao, Cuillas, and Taipi, with many others in order to close the city's exit in that direction with their hordes. From the Cuntisuyu, which is the direction of Cachicachi, came Huaman Quilcana, Curi Huallpa, both superbly equipped and in battle formation, closing a huge gap of more than half a league wide. From the Collasuyu came Llicllic and many other generals with a huge number of men, which was in fact the largest contingent that formed the besieging army. From the Antisuyu came Antallca and Ronpa Yupanqui and many others in order to close the ring around the Spaniards. The impermeability of the completed ring was remarkable. They wanted to attack the Spaniards on that very day but did not dare to proceed as long as my father had not given the orders. For, as I have already explained, he had forbidden anyone, under penalty of death, to make a move. When Vile Oma, the commanding general of the forces, saw all of them completely ready, he sent word to my father, who was staying at Callca at that time, to let him know that the Spaniards were surrounded and in great distress and to inquire whether they should kill them or do something else with them. My father replied that they should be left in their predicament; after all they, too, had caused him much grief, so they should suffer like he suffered. He would get there the next day and finish them off. When Vile Oma heard the message that my father sent him, he was very unhappy about it, for he would have preferred to destroy the Spaniards right away, as he could very easily have done. But he did not dare to disobey the will of my father and announced all around the place that, under penalty of death, nobody was to make a move until he had given the appropriate orders. Moreover, he had all the canals of the city opened in order to flood the fields and roads inside and outside the populated area in case that the Spaniards were to attempt a getaway. This way, they would find the entire land flooded and, once their horses got stuck in the mud, they would easily be overcome by their enemies on foot, for people dressed like the Spaniards have a difficult time in dealing with swamps. All of Vile Oma's orders were carried out exactly as he had commanded. When the Spaniards saw themselves thus surrounded and in such distress, they became convinced that their doom was imminent and, as they could not find a way out, they did not know what to do. While they found themselves so dangerously surrounded, they had to endure the Indians showering them with scorn and mockery, throwing stones on the roofs of their tents and mocking them by lifting a leg at them. Moreover, the Indians began setting the Spaniards' shelters on fire and almost succeeded in setting ablaze the church during one of the raids, if it hadn't been for some blacks who were hiding on the roof. Although they had to endure a hail of arrows shot by the Sati and Anti Indians, they remained unharmed, being protected by God and their shields. As the Spaniards thought themselves lost in such a miserable situation, they entrusted their fate to God. They spent the entire night in the church calling upon God for help, kneeling on the floor and raising their hands folded before their mouths. This is the posture in which they were observed by many Indians. Even those who were waking in the middle of the plaza, as well as many Indians who had been allied with the Spaniards since the events of Cajamarca, did the same thing.

THE SPANIARDS' ATTACK ON THE INDIANS IN THE FORTRESS OF CUZCO

In the early morning of the next day, all the Spaniards left the church and mounted their horses, poised for battle. They looked around and suddenly put their spurs to their horses and, despite their enemies, broke at full speed through the gate, which was sealed like a wall, and made for the hill in the life-and-death flight. When the Indians who were surrounding Cuzco saw them running like this, they cried, "They are fleeing to Castile, they are fleeing to Castile, cut them off." Thus, the entire ring around the city dissolved because some of them were going after them and others tried to cut off the Spaniards' escape route; yet others went to warn those who were guarding the bridge, so that none of them would be able to escape in any direction. When the Spaniards saw themselves pursued by many men, they turned their horses around and went across a mountain called Queancalla in order to attack them from the rear where Vile Oma had taken position. Meanwhile, the latter had climbed up to the fortress of Cuzco, which was called Saczahuaman, in order to take shelter there. The Spaniards fought desperately and took the four gates of the fortress. The Indians hurled many rocks from the mighty walls, shot arrows, and threw lances and spears, which harassed the Spaniards greatly. They killed Juan Pizarro and two blacks as well as many Indians who were allied with the Spaniards. But when Vile Oma's men ran out of ammunition of rocks and other projectiles, the Spaniards, thanks to divine favor, succeeded in penetrating and taking the fortress. Thereby, they killed and crushed many Indians who were inside. Others threw themselves from the walls. The first ones to jump died because the walls were very high; some of those who jumped later survived because they landed on a pile of dead bodies. The battle was very bloody on both sides, because many Indians were fighting for the Spaniards. Among these were two of my father's brothers, Ynguill and Vaipai, as well as many men from his band and Chachapoya and Cañari Indians.

After the fall of the fortress, the battle lasted another three days, for the Indians regrouped on the next day in order to try to retake the fortress. They courageously attacked the Spaniards, who had taken shelter in the fortress; but because of all the guards, consisting of Cañari auxiliary troops as well as Spaniards, they could not harm them. Moreover, these Indians reported the appearance of a white horse, which had been among the first to penetrate the fortress, doing great damage among the Indians. The battle lasted the entire day. At nightfall, the Indians returned to their positions, for they couldn't fight their enemies any longer because of the great darkness. As the Spaniards did not want to give up the fortress, they let them go. The next morning they resumed the battle, which was fought relentlessly on both sides. Finally, when the Indians were attacking the Spaniards with great courage, the Spaniards suddenly broke out of the fortress and launched a fierce counterattack. In the face of this onslaught, the Indians withdrew to Callca, where my father was staying. The Spaniards followed them to the Yucay River, killing or pulling to flight a large number of them. There, the Indians eluded the Spaniards, who went on to Callca, where my father was. However, they did not find him there because he was attending a festivity in a town called Sacsasiray. As they could not catch him there, they returned to Cuzco by another way but lost a large amount of their baggage, which the Indians, who had come out of their hiding place, took from their rear guard. Then the Indians, with their booty, made for the village where my father was celebrating.

After the celebrations in the village of Sacsasiray were over, my father went on to the town of Tambo and spent one night in Yucay on the way. When he arrived at Tambo, he had the entire population of the country gather, for he was planning to build a mighty fort in order to defend himself against the Spaniards, who might attack him. After a very short time all were gathered before my father, and he made the following speech:

The Speech that the Inca made to all his captains in Tambo, whereto he had withdrawn after the failed siege of Cuzco

My beloved sons and brothers, you know how in my previous speeches I have always kept you from doing harm to those evil people who entered my land under the pretense of being sons of Viracocha and whom I permitted to do so. Because of all the very good things I have done for them and because of giving them everything I had—silver and gold, materials and maize, herds, subjects, women, servants, and countless other things—they took me prisoner. They insulted and maltreated me without reason. Then they tried to kill me, which I found out through Antonico, their translator. He is present here; he ran away from the Spaniards because he couldn't bear it any longer. And as you learned during the mobilization of the troops for the siege of Cuzco, I had withdrawn to Callca so that we could deal them a heavy blow without first making them suspicious. As far as I know, everything has been carried out according to my orders. However, I was not able to be present as I had wanted to. This was detrimental to your effort to conquer the fortress of Saczahuaman, which they took from you because of your negligence. Moreover, they then put you to flight, following you to Yucay, without you being able to stop them. It was painful for me to see that you let them get away, despite the fact that you were so numerous and they were but few. Perhaps Viracocha aided them because, as you told me, they worshipped Him all night on their knees. After all, if he didn't help them, what else could explain that they were able to elude you, who were countless in number. But what's done is done. From now on, you must take heed on your life how you deal with them, for you must know that they are our main enemy and that we will always be theirs, because that's the way they have chosen it. I want to take cover in this place and build a fortress that nobody can penetrate. On your life do me this favor, and it may well turn out to be very useful for us one day.

THE SHOCK OF COLUMBUS'S DISCOVERY

The discovery of the New World in 1492 came as an immense shock to Europeans. The clergy, the educated, and the common people had all believed that the scriptures, together with the writings of the church fathers and the ancient authorities, contained the sum of all human knowledge. But it was clear to everyone that neither Pliny nor Aristotle nor, in particular, the Bible contained knowledge of another world across the ocean. God and the church fathers had, it seemed, failed to mention the New World. This absence meant that the scriptures and the ancient philosophers provided no guidance on how the New World should be seen—as an earthly paradise, like Eden before the Fall, or a terrifying place inhabited by satanic creatures from which God had protected his flock. And how should Christian Europe deal with a whole continent of pagan people: were these innocent, ignorant souls awaiting baptism into the welcoming arms of the Holy Roman church, or were they dangerous pagans whose impiety put them beyond salvation? Though well used to condemning non-believers and heretics, for the first time the Church had to ask, What is the Christian view of those who have never known Christ's teaching?

Roger Osborne, Civilization, *A New History of the Western World*, New York: Pegasus Books, 2006, pp. 256–257.

29

UNNAMED INCA

THE BEHEADING OF EMPEROR AMARU

Peru

Editor's Notes: In 1571, 39 years after the Spanish conquistadors first entered Peru, Tupac Amaru, son of Emperor Tupac Manco, became emperor himself. His reign was short-lived. Infuriated by Amaru's efforts to ban Christianity, the Spanish decided to crush the Inca state once and for all. In 1572, a Spanish army marched into the Inca heartland and captured Tupac Amaru. In chains, he and his pregnant wife were taken to Cuzco, the Inca capital. After a sham trial, he was sentenced to death and forcibly baptized. An unnamed Inca witness recorded what next took place.

All the open spaces, as well as roof tops and windows of the parishes of Carmenca and San Cristobal were so full of people that a fallen orange could not have reached the ground, so closely packed were they. When the executioner, a Cañari Indian, brought out the cutlass to behead Tupac Amaru, something wonderful happened. The crowd of Indians uttered such a cry of woe one might have thought the Day of Judgement had arrived ... After receiving last words of comfort from the fathers standing at his side, the Inca laid his head on the block like a lamb. The executioner stepped forward, and lifting the Inca's hair in his left hand, hacked off his head with a single blow and raised it up for all to see. As the head was severed, all the bells of the cathedral rang out and all the other bells, in all the monasteries and all the churches of the city. The execution was the occasion of great sorrow and brought tears to all eyes. The Inca's head was fixed on a pikestaff close to the

Reprinted from *The Vision of the Vanquished: The Spanish Conquest through Indian Eyes, 1530–1570*, by Nathan Wachtel (Sussex, England: Harvester Press/New York: Barnes & Noble, 1977): pp. 183–184.

scaffold. Each day it became more beautiful, for in his lifetime the Inca had had a comely face. At night the Indians came out to worship him, until one morning, at dawn, Juan de la Sierra, standing by chance at his window, saw the idolatry of the people. The viceroy was informed. He ordered the head to be buried, with the body, in a chapel in the cathedral.

30

WAMAN PUMA
THE CONQUEST OF THE INCAS—POSTSCRIPT
Peru

Editor's Notes: Waman Puma, the Incas' most famous historian, lived in Peru's post-conquest era. Born in 1533, he was witness to the disastrous after-effects of the Spanish invasion and conquest of the Incan Empire. Waman spent 30 years, from 1585 to 1615, completing his book with its 1,200 pages and 400 drawings. He describes in great detail the history of the conquest, based on extensive travels throughout the Andes, interviewing people who had personally experienced the Spanish conquest which had lasted 42 years. The voluminous details describe incidents of murder, extortion, bribery, rape, corruption, and destruction of public works. In this selection, Waman describes the status of Incan society after the Spanish had executed the last emperor, Tupac Amaru in 1572, and had completed the destruction of the empire.

You should consider that in the time of the Incas ... people had much faith in God and were loyal, and very charitable, and humble, and they raised their Sons and daughters with discipline and teaching ... And [now] the people of this life are lost. There is no justice. Everything is by self-interest and the lust for aggrandisement. . . .

In the time of the Incas there was none of this greed for gold and silver. But now there are many thieves: Indians, Negroes, and most of all the Spaniards, who flay the poor Indians and injure them and rob them. And not only that, for they take their wives and daughters—especially the priests. . . .

And consider ... Don Francisco de Toledo, the viceroy, who in his pride wanted to be greater than a king ... and who passed judgment on the King of

---

Reprinted from *Stolen Continents: The Americas through Indian Eyes since 1492*, by Ronald Wright (Boston: Houghton Mifflin, 1992), p. 192.

The execution of Tupac Amaru, as depicted in Felipe Guaman Poma de Ayala's *El primer nueva corónica y buen gobierno* (1615/1616), p. 453. (*Source:* København, Det Kongelige Bibliotek/Copenhagen. Courtesy of The Royal Library, GKS2232 4o, http://www.kb.dk/permalink/2006/poma/info/en/frontpage.htm.)

Peru! If only Your Majesty had sent a judge here then to behead *him* on the same scaffold!

Consider the poor Indians and their works ... that in every town they built irrigation canals from the rivers and springs, the lakes and reservoirs. In ancient times they built them with so much effort ... and with the greatest skill in the world, so that it seems as if every Indian [that ever lived] raised up a stone. And all this was sufficient for the large number of people that there used to be here. And thus throughout the kingdom all the land produced food, whether jungles, deserts, or the difficult mountains of this realm....And the Inca kings ordered that ... nobody should damage or remove one stone, and that no livestock should enter the said canals....

But now this law is no longer kept, and so all the fields are ruined for lack of water. Because of this the Indians lose their farms ... For in these times the Spaniards release their animals, their mule trains, cows, their goats and sheep, and they cause great damage. And they also take the water, and break the irrigation canals, so that they could not be repaired now for any amount of money. And the little water that remains, they take even that from the poor Indians. And so the Indians abandon their towns.

THE MOST IMPORTANT LEGACY

[T]he crown insisted that all the [conquistadors] be married. The trickle of Spanish women in the first half of the sixteenth century swelled to 28 percent of all migrants by the 1570s. Nevertheless, the continued shortage of women from the home country encouraged intermarriage, the taking of native mistresses, or sexual enslavement. The male children of these unions were known as *mestizos*. When the blacks arrived, their male offspring with whites were known as *mulattoes*, and with Amerindians as *zambos*. Some authorities consider this interbreeding to be the most important and lasting legacy of the encounter between the Old and the New Worlds.

Marvin Lunenfeld, ed., *1492: Discovery, Invasion, Encounter*, Lexington, MA: D.C. Heath, 1991, p. 327.

FIRST ENCOUNTERS TIMELINE

South America

1492	Spain defeats the Moors
1513	Vasco Núñez de Balboa reaches the Pacific Ocean
1517	Four ships disassembled and dragged over Panama isthmus
1521	Hernán Cortés conquers Mexico
1526	Francisco Pizarro's first voyage to Peru
1530	Pizarro enters Incan territory
1533	Pizarro captures and executes Incan emperor Atahualpa
1545	Assassination of Emperor Manco Inca Yupanqui
1560	Coronation of Emperor Titu Cusi Yupanqui
1571	Execution of Emperor Titu Cusi Yupanqui
1571	Succession of Emperor Topa Amaru
1572	Execution of Emperor Topa Amaru; end of Inca Empire
1585–1615	Historian Waman Puma completes a history of Peru
1617	El Inca Garcilaso de la Vega publishes *The General History of Peru* about the Conquest
1772	Pacification of Incan territory by Spain

Part Four

FIRST ENCOUNTERS IN GREATER AUSTRALIA

INTRODUCTION

Greater Australia is the name for Australia and the islands of Tasmania and New Guinea. This term was introduced in the 1970s to differentiate these islands, which were once part of one continental land mass with Australia, from the much larger area called Oceania or Australasia which includes New Zealand and many islands in the Pacific.

Greater Australia was first settled between 40 to 60,000 years ago by successive waves of hunter-gatherers from Southeast Asia, some driven south by the Ice Age. The first Europeans to explore the area were Portuguese and Spanish navigators in the early sixteenth century, well before Captain James Cook's little fleet circumnavigated the globe, 1768 to 1771. It was Cook who first confirmed the fact that the island of New Guinea was an island separate from the continent of Australia.

Today New Guinea, the second largest island in the world, is divided into two parts. The western half originally was colonized by the Dutch and is now an Indonesian province. The eastern part, constituting the independent country of Papua New Guinea, was colonized in turn by Germans, British, and Australians, until finally in 1975, it achieved its independence.

There are no selections in this anthology from Australia or Tasmania because of the paucity of accounts by indigenous people who witnessed the arrival of the Europeans. But from Papua New Guinea, there are two extraordinary twentieth-century reports by participants in first encounters. One comes from the autobiography of a man who attained a position in the highest levels of government after having been born into a head-hunter, cannibal society. The other consists of interviews with indigenous people who remember vividly their first encounters with white men, gold prospectors from Australia, with whom they then co-existed peacefully, possibly a unique event in the history of colonialism.

A large part of Papua New Guinea is composed of one of the most inaccessible regions of the world, with towering, jungle-covered mountains, swamps, ravines, and streams. For centuries, colonial settlers assumed that the area was too wild for human habitation and avoided it. In 1930, these highlands were first explored by Australians seeking gold. To their astonishment, they discovered thousands of indigenous people in the wide valleys, living in villages surrounded by fertile gardens.

Some 45 years later, Australia withdrew and granted independence to Papua New Guinea. In the history of colonialism around the world, this is perhaps the shortest period of colonial exposure. One can only speculate whether the delayed first encounter with Europeans was a blessing because of the extra years of peace and freedom, or a curse because of the delayed access to the benefits of European technology, medicine and education.

31

ALBERT KIKI

GROWING UP IN NEW GUINEA
Papua New Guinea

Editor's Notes: Albert Kiki's autobiography is one of the only published accounts ever written that spans childhood in a stone age head hunter society through adulthood as an educated professional in a modern culture. Kiki (1931–1993) became a well-known political figure and organizer of one of New Guinea's political parties. Ultimately he became the country's deputy prime minister. His first encounter with the white man was both drastic and painful. Hunted down and captured by missionaries who then used force to keep him in school, he was cut off from family and tribe at an early age. The turning point in his introduction to modernity came when he finally realized that people, not the spirit ancestors and their tribal gods, created machines, tools, and dams through the application of technology.

The very first thing I can remember is the day on which they brought back my dead uncle. Like a hunted boar, they had tied his hands and feet to a long pole that was laid across two men's shoulders. I remember that day better than any other in my life, for it was the same day on which I first, consciously, watched a sunset. Standing on the top of a hill, I could see the red ball of the sun set— virtually at my feet. It was the sudden outbreak of wailing and crying that made me run back to the village. With some bewilderment I watched the little procession. As it arrived in the middle of the village my uncle was untied and laid out on the ground. My mother was prominent among the women who cried in loud wailing voices. All the children, even the tiny ones like myself, were brought to look at him. There was a large gash across his clavicle and the blood was still red and fresh. The men took pains to explain to us that he

Reprinted from *Kiki, Ten Thousand Years in a Lifetime—A New Guinea Autobiography*, by Maori Albert Kiki (Melbourne: F. W. Cheshire, 1968): pp. 5–6, 13–22, 48–95, 162–164, 187.

Albert Kiki and his uncle Haure. (*Source:* Albert Maori Kiki, *Kiki: Ten Thousand Years in a Lifetime*. Melbourne: F. W. Cheshire, 1968.)

had been killed by a man of the Rei people, who lived further up in the mountains. No doubt we were expected to keep a kind of mental account of the continual war between us and our neighbours. The men's chief occupation was to think about and carry out the "payback", which would of course inevitably lead to further retaliation from the other side. . . .

My mother's people always referred to the dead as "going to the West", because they did not bury the dead in the ground but placed them high up in the branches of a tree, facing the sunset. They did not believe in the last judgment and they had no concept of heaven or hell. But they believed that the dead are ever present and that they can be called upon to help in any dangerous situation. I have never grown out of this belief myself. Even though I know that God is with me, I also know that my mother is with me. . . .

My mother's people lived in tiny villages. On the coast a village could easily be some two hundred strong, but among the Parevavo a village of 20 or 30 people was already considered a large one. In the steep mountain area between the Purari and Vailala rivers life was harder than on the coastal plains. My mother's people had to be continually on the move, because after spending six months to a year in a certain area the game would move away. We then packed our few belongings and moved through the forest to a new homestead, some thirty or forty miles away, where new gardens had already been prepared by some of the younger men who had moved ahead. Thus we would move around three or four homesteads until in the end we came back to the original site. This constant movement determined our whole way of life. It was pointless to build solid, permanent homes. We put a few sticks together, tent fashion, and covered them with leaves. While on the move we would simply dig a hole under a fallen log or put some large pieces of bark against a tree trunk. It would have been quite impracticable to make pots. Our only utensils were gourds and string bags, stone axes and bows and arrows. Our only clothing was a piece of barkcloth which covered the head like a cap and hung down the back nearly to the ankles. Our economy also had to be adjusted to this form of life. We kept hunting dogs, but no pigs, which would have been impossible to move on our long treks. We relied on a few quick-growing crops like sweet potatoes and bananas, but mainly we lived on game: wild pigs, cassowary birds, birds' eggs, snakes, lizards. Occasionally we could smoke out a nest of bees and get the honey. All our food was roasted. Making fire was a somewhat laborious business. One sat on a large piece of wood, holding the other end down with one's feet. Then one started rubbing the log somewhere between one's knees with the hard rubbing stick. A fine dust was used to cause extra friction.

I think it must have been the constant movement of the tribe that made them restrict the number of their children. When a woman had borne two children she was given a root to chew that would destroy her womb. In both Parevavo and Orokolo a plant is used to prevent conception. It is a grass called *ero'o* in Parevavo and *heroha* in Orokolo. Heroha is cultivated, it does not grow wild. If you find it in the bush it is an indication that you are standing on an abandoned village site. Women drink a kind of tea brewed from this grass once or twice a week. Since the tea has a bad taste they usually add the juice of *havai* leaves for flavour. During the period nothing is taken, but immediately afterwards women chew the root of the same plant. This tea is also the first thing a woman is given after childbirth, to clean out all the "bad blood" from the womb. There is also a rather dangerous vine called ii which is cultivated in Orokolo. It is mainly used to kill fish. The root is squashed and the juice dropped into the water, killing the smaller fish and numbing the big ones, so they can be caught easily. *Ii* is now popularly known as "Papuan dynamite". Women use it to abort, but it is so dangerous that some have been known to die from an overdose.

In any case, the men practised considerable sexual abstinence. It was believed that a man who spent too much time with his wife would become effeminate and he would become a danger and a liability to the tribe. It was thought that the enemy might easily pick out such a man, that he was likely to be killed more easily and would put us at a disadvantage. A man's life was mainly with other men. They went hunting together, and fighting together, or else they prepared themselves for either activity. In a sense it was the war with neighbouring peoples, the constant watch out for enemy activities, the "payback" expeditions, the preparations of weapons, that provided the major content and the excitement of our lives. I have sometimes been asked by Europeans whether there was any way of breaking the vicious circle of revenge and counter-revenge and arriving at some kind of peace. I think we did not really want peace because we *enjoyed* the fighting. The village leader was always the man who had killed the most people. He was not chosen or elected, he simply asserted himself and his leadership was accepted without query. The war had to be fought according to strict rules. Although we killed animals with poisoned arrows, we never used poison on a man. This was considered cowardly and it was believed that a real man had to kill the hard way. It was a man's obligation to always avenge his mother's relatives, not his father's. The payback had to be carried out according to the "eye for eye, tooth for tooth" principle. When the enemy had killed a man and left his body untouched, we also would not touch the one we killed in revenge. If his head had been cut off, we too had to cut off the head of our victim. If they had eaten our relative it became our duty to eat the one we had killed for his sake. When the first man was killed during an engagement with the enemy, the bereaved was immediately called. It would be his duty to cut off the head or decide whether the body should be treated in any other way. . . .

Today I sometimes wonder how, under these hard conditions of life, in a state of perpetual war and being constantly on the move, our people could still find time to celebrate and rejoice. A small feast was given by every mother a month after childbirth. During the first month she was confined to her hut. It was usually her brother's wife who looked after her during this time. Symbolically, she was called in to "clean the child's first faeces". After one month the mother took over herself, and she had to prepare a feast for her sister-in-law.

The happiest time of the year was the Laula festival. It was celebrated when the first fruit began to appear on the laula trees. This was to us the best time of the year, for fruit would be plentiful on the trees, there would be more birds around and more birds' eggs to eat and more game to hunt. We celebrated this by exchanging gifts of food among the clans. . . .

Compared with the life at Orokolo, let alone Moresby, it was a tough life by the Purari river. We were struggling for mere subsistence and survival. There were no comforts and no luxuries and yet what stands out in my mind about this period of my life is not the hardship, but the happiness of the life. The sense of exhilaration when I was first allowed to wake up with the men at night while expecting or suspecting an enemy attack, the feeling of triumph when I caught my first bird, killed my first pig. There was anxiety too, and constant danger, but there was also the comfort that came from Maruka Akore, the ancestor of the clan, who would never desert me and who watched over every action. When I went hunting, he would guide my hand. When enemies were near, he would protect me from their sight. . . .

My first impression of Orokolo was that it was full of people. Coming from the tiny Parevavo community that wandered through the thick forest with their scanty belongings, Orokolo seemed like a modern metropolis. There, people lived in solid houses, close together, and the place was buzzing with noise and activity. The vast number of pigs roaming about everywhere also astonished me because my mother's people did not keep any tame pigs, whereas in Orokolo the pig population was larger than the human one. My mother told me later that she felt a wonderful sense of security in Orokolo, where one could sleep without fearing a night attack by the enemy. But to me the experience was altogether disturbing and worrying. At night I missed the humming noises that had lulled me to sleep at home. The formidable sound made by the crickets in the forest was reduced to a feeble chirping there and the cries of the night birds were altogether absent.

To me, the most frightening thing was the sight of the sea, the unbelievable, roaring expanse of water. Throughout that first year in Orokolo I could never be induced to swim in the sea, nor would I enter a boat. . . .

Why did my people abandon their festivals? The missionaries get a lot of the blame. It is true, of course, that they did not like the initiation rites and rather tended to discourage them. But at that time their influence was not all that great in Orokolo.

I believe that taxation was a major factor. Even though the tax was only ten shillings per head at first, and one pound later on, the young men had to go out and earn it for themselves and their fathers. So they drifted off to Kerema and maybe Moresby, seeking employment in shops or with white masters. While they were earning the money nobody remained at home to take an active part in the ceremonies. Many of them lost interest when they saw other, more *respectable* ways of life. . . .

[It] seems to me that the breakdown of our social and religious life in Orokolo left a vacuum in people's minds that caused a great deal of confusion and some of the people started to develop strange ideas. In their desperate need for some kind of belief, for some creed and security, these people clung to the most absurd notions. Some of their ideas were evolved from the most trifling accidents, such as some superficial resemblance of words. Jehovah was believed to be the same word as our *ihova* which means *a sign*, and "German" was thought to be the same as *kiavari*, our word for the dead. During the war many people believed that the Germans were our own dead who were coming to bring us our own cargo, and that naturally enough the white men were trying to prevent them. . . .

The first white man I ever saw was a trader called Allen who lived in Orokolo and who bought copra, which he paid for in beads and twist tobacco. I remember being surprised and even a little disappointed because he looked so much like a normal human being and not at all like someone come back from the island of the dead. For our people had strange notions about Europeans in those days. They were supposed to be our dead relatives who had to change their appearance when they returned to live with us. . . .

However, it was not until they dragged me to school that I came into contact with the hard reality of the white man's world. There was only one school in Orokolo then and it belonged to the London Mission Society. Though the administration had no policy about compulsory schooling, the mission made great efforts to bring all of us into school, and since most of us were reluctant to go, they would make periodical raids on the village to snatch truants. When I came down from my mother's village to Orokolo I was already about ten years old and felt reluctant to go and sit on the same bench with younger boys. Therefore I avoided school. But one morning I was caught. I can remember that day very well. It was a fine morning and it was one of those lucky days when fish were very plentiful right near the beach. The women had come back with a big catch and one of them gave my mother some. She wrapped one up in sago for me and I was eating it. Then someone called out from the other end of the village that they were again looking for boys who did not go to school. I hid under a pile of coconut leaves which my father had put aside. They were going to be burned to provide light on one of his nightly fishing expeditions. But someone must have betrayed my hiding place. I was discovered and carried—screaming and kicking—to the school. Immediately on arrival I was given a sound beating by the teacher because I had refused to come earlier. An English missionary, the Reverend Dewdney, was in charge of the mission and the school, but his assistants and teachers were Samoans. My own teacher was born in Papua, because his father had come to the country long ago for the London Mission Society. He spoke our language very well.

The first lesson I attended was given by his wife. She wrote the numbers one to ten on the blackboard and we were asked to copy them. I wrote them all very well, except 2 and 7, which I wrote back to front. I never liked the school. Our teachers were very ready with the cane, and beat us for the slightest mistake or offence. We were taught simple English and arithmetic, but by the time I left I could not speak much English, except for "come" and "go" and such simple, basic things. Much of our time was spent cleaning the mission yard, making fences and looking after the missionary's cows. I became quite an expert in milking them. I was most grateful to the Reverend Dewdney, however, when he taught me a little bit of first aid. It started my great interest in medical work, which was to become a leading influence on my life. The missionary forbade me to go and visit my mother's village, because he knew well that my mother's people were against school and that there I was out of reach. However, I did manage to abscond now and then. I found school no good for me. I liked it better with the birds at home. Often, sitting on the hard school bench, I was thinking of the tame hornbills at home that ate out of your hand and followed you around everywhere. Sometimes, on a Thursday after school, I would tell my friends that I was not feeling well. I would set out for my mother's village in the night. I would walk all Friday and all Saturday and by Sunday I would be running. I would get home sometime Sunday night, and by the time I got back to Orokolo I had missed a whole week of school. I paid for these excursions with another beating.

At first I went to school stark naked because even at that age most children in Orokolo did not wear any clothes; only the girls came in their grass skirts. However, some of boys at school received bits of clothing from their elder brothers who were working in Kerema or Moresby and naturally, I too wanted some clothes. The first garment my mother made for me was made from an old sack. She simply cut two armholes into it, and a larger hole for the head. The sack was quite comfortable, except in the rains, when it became terribly heavy. . . .

We were forced to attend church and Sunday school, but Christianity never came to mean anything to me. I was more deeply impressed by what my mother had taught me when I was young than by this later teaching. To this day talking to a river or to a tree is far more important to me than sitting down and listening to somebody else talking about God. Neither my father nor my mother ever became Christians. I was supposed to bring them to the big evening service on Sunday, and I tried very hard indeed because I was beaten if they didn't come. Occasionally my father went for my sake, but my mother did not even go once. I used to receive fifteen lashes when neither of them attended, and seven and a half when only one did not attend.

Considering how irregularly I attended school I am surprised that they could teach me anything at all. . . .

In spite of everything, I passed out of primary school with Standard V in 1946. My teacher felt that I would make a good missionary and he gave me a letter to take to the Rev. Rankin in Saroa, who would arrange for my training. I set out for the Vailala River, from where I was to take a boat to Moresby. But I did not want to become a missionary. . . .

Early in 1947 I got my first job as *doctor boy*, that is, medical orderly in Kerema hospital. I had been very anxious to become a doctor boy. I was dreaming of learning how to treat sores and then go back and treat my people at home, because though they were a healthy and strong people in many respects, they suffered much from tropical ulcers. However, I was horrified when my first assignment was to carry a patient's faeces. For in my village we were taught that a young boy who comes into contact with an older man's faeces will stop growing, that he will be unable to receive the power from the bush, that he will become an easy prey to evil spirits. . . . I ran away from that job the same afternoon and the medical assistant never forgave me.

The next day I wrote a letter to the district officer asking for an office job and I was accepted as *tea boy*. Now this was my first real job, it was the first time I worked for and was in close contact with a white man. And I shall never forget the very important lesson I learned in that office. The first thing I was taught was how to hold a cup and saucer well together. I was told: something round there, is called saucer. And the one that stands on it is called cup. I have never forgotten it to this day. And I was further told that when I make tea I must not spill anything into that thing called saucer. One day, however, I *did* spill some tea on the saucer and the white officer picked up the tea and threw the boiling hot tea onto my bare chest. I was badly scalded but I shall never forget how to make tea properly. I learned many other lessons in that office, how to stand with my hands behind my back, without moving, waiting for the officer to tell me what papers he wanted me to pass to him. It was a strange, bewildering world to me. On one occasion I was told to sort out the inwards and outwards telegrams. I did not dare to say I did not understand what was meant by "inwards" and "outwards"—I looked at the telegrams, wondering by what criterion to sort them into two piles, and finally decided to put all the clean-looking forms on one pile and all the dirty or crumpled ones on the other. This time the officer took great pains to explain to me: "inwards", he said, pointing towards himself; and "outwards" pointing away from himself. I still did not understand, but I remember going home from the office repeating "inwards"—"outwards" and pointing backwards and forwards, like something out of a Charlie Chaplin film.

My worst experience with a white man in those early days came when my boss at the office sent me with a letter to the medical assistant at the hospital. He was not in the office and I was directed to his house. Now I had been taught at home to always use the back entrance of a house, the front entrance being reserved for important people. But the missionaries had taught me to go up to the front, and I thought that this was a white man's house and I ought to follow their custom. Now whether it was this or another thing that annoyed him, or whether he was angry because I had run away from his job earlier, I don't know. What he was shouting at me as he took the letter I did not understand. But he set his dog on me to drive me away and the dog bit me, drawing blood from my leg, and the scar is still faintly visible to this day.

I must have become very proficient in making tea without spilling it on the saucer, or I must have impressed my superiors in some other way, because after about a year I was made interpreter to patrol officer Bill Maddock, who was to open a new station at Ihu on the Vailala River. My English was barely good enough to do this work. I could cope well enough with the routine work: the patrol officer told the people to keep their village clean, to build their houses farther apart because of fire, to build a road, to form a co-operative for selling copra. He recruited labour for road building and for work on the station. But sometimes I could not understand what he said, and fearing to admit it, had to improvise.

The most interesting experience was an expedition into Kukukuku country. It was not very successful because the people ran away whenever they got news of our coming and we found nothing but deserted villages, with just a few dogs and tame hornbills strolling around. However, we did manage to meet the odd small group of warriors and were able to give them the message of the government and the good news about the civilised life they would be taught to lead. The patrol officer told them: you must not run away when we come to talk to you; you must not fight your next-door neighbours, the killing of people is against the law of the people on the coast and they don't like it; you must learn to stay together and you must stop moving around, you must settle in one place. This last injunction must have sounded stranger than any other to the Kukukukus. But I did not feel bold enough to explain to the patrol officer that moving around is a necessity of life in those parts. That we move, not because we are simply restless, but because we have to follow the game.

I worked for the patrol officer for a year, got fed up and ran back to Kerema. The idea of doing hospital work had not left me, and learning that there was a new medical assistant I applied once more for a doctor boy job. The interview given to me by Mr. Albert Speer is one of the most memorable events in my life. He was the first white man who ever asked me to sit down in his presence. I was afraid to accept, but he finally made me do it. I sat there stiffly, with my hands clasped rigidly between my knees while he talked to me. He asked me whether I knew what it meant to become a medical orderly. Would I be prepared to do night duty? Observe the rules? Above all he warned me, that I was going to work with women, and that I must respect these women. In those days there were no Papuan nurses, only orderlies, and they were all men. Many of the women patients were frightened of the men, who treated them roughly. Some came down with their husbands, and many ran away before their treatment was finished. Mr. Speer was greatly worried about this. I promised to do all I was told, and was accepted at a salary of £1 a month. This was quite a lot in 1947—as tea boy the previous year I had earned only half as much.

I learned a great deal from the medical assistant. Not only did he teach me to dress wounds and to look after patients, but he made me do office work and sometimes I typed all his correspondence. He was the first person to take a serious interest in my career. Often he took me home, showed me pictures of Australia and told me about the countryside where he lived and which he loved. I remember seeing a photograph of sheep for the first time in my life— though the image of sheep had pursued me through Sunday school class. He spoke about the beauty of Sydney and about the cold in Australia, but I said I was not frightened of any cold because in my mother's village it could become very cold at night and we had no clothes there to protect us. We went fishing together and we talked about the water, about fish, about crocodiles and all sorts of things. I told him I wanted to go back to my village, to settle down, but he said, no, there is something important for you to do: you must go and get knowledge and take it back to your people, do not go back empty handed. I said: my mother is getting old, I must look after her. And I know how to shoot birds. I can spear a pig and build a house. He said, these things are very important, but it is also important to learn to build the country. Your country will need men, and I think you are one of them. I want you to get more training, learn more about the white man. These were strange words to me indeed. I had never thought about my country. I knew my loyalty to my mother's people and again to Orokolo. But it was Albert Speer who first made me conscious of Papua New Guinea. Sometimes he spoke to me about the future of this country. He told me that in future black men will rule this country. I could not believe him. He was the first man ever to say such a thing to me. The missionaries had never said anything like it. But he told me that many things he was saying I wouldn't understand until later, in years to come. . . .

The urge in me to go home and settle down was strong. My mother had always thought I was learning bad things at school. She kept saying you have forgotten the secret of your people. My uncles also wanted me to return. They thought I had become a good specimen for a front man.

I loved my mother more than anybody. But in the end I listened to Albert Speer. He had great influence over me. I did not believe him when he told me that one day I would lead my people. But he was the first white man who ever *ate* with me. The first white man ever to become my friend. I found it impossible to disappoint him and so I dropped the idea of marriage.

Some time after that he told me: you can do something better than this, I shall send you to my home at Golbourne, where you will attend a secondary school. My parents there will look after you. He tried very hard to send me to Australia. If the minister for territories had given permission I would have been the first Papuan to be educated in Australia. But he refused and suggested that I should be sent to Sogeri school instead.

I did not understand until much later that it was then the official policy of Australia to educate Papuans and New Guineans only up to a certain point and no further.

So Mr. Speer decided that going to Sogeri would be better than nothing. In December 1948 we set out for Moresby together and I spent a week there with him before going to Sogeri school. Port Moresby made a tremendous impression on me. We arrived there on the day Prince Charles was born and all the huge ships in the harbour (I had never seen such ships in Kerema) were brightly decorated with flags and coloured lights. I remember that Mr. Speer took me shopping in the large Burns Philp store. I looked at this huge building with some pride because my father had worked on its construction as a labourer. Among the confusion of goods inside I was most impressed by the tailors' dummies, and felt a great temptation to steal one. As we came out of the building Mr. Speer stopped a police van to beg a lift, for there were no buses or taxis then. He sat in the front next to the white police officer. I hopped on the back with the constables but could feel they didn't like me there. When the van stopped the white police officer saw me sitting in the back and he shouted "Catch him!" And immediately I was grabbed by the constables and handcuffed. All this happened within seconds, before Mr. Speer could explain that I was with him. Though I was released at once, it made me feel very uncomfortable throughout the rest of my stay in Moresby.

I spent from 1949 to 1951 in Sogeri school. It was there that I learned to speak English properly. All our teachers were Australians, with the exception of a few Papuan tutors who were ex-students of Sogeri themselves. I enjoyed my stay in Sogeri very much. It was away from the coast and was real forest, reminiscent of home. There were many birds and wallabies. I enjoyed games like baseball and cricket but was most keen on the debating society. I can remember a debate on equal rights for women in which I passionately argued against equality. I was still very much influenced by our traditional thinking on this matter. I also enjoyed the concerts and can remember standing on a platform singing songs in my mother's language. Pretty tunes to the others, but a tremendous private joke to myself, because I was abusing everybody in the audience.

Many of the students were restless and troublesome. They argued about what they thought was bad food in the institution and they complained about the low wages awaiting them after training. But there was no political consciousness yet, nor did we think at all about racial discrimination. This question simply did not arise because our Australian teachers were there on one level, and we were on another and it did not even occur to us that we might aspire to the same level.

The biggest thing Sogeri did to me was that it brought me together with other boys from all parts of Papua and New Guinea and I learned to know and like them. Many of them have remained my friends throughout life.

In the final year at Sogeri we all automatically took a teachers' course that would enable us to take a teaching job, though we were not yet regarded as qualified teachers. However, I was never to become a teacher. When I finished at Sogeri I saw an advertisement inviting applications for ex-Sogeri boys to receive medical training in Fiji. I applied to the director of medical services, Dr. Gunther, and as I was supported by Mr. Speer, I was accepted. . . .

The thing that stands out in my mind when I think of this first visit to Sydney, the thing I shall never forget, was my seeing the first beggar. I had read about beggars at Sogeri school, I think. But to actually see one gave me a terrible shock. We were being taken on a sightseeing tour by a retired medical officer. And there was this blind man by the roadside, stretching out his hand. "Who is this man?" I asked and the man who was leading us said "Leave him alone!" and tried to hurry on. But I stopped dead in the street and I said: "I cannot leave him alone. Let's go back and find out what he wants." So he agreed to take me back and he said: "Well, put some money into that hand." Fortunately we had been given some pocket money and so I was able to give him some coins. I could not sleep that night. I kept thinking and picturing his face. I had never seen anything like it at home . . .

The medical course proved too hard for me. I had great difficulties because my English was not yet good enough. I remember the lecturer talking about involuntary muscles, and I didn't know what "voluntary" was, let alone "involuntary". What I really enjoyed was the anatomy class. Partly, perhaps, because we had a brilliant Indian lecturer, and since he was coloured I was greatly encouraged and excited by his intelligence and success, and I kept thinking that if he had succeeded I should also be able to succeed.

It fascinated me to dissect the human body and see how it worked. I was convinced that somewhere we would come across the spirit, but we dissected the body right down to the bones and there was nothing, nothing happened. Many of my old beliefs were seriously challenged there. I had grown up believing that diseases were mostly caused by witchcraft and sorcery but here I was taught to identify germs and breed germ cultures and I began to believe the things I could see with my own eyes rather than the things I was taught at home. Many of the Fijian and Indian students there were much more sophisticated than I, but deep down even they had some of the old notions left in them.

This was demonstrated rather curiously one day in the anatomy class. I was playing ball outside while another class was in the anatomy. The bodies had been stripped right down to the bones when one of the numerous Fiji earthquakes occurred. The bones rattled and shook on the benches and the students started to scream—many of them thinking that the bodies were about to rise. They rushed out of the classroom and broke into laughter when they realised what had happened.

The medical course was too hard for me. I failed my exams twice and was told to go back home. I remember that I was very depressed and unhappy and I wrote in my diary: "This is the darkest hour of my life. I should have tried more . . . I got several unpleasant letters from Moresby. The people who had sponsored my trip were naturally annoyed and accused me openly of spending too much time on outside activities. Only the man I was most concerned about at this moment was very kind. I was very worried how Albert Speer would take to the news of my failure after all he had done for me. But he comforted me and said: "Sorry you could not make it. But you haven't lost anything—you haven't lost friends. And maybe you are better suited for other jobs."

I was brought up before the committee and told that I would have to return to Port Moresby. But I refused to go back. I said that I could not go back empty-handed, and that if I had failed in the medical course I would try the laboratory course and return home as a pathologist. In the end they accepted me and that time I was successful and qualified in the normal period of three years. . . .

It pained me to see that Fijian-Indian relations were getting rather strained. The older people would get on well together and in the countryside relations seemed to be very cordial. But the younger, sophisticated Fijians in the city resented the Indians, who seemed to do most of the trading. Some of them had become wealthy and they owned most of the stores in Suva. They were also growing in numbers at an alarming rate and the Fijians felt that they were being swamped by these strangers who had been imported by the British as labourers. The Indians, of course, are very hard workers. The Fijians are more like ourselves. They prefer the island style, work today and sit around for the next two, for we have grown up in conditions where food is never really short.

When I needed money in Fiji I used to go out for a few weekends to work on a banana plantation. I helped to cut bananas and pack them in boxes for export.

I suppose all these were the "outside activities" I was accused of at home. Or maybe they had also heard that I was going to trade union meetings. For one night after the cinema a Fijian friend asked me to accompany him to a meeting. I asked him what the meeting was about and he said it was a meeting of the Suva Trade Union. I didn't know what a trade union was. There weren't any in Papua and New Guinea at that stage. The meeting fascinated me because everyone talked and shouted at once, unlike home, where everyone listened quietly when one man talked. That meeting was very lively. After a while I began to understand what it was all about. They were discussing the dock workers' wages, which were very low, and it was pointed out how hard the work was, especially the loading of copra. All this excited me a great deal. I remembered that at home my brother Heni was still earning £1 a month as an untrained carpenter. It had not occurred to me before that one could seriously try to do something about it. I went to listen to many trade union meetings after that. I did not join and could not vote in any of these meetings but I wanted to see how they were run and what they might achieve. The more I saw of them the more convinced I became that we had to start organising ourselves at home. I began to dream of all kinds of things I would do when I got back. . . .

My mother hated white people. She often told me how she ran away into the bush when the first gavamani (government officials) came to her village. On that occasion the whole village was deserted and they never met anybody. The second time gavamani came to her village, she met the village constable from Orokolo and followed him. But even though my father himself represented government in the village she continued to hate white men. She considered them to be cruel and never forgave the many insults that accompanied their visits.

I remember the day when she went gathering firewood on the day the patrol officer came. We were late for line-up and the patrol officer fined us one chicken. She never forgave such incidents.

The occasion she hated most was the day when the *gavamani* came to conduct a medical survey on inguinal glands. No doubt they were making a serious medical investigation; but they showed little consideration for the people who were meant to benefit from their work. All the women were simply lined up and the *gavanumi* put their hands under their grass skirts to feel their glands. This incident made all the women of Orokolo furious. . . .

The five years I spent in Moresby after my return from Fiji were full of fights. But they were not spectacular and exhilarating like the fight with the army. They were the slow, nagging, continuous protests against discrimination. Before I went to Fiji I simply accepted things as they were. I was grateful for special opportunities given to me by the administration and I did not really question the established order. My trip to Fiji changed many things for me. For the first time I had the possibility to compare. The first big shock came to me, however, when I had to get a special permit to leave the territory. The permit read as follows:

Territory of Papua and New Guinea
Native Emigration Restriction Ordinance
1935 of the Territory of Papua

PERMIT TO REMOVE NATIVE

FROM THE TERRITORY OF PAPUA

I, Jack Keith Murray, Administrator of the Territory of Papua and New Guinea by virtue of the powers conferred by *Section 3 of the Native Emigration*

Restriction Ordinance, 1935 of the Territory of Papua, and all other powers me enabling, and acting with the advice of the Executive Council, hereby permit the removal of the native MAORI KIKI of OROKOLO by SKYMASTER of Q.E.A. subject to conditions set out hereunder.

Dated at Port Moresby this 19th day of January One thousand nine hundred and fifty two

signed J. K. Murray
Administrator

This extraordinary ordinance is still in power to this very day. . . .

I soon discovered that the administration considered us to be irresponsible and treated us like children. A law forbade us to drink or purchase alcohol. It was argued that alcoholic drinks were not part of our traditional culture and that we must be protected from its evil effects. Some of the missionaries also argued that if we were enabled to drink we would spend all our money on beer and neglect our families. It was not until 1962 that this obnoxious regulation was removed. I agitated like the rest of us for its removal, even though I don't care for alcoholic drinks myself and never touch them. Of course some of our people do get drunk on pay day, but I don't think I have seen as many drunks in Moresby as I have seen on the streets of Sydney or Brisbane on Saturday nights . . .

The paternalistic attitude of the administration was somewhat onesided, however. While we were told many times that we were like children and that others knew what was best for us, we were not being looked after like children. The government drew thousands of people into Moresby to work as clerks and labourers but made no effort to house them. A European civil servant could expect a house to be part of his emoluments but we had to manage as best we could. Most of us lived in real slums. My first house in Moresby was a shack knocked together from corrugated iron sheets left behind by the army.

Needless to say our wages were very much lower than those of white people doing similar jobs. This policy has persisted until today, and it is argued that native wages should be related to the economic capacity of the territory. Thus a Papuan patrol officer today would receive A$1,070–A$1,710 per annum as against the A$3,555–A$4,944 per annum which a white man would receive for doing exactly the same job. But the Papuan would be expected to entertain at the same level as the white man.

Apart from these serious grievances, some of which have persisted to this very day, there were the numerous small daily insults of discrimination and segregation. There were cinemas for whites only and other cinemas for blacks. The administration ran separate bus services for Europeans and natives. The district office in Moresby still has four toilets labelled: Gentlemen (for white men); Ladies (for white women); Tatau (for Papuan men) and Hahine (for Papuan women) the latter two being the appropriate Motu words.

In New Guinea many offices or hotels have separate toilets for gentlemen and *boys*; ladies and *meries*. The ladies' and gentlemen's toilets have seats, in the others you have to squat.

Many of the big stores would not serve "boys" together with the respectable white customers . . .

But the thing that made us dislike Europeans most was their attitude to our women. Many bachelors in the administration were making use of native women to have "a sexual outlet". Before the coming of the white man we did not know prostitution. What I find most offensive is the way Europeans have native women and despise them at the same time.

In 1962 the government removed racially discriminatory provisions from more than fifty laws. But even though the stated policy of the administration opposes discrimination, many individuals still feel the same as before and practice discrimination whenever they feel they can get away with it.

Soon after my return from Fiji I came to realise that there was no point in frittering away one's energies in numerous little incidents and arguments. What was needed was that our people should come together and organise themselves. I thought that the first thing was to organise my own people and gain their confidence as a basis for a larger countrywide organisation. So I teamed up with Olaerape Mairue who was a Welfare Assistant in the Department of Social Welfare, and together we founded the Kerema Welfare Association. Some five hundred people attended our first meeting and I was elected president of the association . . .

(Kiki went on to become founder and president of a political party, the country's leading voice for human rights and self-government.)

Life in Orokolo has become dull and uninspiring. What have our people gained from the cultural contact that has destroyed their customs? We now have better wells in our villages, there is a mission hospital and a fair proportion of the people have learned to read and write. We have a rough road linking us to some other villages, but no cars can drive on it, only the local government tractor, the co-operative society's tractor, and the mission Land Rover. The road was built by community effort. An airstrip at Ihu links us with Moresby and there are regular trading vessels. People now earn some cash from planting and drying copra. What luxuries can they buy for their money? The co-operative stores have a limited range of goods: kerosene, some rather old-fashioned clothes, tinned fish and meat, rice and some oddities. The store in Hopaiku village has a whole shelf full of Worcestershire sauce. Some smart businessman must have succeeded in getting rid of his old stock by talking the co-operative society into buying this useless article.

Of course we also have Christianity now, but it does not fill the gap left by the destruction of our own culture. Many of our people are Christians and good church-goers, but they put the Bible aside on week-days. When they go hunting and fishing and gardening they still rely on the old magical incantations they have learned from their forefathers. We have been made to abandon all communal religious activity: initiation, masks and the rest. But we cling to our private and personal magic. We still fast, chew bark, speak the sacred words as in the olden days. I cannot imagine Orokolo people ever giving up these things.

There is little initiative in Orokolo now. The people are disappointed and frustrated. They remember with some bitterness the famous government rice scheme of the 1920s. Everyone planted rice with great enthusiasm, but after a lot of work and effort they were told that their rice could not be marketed. More recently the government induced people to plant coffee. And once more the people worked for nothing. Their coffee could not be sold. Everywhere around Orokolo today one can see the coffee beans dropping off the trees, unheeded. The people had given up their culture because they were ready for change, for a new kind of life. But nothing happened. So the impatient ones leave for Moresby and the ones who stay on are bitter and distrustful of the government . . .

At this moment in our history I can see my country's future mapped out. We know where we want to go and I think we know how to get there.

As I look back at my early childhood in my mother's village in Parevavo, I feel I have come a very long way. And yet the long way I have travelled has not separated me from my people. The support and understanding I get from these allegedly "primitive" and "backward" people gives me much strength. Only a few weeks ago I stayed in my mother's village with my maternal uncle Haure . . .

"Many people talk about you," he said. "Many people tell me about your aggressiveness. You get up and argue with people. You argue with the white men because you do not like many of the things they do. I am glad to see you battling like this. If there are plenty of Maori Kikis this country will achieve something. White men have lived in this country for a long time—but they have never shown us the way properly. If you keep fighting, others will follow you. If you keep on fighting victory will come to you later. You can see that the wrong road is easy. It is a wide road. Many people will follow you to travel on it, many people will join you in the line. But in the end, you will find it led you to the wrong place. But the right road is hard and narrow. It is a difficult road and few will travel with you. Very few. But at the end of the road you will find a new future for your country New Guinea. So go on fighting. Never mind what they say about you on the long way. You just fight on till you reach the end of the road."

I can feel the strength of the old man right in my blood, and I shall certainly go to the end of the road.

FRIZZLE-HAIRED ISLANDERS

The first Europeans to sight New Guinea were probably the Portuguese and Spanish navigators sailing in the South Pacific in the early part of the 16th century. In 1526–27, Don Jorge de Meneses accidentally came upon the principal island and is credited with naming it "Papua," a Malay word for the frizzled quality of Melanesian hair. The term "New Guinea" was applied to the island in 1545 by a Spaniard, Ynigo Ortis de Retez, because of a fancied resemblance between the islands' inhabitants and those found on the African Guinea coast. Although European navigators visited the islands and explored their coastlines for the next 170 years, little was known of the inhabitants until the late 19th century.

Background notes: Papua New Guinea, U.S. Dept. of State, November 2000. Bureau of East Asian and Pacific Affairs.

32

PAPUAN HIGHLANDERS
First Contacts
Papua New Guinea

Editor's Notes: First encounters in the unexplored highlands of Papua New Guinea, represent a unique type of meeting between Europeans and native peoples. In the 1930s, an Australian prospector, Michael Leahy, while exploring for gold, stumbled upon native villages cut off from the outside world in a rugged, mountainous part of the island, located directly north of the Australian continent.

Leahy accomplished something unparalled in history. He documented his contacts with native villagers by shooting many reels of film, taking thousands of photographs, as well as producing detailed accounts of the meetings in village after village in his diary.

This treasure trove of photographic record and diaries lay undisturbed for 50 years. Then between 1981 and 1983, Australian filmmakers Bob Connolly and Robin Anderson, retraced the steps of Michael Leahy and recorded over 100 hours of interviews with those Papuans still able to remember the coming of the Australians, 50 years earlier. The result is an unusual record of native voices describing the first meeting of two cultures.

"I saw them with my own eyes when they first came," says Kirupano Eza'e, "and I've not forgotten it. We were living in our old village then. My mother had stopped breastfeeding me, I was walking around like any other boy. I was with my father when I first saw them. . . .

"I was so terrified, I couldn't think properly, and I cried uncontrollably. My father pulled me along by the hand and we hid behind some tall kunai grass. Then he stood up and peeped out at the white men. . . .

Bob Connolly and Robin Anderson, *First Contact: New Guinea's Highlanders Encounter The Outside World* (New York: Viking, 1987), pp. 4, 6–8, 36–38, 43–44, 46, 116, 242–244. By arrangement with the Licensor, Bob Connolly and Robin Anderson c/- Curtis Brown (Aust) Pty. Ltd.

Papua New Guinea highlanders encountering Micheal Leahy. (By permission of Jeannette Leahy.)

"Once they had gone, the people sat down and developed stories. They knew nothing of white-skinned men. We had not seen far places. We knew only this side of the mountains. And we thought we were the only living people. We believed that when a person died, his skin changed to white and he went over the boundary to "that place"—the place of the dead. So when the strangers came we said: 'Ah, these men do not belong to the earth. Let's not kill them—they are our own relatives. Those who have died before have turned white and come back.'"

"We heard the white men were in the Waugla people's country. We couldn't go and see them because we were enemies of those people. But we were very keen to meet them. We were so anxious that night we couldn't sleep at all. We met them early next morning—there were many of them, advancing in a line. All dressed in white. At first we thought they were our enemies coming with new-made shields. They came down to the river—there'd been heavy rain and it was flooding—and as they crossed the river all of us gathered around them. We were howling and shouting in excitement! And we were saying—these are our dead people, come back . . . !"

It was at this time that Sole Sole of Gorohonota Village in the Goroka Valley heard news of the strangers. "We believed that when people died they went in that direction," he said, pointing to the east. "So we immediately thought they were ghosts or dead people." When the strangers were interpreted to be the returning dead, they were greeted with tearful elation—fear of the spirits, joy at the return of loved ones or revered ancestors. It was only a short step for the highlanders to imagine that they recognized particular individuals— prominent men, fathers, brothers, sons. . . .

"So we sent messages out in all directions," says Sole Sole, "telling everybody around. And everybody came, and we all gathered to look at them. This was the time when we gave them a pig and also one of our men stole a knife from them. We all gathered around to look, we were pointing at them and we were saying, 'Aah, that one—that must be' . . . and we named one of our people who had died before. 'That must be him.' And we'd point to another one and say that that must be this other dead person we knew had died before . . . and we were naming them."

Gopie, from Gama Village near Goroka, heard the calls that strangers were coming and rushed down to where they had camped. He was confused about the identity of the white men but had no doubt who the black carriers were. They were dead clansmen. One was his late cousin Ulaline. The evidence was overwhelming. "My cousin had been killed in a tribal fight. When he came towards me I saw half his finger missing, and I recognised him as my dead cousin. The reason his finger was cut off was that [when alive] he'd had too many children with his wife. His people had punished him by cutting off his little finger. When he came towards me I said to him, 'Cousin!' And he lifted his eyebrows. So I knew it was definitely him. He was the same colour, the very same man. His facial expression, the way he talked, laughed—exactly the same. And it wasn't only me who thought this, everyone did. Today I tell this story to the pastors at the Seventh Day Adventist Church—but they just laugh at me. . . . "

The highlanders were anxious to detect any areas of similarity between themselves and the strangers. Did they eat? Drink? Sleep? Defecate? "Because they wore *lap laps* and trousers," says Kirupano Eza'e of Seigu, "the people said, 'We think they have no wastes in them. How could they when they were wrapped up so neatly and completely?' We wondered how the *excreta* could be passed. We wondered much about that. . . . "

A screened latrine pit was dug within the roped-off area. But the highlanders' curiosity could not be left unsatisfied for long. "One of the people hid," recalls Kirupano, "and watched them going to excrete. He came back and said, 'Those men from heaven went to excrete over there.' Once they had left many men went to take a look. When they saw that it smelt bad, they said, 'Their skin might be different, but their shit smells bad like ours. . . . ' "

The strangers' bodies were covered in a strange material. They must have something important to hide. "We had only our traditional dress to cover our private parts," says Gasowe of Makiroka Village in the Asaro. "So when we saw these new strangers, with clothes and belts all over them, we thought they must have a huge penis they were trying to cover up. We thought it must be so long it was wrapped round and round their waists. It was because they were wearing these strange clothes and belts. The thought of that really used to scare us. The women used to be on the lookout and they would run away. . . . "

Many Eastern Highlands people remember speculating about the size of the strangers' penises. Enlightenment came to some when the white men were observed washing in the river. "When they had their bath," says Gasowe, "we used to peep at them and that's when we found out we were wrong. In fact they were just the same as all us men." But the sight of the strangers washing themselves provoked considerable consternation. "When we saw them using the soap in the river," says Gasowe, "and we saw all the foam that was on their bodies, we thought it was the pus coming from a dead person's skin, like the milky part from the rotten flesh. Our minds were in a turmoil when we saw such things . . . !"

"When the white men first came to the highlands," says Kirupano Eza'e, "they filled their dishes with sand and washed that in the water. They washed and washed, poured it out again, washed, poured off, washed, poured off. They did that on and on. And we watched, and thought like this: in the past, our ancestors, our forefathers and foremothers, when they died their bodies were burnt, and we used to pick up the bones and ashes and throw them in the river. And so we thought those ancestors of ours had come back to collect and wash their ashes and bones.

"Some men thought like that, and others thought, 'Did they want to wash the bones to make them come back to life?' We weren't clear on things then. But we know now. They got money from our ground. Now we think straight—that's how they made money, but before we didn't think like that. We had many wild thoughts. . . ."

"At first," says Ndika Wingti, "we used to wonder why they had come. We thought, 'Who are these people?' But when we saw the things they were trading we thought, 'We must befriend them now. They must be our people.' When we saw them giving out things we just knew they must be really close to us, part of our own people. . . ."

Kopia Rebia—who had become one of Leahy's main interpreters—says young boys like himself were often used as go-betweens by the white men, taking messages to particular women or their male relatives. "The white men used to point out a woman to me and say go and tell her to come to me. I'll give her axes and shells and things. But I was frightened of the husbands, and I'd tell the white man I was going to do this, but often take my own time about it and not tell them. Sometimes I'd go back to the white man and pretend I'd spoken to the woman. I'd make something up and say: 'Oh that woman doesn't want to come to you.' I didn't like doing this very much. Sometimes when they'd ask I'd say no. But there were others who did it all the time.

"Generation and generation before the white man came," says Kopia Rebia, "there was no such thing—for a man to take his wife to another man in exchange for something—never. There were tribal fights over women, but men would never give wives to other men. They did this only with the white men. And they did it because of the shells. We would not do this with a wealthy man of our own race. That is certain. We did say that the white men were different."

As Mokei Wamp, Kopia Rebia and Dan Leahy imply, there was no set pattern or uniform response. People acted individually. Men had great control over their women and could compel them to do as they wanted up to a point. Many disapproved of prostituting their womenfolk but others were overcome by their desire for what their wives could get for them. And sometimes this led to shame and suffering for those involved. One young man suggested to his new wife, Yamka Amp Wenta from Korabug, that she go along to the white man. They lived close to Kuta so it was a short journey. "My husband told me the white men were giving out good things for women," says Wenta today, "and he asked me to go to them. He took me there at night. I went there three times, and when I got the things, my husband took them all.

"I didn't mind going. I was attracted myself to all the different things he had. Seeing the white man had paid for me I thought it was all right. My husband told me to go, so I had no choice in the matter, anyway. The white man liked me. He gave me a lot of shells and pork and things like that. He'd show me a place to sit down in his house, and put the trade goods in front of me. We just made sign language. He just thought about things to himself and I did the same."

Yamka Amp Wenta. (By permission of Jeannette Leahy.)

Wenta says the white man was Michael Leahy. She remembers him taking photographs of her, and these exist today. She appears as a young girl of fifteen or sixteen, alternatively apprehensive and smiling, wearing a necklace of giri giri shells, a woven string bag around her head.

Wenta's brief association with the white man would have passed unnoticed were it not for the fact that she later gave birth to a mixed- race son. "When I saw he was different," she says, "I knew that it must be the white man's son, from the times I had been there with him. When I was expecting the baby, everyone thought it was my husband's child. Then people said, 'She's had a white son!' She must have been with the white man! And my husband said nothing to defend me."

Wenta was upset by her husband's failure to declare that it was he who suggested she go to the white man. Now it looked for all the world as though she had gone on her own initiative and this she found utterly shameful, and so did others. There was much snide gossip. Humiliated, she left her husband and fled with her baby to her relatives in another village.

"I was hurt and embarrassed, and at the time it was very hard. My son was quite a grown boy when I went back to my husband. Other men wanted to marry me during that time, but if I had done that, my son would never have been a Kopia now [the clan of her husband]. When I brought him back my husband was good to him. He was quite grown then about three of four years old. But those early times when my son and I were separated from my husband created a scar which is lasting even now."

FIRST ENCOUNTERS TIMELINE

Greater Australia
(Papua New Guinea)

60,000–40,000 BC	First humans arrive from Southeast Asia
1526–1545	Portuguese and Spanish voyagers pass and name the island
1769–1770	Captain James Cook circumnavigates the island of New Guinea
1828	Dutch annex west half of New Guinea; British take the southeast coast, Germans the northeast coast.
1905	British give territory of Papua New Guinea to Australia
1914	Australia seizes German New Guinea
1930s	Michael Leahy records his encounters with isolated indigenous people in highlands of New Guinea
1931	Birth of Albert Maori Kiki
1949	Australia forms territory of Papua New Guinea
1968	Kiki publishes his autobiography
1975	Australia grants independence to Papua New Guinea; death of Kiki
1980s	Bob Connolly and Robin Anderson make film and publish book on Leahy's 1930s encounters

Part Five

FIRST ENCOUNTERS IN ASIA

INTRODUCTION

With only a few exceptions, first encounters in Asia differ greatly from those taking place in other parts of the world. Elsewhere, the European usually appeared as intruder, trespasser and conqueror. In Asia, however, the Europeans arrived, not as intruding interlopers, but as unobtrusive visitors, traders, and missionaries. For years, and even centuries, the Europeans who showed up on the coasts were regarded as inferior barbarians, unwelcome visitors, and over-inquisitive travelers. They were generally shunned, ignored, and confined to the coasts. Consequently, from the early 1500s to the mid-1800s, there were few, if any, encounters which provoked a reaction by native voices. Only later, when missionaries had unobtrusively penetrated the countries of the East and were becoming successful in spreading Christianity, were native voices raised in protest. These voices were those of scholars, religious leaders, and travelers who were in a position to view the larger picture and perceive the subtle encroachment of the Europeans. Unlike the native voices in the rest of the world, these were usually scholarly voices responding to the rhetoric of the missionary.

The Portuguese navigator Vasco da Gama was the first European to open up the sea route to Asia. Setting forth in 1497 with four ships and three years' worth of supplies, he sailed around southern Africa and headed east, landing on the west coast of India in 1498. He had disproved, once and for all, the myth that the oceans and seas of the world were land-locked. The English, French, and others soon followed. Small trading centers were established along the Indian coast opening up what was soon to become a thriving business. Previously, Europe's need for spices to break the monotony of its diet and hide the taste of spoiled meat, had to be met by transport over land which was long, arduous, and expensive. Now Europeans could engage directly in this trade and become rich in the process.

The English took the lead in establishing trade links with India and, with the creation of the East India Company early in the seventeenth century, the way was being prepared for the later incorporation of India into the British Empire. The Indian subcontinent had no strong central government and the various independent states were often at odds with each other. Using the tactic of divide and rule, the company gradually and almost imperceptibly increased its possessions and its control. For 100 years, from 1757 to 1858, India was, in essence, ruled by the East India Company. After a rebellion in 1858, the British Crown took over; the British ruled for another hundred years, until India became independent in 1947.

During the sixteenth century, European ships made some visits to the Far East, but it was not until the seventeenth century that regular trade routes were established with China to satisfy the newly developed taste for tea and silks. In return, China showed some interest in acquiring clocks, organs, telescopes, and eyeglasses. But these European goods were of much less interest to them than tea and silk were to the Europeans and, as a result, a growing trade imbalance developed which would, in later years, have catastrophic results for the Chinese. Between 1600 and the mid-nineteenth century China deliberately and systematically avoided contact with other countries, except for these European traders who were carefully confined to the coasts where they could engage in trade with local merchants. During these years, the Chinese showed very little curiosity about the Europeans who were characterized as uncultured barbarians, outside the pale of civilization. But Confucian scholars did notice the growing influence of Jesuit missionaries who brought scientific ideas as well as a new religion with them. Their vigorous criticisms of Catholicism centered on its emphasis on the afterlife.

In contrast to China, Japan did not initially feel threatened by the advent of foreign traders and missionaries who started to arrive in the middle of the sixteenth century. But when Christianity spread rapidly, especially among peasants, the government banned it in 1612. And in 1640, all foreigners were expelled; only the Dutch and Chinese were allowed to continue trading from a small island off the coast. Japan shut itself off from the rest of the world.

Chinese and Japanese isolationism, born of a combination of superiority and fear, was broken into by foreign invasions at about the same time in the middle of the nineteenth century. First came the Opium War (1839–1842). The East India Company had found a way to deal with their huge trade imbalance with China by smuggling opium, grown in India, into China and then marketing large quantities of it through their only official Chinese trading center, Canton. The Chinese eventually realized the nature of this threat and resisted by blockading British ships in Canton and burning the opium stockpiles. The British retaliated by capturing the city of Canton (now Guangzhou). The war ended with China ceding the island of Hong Kong to Britain and paying a large indemnity.

Japan was opened in 1846 when U.S. warships under Commodore Matthew Perry bullied their way into Japanese ports to force the country to open itself to international trade. The perception of foreigners as intruders never changed after these events.

JAPAN WELCOMED EUROPEANS AT FIRST

[Initially] Europeans got a much warmer greeting [in Japan] than they had received in China. The Chinese had wanted to quarantine them, like an infection. The Japanese, as soon as they realized the mighty powers of these strangers—their ability, for example, to shoot down birds in flight—took them in with open arms and vied with one another to learn their secrets. They also sought to trade with them because the gains were substantial. And the Europeans, on their side, seeing an opportunity to plant themselves in this welcoming society and get rich, scurried to make themselves useful. These wonderfully exotic Japanese had good tradables and placed an inordinately high value on European things and a foolishly low value on their own. Two worlds embraced, and each thought itself fortunate and the other generous.

David S. Landes, *The Wealth and Poverty of Nations*, New York: W. W. Norton, 1998, pp. 351–352.

33

CHINESE EMPEROR QIAN LONG
Scornful Letter to King George III
China

Editor's Notes: In 1793, the King of England, George III, sent his ambassador to the court of Chinese Emperor Qian Long (Ch'ien Lung) in Peking (Beijing) in an attempt to improve commercial relations between the two countries. Specifically, the king was requesting special trade privileges for British goods. Up to that time, absolute deference was expected from visitors in the presence of the emperor. Traditionally, this was accomplished by a visitor's doing the kowtow consisting of three knee bends and three prostrations. It is recorded that the British emissary refused to comply and for some unknown reason the emperor did not insist.

The emperor's reply to the king's requests to open up trade is a classic example of near total misunderstanding of another's culture and status in the world. The letter bristles with arrogance, haughtiness, patronage, and anti-foreign bias. Most revealing, however, is his inability to understand the relatively advanced state of English technology. The emperor expressed no interest in the strange and useless objects produced by English manufacturers.

You, O King, live beyond the confines of many seas, nevertheless, impelled by your humble desire to partake of the benefits of our civilisation, you have dispatched a mission respectfully bearing your memorial. Your Envoy has crossed the seas and paid his respects at my Court on the anniversary of my birthday. To show your devotion, you have also sent offerings of your country's produce.

I have perused your memorial: the earnest terms in which it is couched reveal a respectful humility on your part, which is highly praiseworthy. In consideration of the fact that your Ambassador and his deputy have come a long

Reprinted from *Annals and Memoirs of the Court of Peking*, by Edmund Trelawny Backhouse and J. O. P. Bland (London: Heinemann/Boston: Houghton Mifflin, 1914): pp. 322–326, 328–330.

Hung-li (1711–1799), known by the reign name Qian Long (Ch'ien Lung in the Wade-Giles Romanization system for Chinese), from a watercolor painting by William Alexander, who accompanied Lord Macartney's embassy to the Qing (Ch'ing) court in 1793. Alexander was not present at the audience with the emperor and worked from sketches made by others. In 1793, Qian Long had reigned for nearly six decades. (*Source*: E. Backhouse and J. O. P. Bland, *Annals and Memoirs of the Court of Peking* [1914].)

way with your memorial and tribute, I have shown them high favour and have allowed them to be introduced into my presence. To manifest my indulgence, I have entertained them at a banquet and made them numerous gifts. I have also caused presents to be forwarded to the Naval Commander and six hundred of his officers and men, although they did not come to Peking, so that they too may share in my all embracing kindness.

As to your entreaty to send one of your nationals to be accredited to my Celestial Court and to be in control of your country's trade with China, this request is contrary to all usage of my dynasty and cannot possibly be entertained. It is true that Europeans, in the service of the dynasty, have been permitted to live at Peking, but they are compelled to adopt Chinese dress, they are strictly confirmed to their own precincts and are never permitted to return home. You are presumably familiar with our dynastic regulations. Your proposed Envoy to my Court could not be placed in a position similar to that of European officials in Peking who are forbidden to leave China, nor could he, on the other hand, be allowed liberty of movement and the privilege of corresponding with his own country; so that you would gain nothing by his residence in our midst.

Moreover, our Celestial dynasty possesses vast territories, and tribute missions from the dependencies are provided for by the Department for Tributary States, which ministers to their wants and exercises strict control over their movements. It would be quite impossible to leave them to their own devices. Supposing that your Envoy should come to our Court, his language and national dress differ from that of our people, and there would be no place in which to bestow him. It may be suggested that he might imitate the Europeans permanently resident in Peking and adopt the dress and customs of China, but, it has never been our dynasty's wish to force people to do things unseemly and inconvenient. Besides, supposing I sent an Ambassador to reside in your country, how could you possibly make for him the requisite arrangements? Europe consists of many other nations besides your own: if each and all demanded to be represented at our Court, how could we possibly consent? The thing is utterly impracticable. How can our dynasty alter its whole procedure and system of etiquette, established for more than a century, in order to meet your individual views? If it be said that your object is to exercise control over your country's trade, your nationals have had full liberty to trade at Canton for many a year, and have received the greatest consideration at our hands. Missions have been sent by Portugal and Italy, preferring similar requests. The Throne appreciated their sincerity and loaded them with favours, besides authorising measures to facilitate their trade with China. You are no doubt aware that, when my Canton merchant, Wu Chaoping, was in debt to the foreign ships, I made the Viceroy advance the monies due, out of the provincial treasury, and ordered him to punish the culprit severely. Why then should foreign nations advance this utterly unreasonable request to be represented at my Court? Peking is nearly two thousand miles from Canton and at such a distance what possible control could any British representative exercise?

If you assert that your reverence for Our Celestial dynasty fills you with a desire to acquire our civilisation, our ceremonies and code of laws differ so completely from your own that, even if your Envoy were able to acquire the rudiments of our civilisation, you could not possibly transplant our manners and customs to your alien soil. Therefore, however adept the Envoy might become, nothing would be gained thereby.

Swaying the wide world, I have but one aim in view, namely, to maintain a perfect governance and to fulfill the duties of the State: strange and costly objects do not interest me. If I have commanded that the tribute offerings sent by you, O King, are to be accepted, this was solely in consideration for the spirit which prompted you to dispatch them from afar. Our dynasty's majestic virtue has penetrated unto every country under Heaven and Kings of all nations have offered their costly tribute by land and sea. As your Ambassador can see for himself we possess all things. I set no value on objects strange or ingenious, and have no use for your country's manufactures. This then is my answer to your request to appoint a representative at my Court, a request contrary to our dynastic usage, which would only result in inconvenience to yourself. I have expounded my wishes in detail and have commanded your tribute Envoys to leave in peace on their homeward journey. It behooves you, O King, to respect my sentiments and to display even greater devotion and loyalty in future, so that, by perpetual submission to our Throne, you may secure peace and prosperity for your country hereafter. Besides making gifts (of which I enclose an inventory) to each member of your Mission, I confer upon you, O King, valuable presents in excess of the number usually bestowed on such occasions, including silks and curios—a list of which is likewise enclosed. Do you reverently receive them and take note of my tender goodwill towards you! A special mandate.

Yesterday your Ambassador petitioned my Ministers to memorialise me regarding your trade with China, but his proposal is not consistent with our dynastic usage and cannot be entertained. Hitherto, all European nations, including your own country's barbarian merchants, have carried on their trade with our Celestial Empire at Canton. Such has been the procedure for many years, although our Celestial Empire possesses all things in prolific abundance and lacks no product within its own borders. There was therefore no need to import the manufactures of outside barbarians in exchange for our own produce. But as the tea, silk and porcelain which the Celestial Empire produces, are absolute necessities to European nations and to yourselves, we have permitted, as a signal mark of favour, that foreign hongs [merchant firms] should be established at Canton, so that your wants might be supplied and your country thus participate in our beneficence. But your Ambassador has now put forward new requests which completely fail to recognise the Throne's principle to "treat strangers from afar with indulgence," and to exercise a pacifying control over barbarian tribes, the world over. Moreover, our dynasty, swaying the myriad races of the globe, extends the same benevolence towards all. Your England is not the only nation trading at Canton. If other nations, following your bad example, wrongfully importune my ear with further impossible requests, how will it be possible for me to treat them with easy indulgence? Nevertheless, I do not forget the lonely remoteness of your island, cut off from the world by intervening wastes of sea, nor do I overlook your excusable ignorance of the usages of our Celestial Empire. I have consequently commanded my Ministers to enlighten your Ambassador on the subject, and have ordered the departure of the mission. But I have doubts that, after your Envoy's return he may fail to acquaint you with my view in detail or that he may be lacking in lucidity, so that I shall now proceed . . . to issue my mandate on each question separately. In this way you will, I trust, comprehend my meaning. . . .

(3) Your request for a small island near Chusan, where your merchants may reside and goods be warehoused, arises from your desire to develop trade. As there are neither foreign hongs nor interpreters in or near Chusan, where none of your ships have ever called, such an island would be utterly useless for

your purposes. Every inch of the territory of our Empire is marked on the map and the strictest vigilance is exercised over it all: even tiny islets and farlying sandbanks are clearly defined as part of the provinces to which they belong. Consider, moreover, that England is not the only barbarian land which wishes to establish trade with our Empire: supposing that other nations were all to imitate your evil example and beseech me to present them each and all with a site for trading purposes, how could I possibly comply? This also is a flagrant infringement of the usage of my Empire and cannot possibly be entertained.

(4) The next request, for a small site in the vicinity of Canton city, where your barbarian merchants may lodge or, alternatively, that there be no longer any restrictions over their movements at Aomen [Macao], has arisen from the following causes. Hitherto, the barbarian merchants of Europe have had a definite locality assigned to them at Aomen for residence and trade, and have been forbidden to encroach an inch beyond the limits assigned to that locality. . . . If these restrictions were withdrawn, friction would inevitably occur between the Chinese and your barbarian subjects, and the results would militate against the benevolent regard that I feel towards you. From every point of view, therefore, it is best that the regulations now in force should continue unchanged. . . .

(7) Regarding your nation's worship of the Lord of Heaven, it is the same religion as that of other European nations. Ever since the beginning of history, sage Emperors and wise rulers have bestowed on China a moral system and inculcated a code, which from time immemorial has been religiously observed by the myriads of my subjects. There has been no hankering after heterodox doctrines. Even the European (missionary) officials in my capital are forbidden to hold intercourse with Chinese subjects; they are restricted within the limits of their appointed residences, and may not go about propagating their religion. The distinction between Chinese and barbarian is most strict, and your Ambassador's request that barbarians shall be given full liberty to disseminate their religion is utterly unreasonable.

It may be, O King, that the above proposals have been wantonly made by your Ambassador on his own responsibility, or peradventure you yourself are ignorant of our dynastic regulations and had no intention of transgressing them when you expressed these wild ideas and hopes. . . . If, after the receipt of this explicit decree, you lightly give ear to the representations of your subordinates and allow your barbarian merchants to proceed to Chêkiang and Tientsin, with the object of landing and trading there, the ordinances of my Celestial Empire are strict in the extreme, and the local officials, both civil and military, are bound reverently to obey the law of the land. Should your vessels touch the shore, your merchants will assuredly never be permitted to land or to reside there, but will be subject to instant expulsion. In that event your barbarian merchants will have had a long journey for nothing. Do not say that you were not warned in due time! Tremblingly, obey and show no negligence! A special mandate!

WHY CHINA MISSED ITS BIG CHANCE

Why did China, where so many things were invented, exploit its creativity so poorly? The Chinese discovered paper and movable type, yet the country was virtually illiterate until the 20th century. Gunpowder was also invented in China, yet its cannons were inferior to those made by Europeans. China's bustling cities, despite their vitality, never stimulated the intellectual ferment that in Europe led to innovation. Part of the explanation is the dominant role in China's history played by bureaucracy, which was intensely conservative, and by Confucian philosophy, which emphasized order, continuity and stability. Ricci noted that the Chinese word for their country, *Thienhia*, meant "everything under the heavens." Believing that China was superior to other nations, officials of the imperial court were leery of innovation and humiliated to learn that something had been done better elsewhere.

John Elson, *Time*, October 15, 1992, p. 21.

34

CANTON CITIZENS

DENUNCIATION OF THE BRITISH

China

Editor's Notes: During the Opium War (1839–42), in order to force China to accept the opium trade, British forces marched inland from Hong Kong to the great walled city of Canton (now Guangzhou). Following the payment of a ransom the British withdrew. This first general exposure to foreign incursion resulted in the formation of a popular anti-British movement centered around the city of Canton. This denunciation was written by a group of protestors. Some historians claim that this united show of force may mark the very beginning of Chinese nationalism.

The thoroughly loyal and patriotic people of the whole province of Kwangtung instruct the rebellious barbarian dogs and sheep for their information. We note that you English barbarians have formed the habits and developed the nature of wolves, plundering and seizing things by force. . . .

In trade relations, you come to our country merely to covet profit. What knowledge do you have? Your seeking profit resembles the animal's greed for food. You are ignorant of our laws and institutions, ignorant of right principles . . . You have no gratitude for the great favor of our Celestial Court; on the contrary you treat us like enemies and do us harm. You use opium to injure our common people, cheating us of our silver and cash. . . .

Although you have penetrated our inland rivers and enticed fellows who renounce their fathers and their ruler to become Chinese traitors and stir up trouble among us, you are only using money to buy up their services—what

Reprinted by permission of the publisher from *China's Response to the West; A Documentary Survey, 1839–1923*, by Ssu-yü Têng and John King Fairbank, p. 36 (Cambridge, Mass.: Harvard University Press), Copyright © 1954, 1979, by the President and Fellows of Harvard College, Copyright renewed 1982 by Ssu-yü Têng and John King Fairbank.

good points have you? . . . Except for your ships being solid, your gunfire fierce, and your rockets powerful, what other abilities have you? . . .

We patriots have received the favor of the Celestial Dynasty in nourishing us for two centuries. Today, if we do not exterminate you English barbarians, we will not be human beings. You have killed and injured our common people in many villages, and seriously hurt the universal harmony. You also completely destroyed the coffins in several places, and you disastrously damaged the Buddhist statues in several monasteries. This is properly a time when Heaven is angered and mankind is resentful; even the ghosts and spirits will not tolerate you beasts. . . .

Our hatred is already at white heat. If we do not completely exterminate you pigs and dogs, we will not be manly Chinese able to support the sky on our heads and stand firmly on the earth. Once we have said this, we will never go back on it, even if frustrated ten thousand times. We are definitely going to kill you, cut your heads off and burn you to death! Even though you ask people to admonish us, we will not obey. We must strip off your skins and eat your flesh, and then you will know how tough we are. . . .

We ought really to use refined expressions. But since you beasts do not understand written characters, therefore we use rough, vulgar words to instruct you in simple terms.

35

WEI YUAN

Beware of Western Barbarians

China

Editor's Notes: Following China's defeat in the Opium War, 1839–1842, resulting in the forced trading of opium, awareness of the Western barbarians started to grow. In the mid-1840s the first scholarly book about the West titled, Illustrated Gazetteer of the Maritime Countries, *by Wei Yuan, was published. It issued a warning for China to take seriously the growing influence of the Westerner for whom Wei had nothing but contempt. Up until that time, China had paid little attention to the growing presence of the Europeans, on the assumption that they were inconsequential and not worth bothering with. In this brief summary, Wei urges his country to face the threat and take action, but he is careful to avoid specifying whether this should be accomplished through war or peaceful diplomacy.*

Wei Yuan, 1794–1856, historian and geographer, spent most of his life in Hunan Province as a minor city administrator. His famous Gazetteer *was widely circulated and even translated into Japanese.*

The Western barbarians, bent on power and profit, have devised techniques and machines by which to subvert or conquer the civilized world. China, dedicated as she is to virtue, learning, and the ways of peace, possesses a spiritual and moral strength which can yet triumph over the enemy if only the Chinese awaken to the danger and apply themselves to the practical problems involved. Traditional military science suggests that the first requisite is intelligence of the enemy—of his strengths and weaknesses. The second requisite is to match these strengths and exploit the weaknesses. If the natural abilities of the Chinese are devoted to the study and adoption of Western military methods, and there is not too great an impatience with the achievement of immediate results, the time will come when China can reassert herself. In the meantime, she should seek to exploit the prime weakness of the West—its inherent disunity, which derives from the lack of a common moral basis and consequent anarchy of selfish ambitions among the nations. To play the Western powers off against one another is then the obvious strategy.

36

ABU TALEB
The Evil of Western Materialism
India

Editor's Notes: The first encounters between the native populations of India and the Europeans were nearly imperceptible and gradually extended over several centuries. Following Vasco da Gama's discovery of the sea route to India in 1498, European merchants established trading posts on both coasts of the subcontinent and conducted their business strictly through local native merchants. For several centuries India was so preoccupied with its own internal affairs that who these foreigners were, or from whence they came, was of no or little concern.

Abu Taleb was born in 1752 in Lucknow, India. As a young man, he served in several state governments and later worked for the British where he acquired considerable skill in the English language. Despondent at the lack of opportunities for promotion, he accepted the invitation of a Scottish friend to visit England. Three years later in 1803, on his return to India, he published an account of his travels which includes a description of the twelve worst faults of the British, as well as six of their greatest virtues.

The first and greatest defect I observed in the English, is their want of faith in religion, and their great inclination to philosophy (atheism). The effects of these principles, or rather want of principle, is very conspicuous in the lower orders of people, who are totally devoid of honesty. They are, indeed, cautious how they transgress against the laws, from fear of punishment; but whenever an opportunity offers of purloining anything without the risk of detection, they never pass it by. They are also ever on the watch to appropriate to themselves the property of the rich, who, on this account, are obliged constantly to keep

Reprinted from *Westward Bound: Travels of Mirza Abu Taleb*, ed. by Mushirul Hasan, tr. by Charles Stewart (New Delhi: Oxford University Press, 2005), 145–157.

their doors shut, and never to permit an unknown person to enter them. At present, owing to the vigilance of the magistrates, the severity of the laws, and the honour of the superior classes of people, no very bad consequences are to be apprehended; but if ever such nefarious practices should become prevalent, and should creep in among the higher classes, inevitable ruin must ensue.

The second defect, most conspicuous in life English character, is pride, or insolence. Puffed up with their power and good fortune for the last fifty years, they are not apprehensive of adversity, and take no pains to avert it. Thus, when the people of London, sometime ago, assembled in mobs on account of the great increase of taxes and high price of provisions, and were nearly in a state of insurrection—although the magistrates, by their vigilance in watching them, and by causing parties of soldiers to patrol the streets day and night, to disperse all persons whom they saw assembling together, succeeded in quieting the disturbance—yet no pains were afterwards taken to eradicate the evil. Some of the men in power said, it had been merely a plan of the artificers to obtain higher wages (an attempt frequently made by the English tradesmen); others were of opinion that no remedy could be applied; therefore no further notice was taken of the affair. All this, I say, betrays a blind confidence, which, instead of meeting the danger, and endeavouring to prevent it, waits till the misfortune arrives, and then attempts to remedy it. Such was the case with the late King of France, who took no step to oppose the Revolution, till it was too late. This self-confidence is to be found, more or less, in every Englishman: it however differs much from the pride of Indians and Persians.

Their third defect is a passion for acquiring money, and their attachment to worldly affairs. Although these bad qualities are not so reprehensible in them as in countries more subject to the vicissitudes of fortune, (because, in England, property is so well protected by the laws, that every person reaps the fruits of his industry, and, in his old age, enjoys the earnings or economy of his youth), yet sordid and illiberal habits are generally found to accompany avarice and parsimony, and, consequently, render the possessor of them contemptible: on the contrary, generosity, if it does not launch into prodigality, but is guided by the hand of prudence, will render a man respected and esteemed.

The fourth of their frailties is a desire of ease, and a dislike to exertion: this, however, prevails only in a moderate degree, and bears no proportion to the apathy and indolence of the smokers of opium of Hindoostan and Constantinople; it only prevents them from perfecting themselves in science, and exerting themselves in the service of their friends, upon what they *choose* to call trivial occasions.

The fifth defect is nearly allied to the former and is termed irritability of temper. This passion often leads them to quarrel with their friends and acquaintances, without any substantial cause. Of the bad effects of this quality, strangers seldom have much reason to complain; but as society can only be supported by mutual forbearance, and sometimes shutting our eyes on the frailties or ignorance of our friends, it often causes animosities and disunion between the nearest relatives, and hurries the possessor into dilemmas whence he frequently finds it difficult to extricate himself.

The sixth defect of the English is their throwing away their time, in sleeping, eating, and dressing; for, besides the necessary ablutions, they every morning shave, and dress their hair; then, to accommodate themselves to the fashion, they put on twenty-five different articles of dress: all this, except shaving, is repeated before dinner, and the whole of these clothes are again to be taken off at night: so that not less than two complete hours can be allowed on this account. One hour is expended at breakfast; three hours at dinner; and the three following hours are devoted to tea, and the company of the ladies. Nine hours are given up to sleep: so that there remain just six hours, out of the twenty-four, for visiting and business. If they are reproached with this waste of time, they reply, "How is it to be avoided?" I answer them thus: "Curtail the number of your garments; render your dress simple; wear your beards; and give up less of your time to eating, drinking, and sleeping."

Their seventh defect is a luxurious manner of living, by which their wants are increased a hundred-fold. Observe their kitchens, filled with various utensils; their rooms, fitted up with costly furniture; their side-boards, covered with plate; their tables, loaded with expensive glass and china; their cellars, stocked with wines from every quarter of the world; their parks, abounding in game of various sorts; and their ponds, stored with fish. All these expenses are incurred to pamper their appetites, which, from long indulgence, have gained such absolute sway over them, that a diminution of these luxuries would be considered, by many, as a serious misfortune.

The eighth defect of the English is vanity, and arrogance, respecting their acquirements in science, and a knowledge of foreign languages, for, as soon as one of them acquires the smallest insight into the principles of any science, or the rudiments of any foreign language, he immediately sits down and composes a work on the subject, and, by means of the press, circulates books which have no more intrinsic worth than the toys bestowed on children, which serve to amuse the ignorant, but are of no use to the learned. This is not merely my own opinion, but was confirmed to me both by Greeks and Frenchmen, whose languages are cultivated in England with more ardour than any others. Such, however, is the infatuation of the English, that they give the author implicit credit for his profound knowledge, and purchase his books. Even those who are judges of the subject do not discountenance this measure, but contend that a little knowledge is better than entire ignorance, and that perfection can only be acquired by degrees. This axiom I deny; for the portion of science and truth contained in many of their books is so small, that much time is thrown away in reading them: besides, erroneous opinions and bad habits are often contracted by the perusal of such works, which are more difficult to eradicate, than it is to implant correct ideas in a mind totally uncultivated.

A ninth failing prevalent among the English is selfishness. They frequently endeavour to benefit themselves, without attending to the injury it may do to others: and when they seek their own advantage, they are more humble and submissive than appears to me proper; for after they have obtained their object, they are either ashamed of their former conduct, or dislike the continuance of it so much, that they frequently break off the connection. Others, restrained by a sense of propriety, still keep up the intercourse, and endeavour to make the person they have injured, or whom they have deceived by promises, forget the circumstance, by their flattering and courteous behaviour. I had few opportunities of experiencing this myself in England; but the conduct in India of Colonel Hanny, Mr. Middleton, Mr. Johnson, and Dr. Blane, gave me convincing proofs of it; for, whenever they had any point to carry, they would accept of no excuse from me; and having, by persuasion and promises, prevailed upon me to undertake their business, as soon as they had obtained their wishes they forgot their promises, and abandoned me to the malice of enemies. It might have been unnecessary to quote these instances; for this defect in the character of the English is so evident, that no doubts remain on the subject.

The tenth vice of this nation is want of chastity; for under this head I not only include the reprehensible conduct of young women running away with their lovers, and others cohabiting with a man before marriage, but the great degree of licentiousness practised by numbers of both sexes in London; evinced by the multiplicity of public-houses and bagnios in every part of the town. I was credibly informed, that in the single parish of Mary-la-bonne, which is only a sixth part of London, there reside sixty thousand courtezans; besides which, there is scarcely, a street in the metropolis where they are not to be found. . . .

The eleventh vice of the English is extravagance, that is, living beyond their incomes by incurring useless expenses, and keeping up unnecessary establishments. Some of these I have before alluded to, under the head of luxuries; but to those are now to be added the establishments of carriages, horses, and servants, two sets of which are frequently kept, one for the husband, the other for his wife. Much money is also lavished in London, on balls, masquerades, routs etc.

If the English will take the trouble of reading ancient history, they will find that luxury and prodigality have caused the ruin of more governments than was ever effected by an invading enemy: they generate envy, discord, and animosity, and render the people either effeminate, or desirous of a change. To these vices may be ascribed the subversion of the Roman empire in Europe, and the annihilation of the Moghul government in India.

Their twelfth defect is a contempt for the customs of other nations, and the preference they give to their own; although theirs, in fact, may be much inferior. I had a striking instance of this prejudice in the conduct of my fellow-passengers on board ship. Some of these, who were otherwise respectable characters, ridiculed the idea of my wearing trousers, and a night-dress, when I went to bed; and contended, that they slept much more at their ease by going to bed nearly naked. I replied, that I slept very comfortably; that mine was certainly the most decent mode; and that, in the event of any sudden accident happening, I could run on deck instantly, and, if requisite, jump into the boat in a minute; whilst they must either lose some time in dressing, or come out of their cabins in a very immodest manner. In answer to this, they said, such sudden accidents seldom occurred, but that if it did happen, they would not hesitate to come on deck in their shirts only. This I give merely as a specimen of their obstinacy and prejudice in favour of their own customs.

I fear, in the foregoing chapter, I have fatigued my readers with a long detail of the vices, or defects of the English: I shall, therefore, now give some account of their virtues; but, lest I should be accused of flatter will endeavour to avoid prolixity on this subject.

The first of the English virtues is a high sense of honour, especially among the better classes. This is the effect of a liberal education, and of the contempt with which those who do not possess it are regarded. This sense of honour is carried to such a degree, that men possessing every terrestrial enjoyment, as wealth, estates, wife, and children, will, on the smallest imputation, sacrifice their lives, and the welfare of their families, to recover their reputation, or to wipe off an ignominious slander.

Their second good quality is a reverence for every thing or person possessing superior excellence. This mode of thinking has this great advantage—it makes them emulous of acquiring the esteem of the world, and thus renders them better men. In other countries, this respect is not paid to superior merit: people will therefore not give themselves any trouble on the subject: wisdom, knowledge, and virtue, are consequently banished from among them.

The third of their perfections is a dread of offending against the rules of propriety, or the laws of the realm: they are therefore generally content with their own situations, and very seldom attempt to exalt themselves by base or nefarious practices. By these means the establishments of Church and State are supported, and the bonds of society strengthened; for when men are ambitious of raising themselves from inferior to exalted situations, they attempt to overcome all obstacles; and though a few gain their object, the greater part are disappointed, and become, ever after, unhappy and discontented.

The fourth of their virtues is a strong desire to improve the situations of the common people, and an aversion to do anything which can injure them. It may be said, that in so doing they are not perfectly disinterested; for that the benefits of many of these institutions and inventions revert to themselves.

During my residence in England, and at a time when coals were extremely dear, one of their philosophers invented a kettle, with a small furnace below, which required so little fuel, that a piece of lighted paper, or a burning stick, thrown into the furnace, would cause the water to boil long enough to dress a joint of meat. By means of such machines, and the various conveniences adopted in the fitting up of a house, so much time and labour are saved, that two servants in England will do the work of fifteen in India.

Their fifth good quality is so nearly allied to weakness, that by some worldly people it has been called such: I mean, an adherence to the rules of fashion. By this arbitrary law, the rich are obliged not only to alter the shape of their clothes every year, but also to change all the furniture of their houses. It would bethought quite derogatory to a person of taste, to have his drawing room fitted up in the same manner for two successive years. The advantage of this profusion is the encouragement it gives to ingenuity and manufacturers of every kind; and it enables the middling and lower classes of people to supply their wants at a cheap rate, by purchasing the old fashioned articles.

Their sixth excellence is a passion for mechanism, and their numerous contrivances for facilitating labour and industry.

Their seventh perfection is plainness of manners: and sincerity of disposition; the former is evinced in the colours of their clothes, which are generally of a dark hue, and exempt from all tawdriness; and the latter, by their open and manly conduct.

Their other good qualities are good natural sense and soundness of judgement, which induce them to prefer things that are useful to those that are brilliant; to which may be added, their perseverance in the acquirement of science, and the attainment of wealth and honours.

Their hospitality is also very praiseworthy, and their attention to their guests can nowhere be exceeded. They have an aversion to sit down to table *alone*. . . .

37

RAMMOHUN ROY
Hinduism Is Not Inferior to Christianity
India

Editor's Notes: Rammohum Roy (1772–1833) was born of upper-class Brahmin parents in Bengal, western India. At a young age, there were indications that he would become one of India's most talented linguists, scholars, and philosophers. He mastered several languages and attained fluent English. Among his many achievements were the founding of several secondary schools, the organization of a highly influential religious society, the founding and editing of several newspapers, and the leadership of a campaign against sati *(the practice of burning Hindu widows alive). He joined the British civil service and eventually was promoted to the highest level.*

Roy was among the very first Indian scholars to delve deeply into the literature of the Christian Bible. He developed the idea that Hinduism and Christianity had much in common if one concentrated only on the ethics and humanitarian aspects of the respective religions while rejecting the doctrinal and theological. Protestant missionaries in India were outraged by Roy's rejection of the divinity of Christ and wrote scathing denunciations of his writings. In his counterattacks, Roy emphasized the unfairness of missionary proselytising, reminding his readers that in denigrating Asian people, they were also denigrating Jesus Christ who, himself, was Asian.

For a period of upwards of fifty years, this country . . . has been in exclusive possession of the English nation, during the first thirty years of which from their word and deed it was universally believed that they would not interfere with the religion of their subjects, and that they truly wished every man to act in such matters according to the dictates of his own conscience. Their possessions in Hindoostan and their political strength have, through the grace of God,

From *Sources of Indian Tradition*, edited by William Theodore deBary. Copyright ©1958 Columbia University Press, 578–579, 580. Reprinted with permission of the publisher.

gradually increased. But during the last twenty years, a body of English Gentlemen who are called missionaries have been publicly endeavoring, in several ways,
to convert Hindoos and Mussulmans of this country into Christianity. The first
way is that of publishing and distributing among the natives various books, large
and small, reviling both religions, and abusing and ridiculing the gods and saints
of the former; the second way is that of standing in front of the doors of the
natives or in the public roads to preach the excellency of that of others; the third
way is that if any natives of low origin become Christians from the desire of gain
or from any other motives, these Gentlemen employ and maintain them as a
necessary encouragement to others to follow their example.

It is true that the apostles of Jesus Christ used to preach the superiority of the
Christian religion to the natives of different countries. But we must recollect that
they were not the rulers of those countries where they preached. Were the missionaries likewise to preach the Gospel and distribute books in countries not
conquered by the English, such as Turkey, Persia, &c. which are much nearer
England, they would be esteemed a body of men truly zealous in propagating
religion and in following the example of the founders of Christianity. In Bengal,
where the English are the sole rulers, and where the mere name of Englishman is
sufficient to frighten people, an encroachment upon the rights of her poor timid
and humble inhabitants and upon their religion cannot be viewed in the eyes of
God or the public as a justifiable act. For wise and good men always feel disin-
clined to hurt those that are of much less strength than themselves, and if such
weak creatures be dependent on them and subject to their authority, they can
never attempt, even in thought, to mortify their feelings. . . .

If by the "ray of intelligence" for which the Christian says we are indebted to
the English, he means the introduction of useful mechanical arts, I am ready to
express my assent and also my gratitude; but with respect to *science, literature,*
or *religion,* I do not acknowledge that we are placed under any obligation. For
by a reference to History it may be proved that the world was indebted to *our
ancestors* for the first dawn of knowledge, which sprang up in the East, and thanks
to the Goddess of Wisdom, we have still a philosophical and copious language of
our own which distinguishes us from other nations who cannot express scientific
or abstract ideas without borrowing the language of foreigners. . . .

Before "A Christian" indulged in a tirade about persons being "degraded by
Asiatic effeminacy" he should have recollected that almost all the ancient
prophets and patriarchs venerated by Christians, nay even Jesus Christ himself,
a Divine Incarnation and the *founder* of the Christian Faith, were Asiatics.
So that if a Christian thinks it degrading to be born or to reside in Asia, he
directly reflects upon them. . . .

It is unjust in the Christian to quarrel with Hindoos because (he says) they
cannot comprehend the sublime mystery of his religion [the Doctrine of the
Trinity]; since he is equally unable to comprehend the sublime mysteries of
ours, and since both these mysteries equally transcend the human understanding, one cannot be preferred to the other.

38

HIRATU ATSUTANE

Japanese Are Superior, Dutch Are Inferior

Japan

Editor's Notes: Hirata Atsutane (1776–1843) was born in northern Japan but moved to Edo (Tokyo) as a young man. He trained to become a physician and while expressing admiration for Western medicine and science, violently rejected everything else originating from the Europeans. He became known as an ultranationalistic scholar. His work includes respected scholarship, but also what has been termed irrational bigotry in his attempts to reach the average reader. The first selection, illustrates his belief that Japan is the home of the gods, while the second provides an example of his crude attacks on the Europeans.

THE JAPANESE ARE SUPERIOR

People all over the world refer to Japan as the Land of the Gods and call us the descendants of the gods. Indeed, it is exactly as they say: our country, as a special mark of favor from the heavenly gods, was begotten by them, and there is thus so immense a difference between Japan and all the other countries of the world as to defy comparison.

Ours is a splendid and blessed country, the Land of the Gods beyond any doubt, and we, down to the most humble man and woman, are the descendants of the gods. Nevertheless, there are unhappily many people who do not understand why Japan is the land of the gods and we their descendants. . . .

Is this not a lamentable state of affairs? Japanese differ completely from and are superior to the peoples of China, India, Russia, Holland, Siam, Cambodia, and all other countries of the world, and for us to have called our country the

Richard Minear (ed.), *Through Japanese Eyes* (New York: CITE Books, The Apex Press, 1994), pp. 64–67.

Land of the Gods was not mere vainglory. It was the gods who formed all the lands of the world at the Creation, and these gods were without exception born in Japan.

Japan is thus the homeland of the gods, and that is why we call it the Land of the Gods. This is a matter of universal belief, and is quite beyond dispute. Even in countries where our ancient traditions have not been transmitted, the peoples recognize Japan as a divine land because of the majestic effulgence that of itself emanates from our country.

In olden days, when Korea was divided into three kingdoms, reports were heard there of how splendid, miraculous, and blessed a land Japan is, and, because Japan lies to the east of Korea, they said in awe and reverence, "to the East is a divine land, called the Land of the Rising Sun."

Word of this eventually spread all over the world, and now people everywhere refer to Japan as the Land of the Gods, irrespective of whether or not they know why this is true.

THE DUTCH ARE INFERIOR

As everybody knows who has seen one, the Dutch are taller than other people, have fair complexions, big noses, and white stars in their eyes. By nature they are very light-hearted and often laugh. They are seldom angry, a fact which does not accord with their appearance and is a seeming sign of weakness. They shave their beards, cut their nails, and are not dirty like the Chinese. Their clothing is extremely beautiful and ornamented with gold and silver.

Their eyes are really just like those of a dog. They are long from the waist downward, and the slenderness of their legs also makes them resemble animals. When they urinate they lift one leg, the way dogs do. Moreover, apparently because the backs of their feet do not reach to the ground, they fasten wooden heels to their shoes, which makes them look all the more like dogs. This may explain also why a Dutchman's penis appears to be cut short at the end, just like a dog's. This may sound like a joke, but it is quite true, not only of Dutchmen but of Russians too. . . . This may be the reason why the Dutch are as lascivious as dogs and spend their entire nights at erotic practices. . . . Because they are thus addicted to sexual excesses and to drink, none of them lives very long. For a Dutchman to reach 50 years is as rare as for a Japanese to live to be over 100.

39

TOKUGAWA NARIAKI
War Is Preferable to Peace
Japan

Editor's Notes: In July, 1853, Commodore Matthew Perry, commander-in-chief of all U.S. naval forces in the Far East, delivered a message addressed to His Imperial Majesty, the Emperor of Japan. It proclaimed friendship and requested that trade between the countries be established. The letter was given wide coverage by the Japanese government and the issue of a closed, versus an open trade policy was widely discussed.

Tokugawa Nariaki, one of Japan's most powerful war lords, expressed his strong feelings against the encouragement of trade. In a letter to the Bakufu (the government), he puts forth 10 arguments why war is preferable to peace with the intruding foreign traders.

Among the 10 reasons (seven are discussed here), he declared that national prestige is at stake, that traders would open the doors for proselytizing missionaries to undermine religion, that peace would encourage traders to bring in useless Western goods, and that the Japanese would lose face among the lesser nations of the world.

It is my belief that the first and most urgent of our tasks is for the Bakufu to make its choice between peace and war, and having determined its policy to pursue it unwaveringly thereafter. When we consider the respective advantages and disadvantages of war and peace, we find that if we put our trust in war the whole country's morale will be increased and even if we sustain an initial defeat we will in the end expel the foreigner; while if we put our trust in peace, even though things may seem tranquil for a time, the morale of the country will be greatly lowered and we will come in the end to complete collapse. This has been amply

From *Select Documents on Japanese Foreign Policy*, by W. G. Beasley (1955). By permission of Oxford University Press, pp. 102–107.

demonstrated in the history of China and is a fact that men of intelligence, both past and present, have always known. It is therefore unnecessary for me to speak of this in detail. However, I propose to give here in outline the ten reasons why in my view we must never choose the policy of peace.

1. Although our country's territory is not extensive, foreigners both fear and respect us. That, after all, is because our resoluteness and military prowess have been clearly demonstrated to the world outside ...

... the Americans who arrived recently, though fully aware of the Bakufu's prohibition, entered Uraga displaying a white flag as a symbol of peace and insisted on presenting their written requests. Moreover they entered Edo Bay, fired heavy guns in salute and even went so far as to conduct surveys without permission. They were arrogant and discourteous, their actions an outrage. Indeed, this was the greatest disgrace we have suffered since the dawn of our history. The saying is that if the enemy dictates terms in one's own capital, one's country is disgraced. The foreigners having thus ignored our prohibition and penetrated our waters even to the vicinity of the capital, threatening us and making demands upon us, should it happen not only that the Bakufu fails to expel them but also that it concludes an agreement in accordance with their requests, then I fear it would be impossible to maintain our national prestige [kokutai]. That is the first reason why we must never choose the policy of peace.

2. The prohibition of Christianity is the first rule of the Tokugawa house. Public notices concerning it are posted everywhere, even to the remotest corner of every province. It is said that even so, during the Bunsei period [1818–30], men have been executed for propagating this religion secretly in Osaka. The Bakufu can never ignore or overlook the evils of Christianity. Yet if the Americans are allowed to come again this religion will inevitably raise its head once more, however strict the prohibition; and this, I fear, is something we could never justify to the spirits of our ancestors. That is the second reason why we must never choose the policy of peace.

3. To exchange our valuable articles like gold, silver, copper, and iron for useless foreign goods like woolens and satin is to incur great loss while acquiring not the smallest benefit. The best course of all would be for the Bakufu to put a stop to the trade with Holland. By contrast, to open such valueless trade with others besides the Dutch would, I believe, inflict the greatest possible harm on our country. That is the third reason why we must never choose the policy of peace.

4. For some years Russia, England, and others have sought trade with us, but the Bakufu has not permitted it. Should permission be granted to the Americans, on what grounds would it be possible to refuse if Russia and the others [again] request it? That is the fourth reason why we must never choose the policy of peace.

5. It is widely stated that [apart from trade] the foreigners have no other evil designs and that if only the Bakufu will permit trade there will be no further

difficulty. However, it is their practice first to seek a foothold by means of trade and then to go on to propagate Christianity and make other unreasonable demands. Thus we would be repeating the blunders of others, seen remotely in the Christianity incidents of the Kanei period [1624–44] and before [in Japan] and more recently in the Opium War in China. That is the fifth reason why we must never choose the policy of peace.

6. Though . . . (one) . . . may argue secretly that world conditions are much changed from what they were, Japan alone clinging to ideas of seclusion in isolation amidst the seas, that this is a constant source of danger to us and that our best course would therefore be to communicate with foreign countries and open an extensive trade; yet, to my mind, if the people of Japan stand firmly united, if we complete our military preparations and return to the state of society that existed before the middle ages, then we will even be able to go out against foreign countries and spread abroad our fame and prestige. But if we open trade at the demand of the foreigners, for no better reason than that, our habits today being those of peace and indolence, men have shown fear merely at the coming of a handful of foreign warships, then it would truly be a vain illusion to think of evolving any long-range plan for going out against foreign countries. That is the sixth reason why we must never choose the policy of peace. . . .

9. I hear that all, even though they be commoners, who have witnessed the recent actions of the foreigners, think them abominable; and if the Bakufu does not expel these insolent foreigners root and branch there may be some who will complain in secret, asking to what purpose have been all the preparation of gun-emplacements. It is inevitable that men should think in this way when they have seen how arrogantly the foreigners acted at Uraga. That, I believe, is because even the humblest are conscious of the debt they owe their country, and it is indeed a promising sign. Since even ignorant commoners are talking in this way, I fear that if the Bakufu does not decide to carry out expulsion, if its handling of the matter shows nothing but excess of leniency and appeasement of the foreigners, then lower orders may fail to understand its ideas and hence opposition might arise from evil men who had lost their respect for Bakufu authority. It might even be that Bakufu control of the great lords would itself be endangered. That is the ninth reason why we must never choose the policy of peace. . . .

I have tried to explain above in general terms the relative advantages and disadvantages of the war and peace policies. However, this [policy I recommend] is something that is easy to understand but difficult to carry out. In these feeble days men tend to cling to peace; they are not fond of defending their country by war. They slander those of us who are determined to fight, calling us lovers of war, men who enjoy conflict. If matters become desperate they might, in their enormous folly, try to overthrow those of us who are determined to fight, offering excuses to the enemy and concluding a peace agreement with him. They would thus in the end bring total destruction upon us.

In view of our country's tradition of military courage, however, it is probable that once the Bakufu has taken a firm decision we shall find no such cowards among us. But good advice is as hard to accept as good medicine is unpleasing to the palate. A temporizing and time-serving policy is the one easiest for men to adopt. It is therefore my belief that in this question of coast defense it is if the first importance that the Bakufu pay due heed [to these matters] and that having once reached a decision it should never waver from it thereafter. . . .

40

YI IK
CRITICISMS OF CATHOLICISM
Korea

Editor's Notes: European missionaries arrived in China during the early years of the seventeenth century, after enduring, in some cases, journeys of as much as three years. Korea's first contact with European missionaries was through their books which were imported from China. The early missionaries in China followed a proselytizing strategy which claimed that the obvious superiority of Western technology was proof that their religion was therefore also superior.

This was strongly disputed by Yi Ik (1681–1763), a noted Korean scholar, who, while recognizing the value of Western goods and technical accomplishments, especially in the field of astronomy, refused to take the leap that Catholicism was therefore also valid.

One of Yi Ik's main criticisms was that the belief in heaven and hell was simply a carrot and stick strategy for controlling human behavior on earth. And he objected to the belief that the Lord of Heaven was allegedly concerned with all of mankind universally. If this were so, how is it that only Europeans knew about him directly whereas the rest of the world did not?

They hold out promises of rewards in heaven and threats of punishment in hell to encourage good behavior and discourage evil. And they believe the person who spread these teachings far and wide to enlighten and transform the world was someone called Jesus. Jesus is the Western word for savior.

They say that people have known about Jesus for quite some time. As mankind gradually lost its original purity and honest simplicity, and sages and

From *Sources of Korean Tradition*, Vol. II, ed. by Peter H. Lee and William Theodore de Bary, et al. Copyright © 2000 Columbia University Press, pp. 125–127. Reprinted with permission of the publisher.

saints disappeared from the earth, as the pursuit of pleasure grew stronger and the adherence to moral standards grew weaker, the Lord of Heaven felt compassion for mankind and descended to earth personally in order to save this world. He chose a virgin as his mother and, borrowing that womb, which had never known sexual relations, was born in the land of Judea under the name of Jesus. After preaching his message for thirty-three years in that Western land, he returned to heaven. His teachings subsequently spread to the various nations of Europe. There are five continents in this world. Asia sits in the center and Europe is off in the West. China occupies just one-tenth of Asia. Judea is a country off in the far western corner of Asia. . . .

If the Lord of Heaven truly felt compassion for mankind and descended to this earth in human form, walking and talking among men like any other man, then, since in the million places on this earth there are an infinite number of people deserving of his compassion, he should have admonished them all one by one. But how could the Lord of Heaven, in the form of just one man, do all that? Those living outside of Europe, those who have never heard of these European teachings, have seen no signs of his having visited them. What is so special about Europeans that he has so favored them with his visits? And what about all these miraculous signs of the Lord's presence that Europe claims? How do we know they are not simply the tricks of evil spirits?

The Europeans have made some drastic changes in their practices and their ideas over the years. Whereas they once believed that proper behavior generates good fortune, just as improper behavior engenders misfortune, they gradually lost faith in that notion. The written record of the teachings of the Lord of Heaven was at first no different from what we can find in the *Classic of Odes* and the *Classic of Documents*. But out of concern that people were drifting away from those teachings, this story of heaven and hell was created to keep them on the straight and narrow. Subsequently, this talk of heaven and hell gradually evolved into the elaborate tales of spirits and their miraculous activities the Europeans believe in today, though these miracles are more like what is called elsewhere tricks of evil spirits.

Generally speaking, the Chinese only accept solid evidence. If there is no solid evidence for some assertion, then even the most ignorant do not believe it. But the Europeans embrace the miraculous and the mysterious. The more perplexing the evidence, the more easily the ignorant are seduced by it. This being the case, they have no right to complain that only evil spirits delude people. The teachings of their Lord of Heaven do at least as much damage to the hearts and minds of people. Their stories of heaven and hell are no different from the reports of memories of previous lives that appeared in China after the arrival of Buddhism.

There is no subject these Westerners have not exhaustively explored and nothing too profound for them to understand, so it is really a pity that they have become mixed up with such nonsense.

41

AN CHONGBOK

THE WEAKNESS OF CATHOLICISM

Korea

Editor's Notes: An Chongbok (1712–1791), a noted Confucian scholar, denounced Catholicism just as the first Catholic converts were appearing during the 1780s. The following debate on religious belief probably took place between An and his step-son, Kwon, just after the latter had converted to Catholicism. Despite his stepfather's warnings, Kwon persisted in his new faith and died at the hands of governmental officials who were concerned about the spread of Catholicism.

An Chongbok's main argument against Catholicism is that it concentrates on the next world, at the expense of doing good work and avoiding evil in this one.

Someone said to me, "These European priests live celibate lives, and that is more than virtuous Chinese scholars are capable of. Moreover, the breadth and depth of their knowledge make them truly exceptional men. They are able to map the heavens, calculate calendars, and make such useful items as a cannon that can pierce the nine layers of heaven.... These Europeans are also able to circumnavigate the globe. When they enter a strange country, they are able to speak and read that country's language after just a short while. And their astronomical calculations are accurate in every particular. They truly are sagelike men. Since they are sagely, then how can you not trust them?"

I replied, "What you say may be true, but let's look at where they come from. Europe lies at the foot of the Kunlun mountains. Therefore the climate is invigorating, the people are unusually sturdy and tall, and there is an abundance of natural resources there. It is like the abdomen in the human

From *Sourcebook of Korean Civilization*, Vol. II, ed. by Peter H. Lee et al. Copyright © 1996 Columbia University Press, 141–144. Reprinted with permission of the publisher.

body—the blood collects there to drink and dine and then goes back to serving as the foundation of human life.

China, on the other hand, is in the southeast corner of the world. The sun's light is concentrated there. As a result those who are born with an endowment of the material force of that place are sagely men such as Yao, Shun, . . . the Duke of Chou, and Confucius. China is like the heart in man's chest, which is the site of intelligence and out of which the myriad transformations come. If you look at it this way, then you can see why the sagely learning of China is sound but the "heavenly learning" of Europe, though there are some who call it the true way and a sagely teaching, is not what I call sagely teaching. . . . "

My questioner continued, "Jesus is the name of the Messiah, the savior of the world. He was just like the sages in that he wanted to promote moral behavior. There is no difference."

I responded, "How can you say that? When Jesus worked on 'saving the world,' he focused on a world after this one. He tantalized people with promises of heaven if they did good and threatened people with hell if they did evil. In promoting moral behavior, the sages, however, focus on this world. They illuminate virtue and revitalize the people in order to educate and transform them. Jesus encouraged selfishness and the sages' foster selflessness. Therein lies a difference.

"If what the Westerners say is true and there really is a heaven and a hell, then those who do good and avoid evil in this life will go to heaven anyway, and those who are not virtuous and who act improperly will end up in hell anyway after they die. In the meantime, people should simply continue to do what is right and not turn their backs on the moral nature heaven has given them. They should not pay the slightest attention to the possibility of some reward in the next life for what they do in this life. Master Ch'eng said that Buddhists seek escape from the never-ending cycle of birth, death, and rebirth only because that is in their own self-interest. Don't the prayers of Catholics to avoid hell also represent their pursuit of individual self-interest? . . . "

He continued, "These Europeans warn us about the three enemies of man. The first is our own body. The sensations of sound and sight, of taste and smell, along with our tendencies toward lust, laziness, and licentiousness, quietly weaken us internally. Our second enemy, according to them, is the mundane world. Through the lure of wealth, fame, amusements, and frivolities, it openly attacks us from the outside. The third enemy of man is the devil. He uses our own pride as well as external allurements to bewitch and confuse us and attacks us both internally and externally. How can you not agree with this? Doesn't this make a lot of sense?"

I answered, "You have really been deluded. This notion that our body is our enemy is a terrible perversion of morality. It is true that because we have bodies we are beset with desires of the flesh. That is why we Confucians stress the need for self-control. But where do you think your body comes from? We get our bodies from our parents. So, if our bodies are our enemies, then our parents who gave us those bodies must be our enemies as well! . . . "

Moreover, since we are all born into this world, it is only natural that some of us will be rich and others poor, some of us will be well known and respected and others will not, some of us will be successes and others failures, and some will do well in life and others will do not so well. That is just the way things are. But if you don't know how to gain the strength to resist the temptations of this world by engaging in self-examination and exercising self-control but take the world with all its rewards and disappointments as your enemy instead, then you will render all the moral obligations of that world, such as the moral ties between rulers and subjects, meaningless.

As for their talk about a 'devil,' that is really ridiculous. . . . Who can see this devil? If he does happen to exist, he is out there somewhere in the world around us. It is true that temptations from the world around us can cause us to lose our original nature. But the absence of good in man is due to imperfections in his physical endowment, that's all. How can we blame our faults on this devil? Their approach of looking for internal and external enemies to blame is quite different from our Confucian approach of simply exerting self-control. When these Europeans blame the devil rather than their own physical endowment for their moral failings, they are missing the point. Their ideas are really not worth discussing. . . . "

He continued questioning me, "Jesus the Savior was crucified. Even though he had power to move Heaven and Earth and all of creation, he did not harm in the least bit the people who nailed him to the cross. Does that not show the greatest possible love for mankind?"

I responded, "What you are talking about is the so-called 'love your enemy and forget your hatred' precept. . . . Generally speaking, there are two kinds of enemies. In the case of those enemies who have harmed us personally, there are many cases of admirable gentlemen in ancient times who followed this precept you mention in dealing with such enemies. However, the second kind of enemy is the enemy of your ruler or of your parents. To follow the example of Jesus and love that kind of enemy would be a grave violation of your moral obligations and a betrayal of your ruler or your parents. . . .

He then said to me, "As I understand it, you are saying that this Catholic religion is without a doubt heterodox. Our Confucian efforts to illuminate virtue and transform the people all focus on this world. These Europeans, on the other hand, are only thinking about the next world when they talk about doing good and avoiding evil. According to you, since people are born into this world, they should expend all their energy on things of this world and try to do their very best without concerning themselves the least bit with possible rewards in the next life. The Catholic approach is really different from our Confucian approach. Their ideas all have their roots in individual selfishness. How can this compare with our Confucian concern for doing what is right for the common good? From now on, I will listen to what you have to say."

Hearing this, I smiled, and after my guest had left, I wrote down this account of our conversation.

42

YI HANGRO

CHINA IS THE CENTER OF THE UNIVERSE

Korea

Editor's Notes: During the mid-nineteenth century, European Catholic missionary activity in Korea was producing an increasing number of converts. Yi Hangro (1792–1868), noted scholar, teacher, and one-time government official, viewed these conversions with extreme alarm. He was a forceful critic of Catholicism who found it inconceivable that supposedly intelligent men, educated in the West, could attempt to undermine the long Confucian traditions of China and Korea.

The core of his beliefs was that China was the center of the universe. All other countries were barbaric and subsidiary. He urged his king to wage a war of resistance against the influence of the West, not only to boycott European goods in the future, but also to destroy all that had already arrived.

When Chinese civilization encounters a barbarian people, those barbarians are transformed by Chinese ways into a civilized people. Barbarians look up to China and are delighted to receive its civilizing influence. This is the way things are in the natural order of things. This is the way human beings ought to feel. China is like the roots of a plant supplying nourishment for the branches and leaves. It is like the hands and feet that protect the belly and chest of the human body. This should never change. . . .

Europe has . . . been saturated with a lot of misleading notions, and Europeans as a result tend to spout a bunch of nonsense, criticizing the teachings of the earlier Confucian sages and condemning the teachings of later Neo-Confucian philosophers. It appears to be next to impossible to awaken those men to their true inner nature and get them to change their mistaken practices. Europeans do have a remarkable talent for technology. They easily surpass the Chinese in that area. But that achievement makes them arrogant, and they think that they can convert the whole world to their way of thinking. They need to think again!

The heavens are so vast that the universe appears boundless. Yet we can locate the center of the universe, that point around which it revolves. That is the North Pole. The earth is also quite large, extending so far in all directions that it too appears infinite in size. Yet it also has a center, the site from which the entire earth is governed. That terrestrial center is China. There are also many different ways human beings can behave and interact, so many that they appear countless. But above them all is the Supreme Ultimate, the Way of ways.

The North Pole rules over the multitude of stars, so the multitude of stars all bow in the direction of the North Pole. The center of the earth rules the ten thousand regions, so all of those regions recognize the paramount position of China. The Supreme Ultimate reigns over all creation, so all creation is brought together under the Supreme Ultimate. This is the one principle that unites everything in Heaven, on earth, and among people.

The key to eradicating the disaster brought about by the Western barbarians lies in Your Majesty's heart. The only recommendation that might assist Your Majesty is to purify the heart and remain firm, resisting the influence or temptation of things foreign. Although foreign things are of so many varieties that not all of them can be enumerated, the Western commodities are the most obvious. I beg Your Majesty to make a firm decision and burn any Western goods that may be found among your clothes, food, and items of daily use. It will serve to show what you like and dislike. It will prove your self-discipline and rectitude. And your lifestyle will conform to the established norms.

The royal household, royal relatives and in-laws will thus be informed and warned to follow your example. Once the court is in order, the entire state, even in remote villages, will be in order following the example of the court. If personal virtues are cultivated, family life is well ordered, and the country is properly governed, there will be no need for Western goods, and the trade in these goods will cease. Without trade, their novelty and wonder will be unrecognized. If their novelty and wonder are unrecognized, the Westerners will surely stop coming because there will be nothing for them to do.

THE HERMIT KINGDOM

The West referred to Korea as the "hermit kingdom" because it had for centuries essentially rejected all outside contact. Rejection of the West had been based on a general disdain for foreigners combined with the belief that Confucianism was the only valid belief; thus any civilization that thought differently should be kept out. Relations with the Western barbarians would mean abandonment of those values upon which all of civilization rested. Until the nineteenth century, foreign relations consisted of an annual tribute mission to Peking and limited contact with Japan. In the nineteenth century the West and Japan forced Korea to end its long entrenched policies of isolation. Once opened to the world, it encountered a variety of challenges; exploitation, war, and the potential loss of national sovereignty.

Mary E. Connor, *The Koreas: A Global Studies Handbook*, ABC-CLIO, Inc., 2002, p. 29.

FIRST ENCOUNTERS TIMELINE

Asia

1271–1295	Marco Polo visits China
1498	Vasco da Gama (Portuguese) lands on the west coast of India to trade
1514	Portuguese reach China and are later permitted to dwell on Macao Island under guard
1542	Portuguese reach Japan, opening a century of trade and contact with the West
1581	Korean scholars travel to China and encounter Western missionaries
1612	Japan bans Christianity
1628	First of several Dutch shipwrecks off Korean coast; most sailors never return home
1640–1853	Japan isolates itself; only Dutch traders allowed
1752	Yi Ik, Korean scholar and religious philosopher, condemns Catholicism
1790	An Chongbok, Korean Confucian scholar, criticizes Catholicism
1791–1850	American and Russian ships, separately, unsuccessfully try to open up trade with Japan
1793	Chinese Emperor Qian Long writes British King George III, rejecting relations
1803	Abu Taleb Khan publishes his criticisms of the British
1803	Raja Rammohun Roy, Indian philosopher, denigrates Catholicism
1831	Hiratu Atsutane, Japanese patriot, praises Japan and ridicules the Dutch
1839–1842	British-Chinese Opium War
1842	Canton-Chinese citizens condemn the British invaders
1844	Wei Yuan, Chinese scholar, describes the Western Barbarians

1846	U.S. warships demand the opening of Japan to Western trade
1853	American Commodore Matthew Perry, with warships, forces open Japan to trade
1853	Tokugawa Nariaki, Japanese warlord, urges war against foreigners
1860	Yi Hangro, Korean scholar, extols Chinese superiority

BIBLIOGRAPHY

Achebe, Chinua. *Things Fall Apart*. Oxford: Heinemann Educational Publishers, 1996.
A powerful novel written in the 1950's by one of Africa's most eminent writers. He describes life in a traditional Nigerian village prior to the arrival of a European missionary which brings shattering social consequences.

Andrews, Susan B. and John Creed. *Authentic Alaska: Voices of Its Native Writers*. Lincoln: University of Nebraska Press, 1998.
Views of Alaskan life written by indigenous writers including descriptions of changing cultures.

Armstrong, Virginia Irving, ed. *I Have Spoken: American History Through the Voices of the Indians*. Chicago: Sage Books, 1971.
A collection of speeches by Indians from 1609 to 1970 which tell the sad story of Indian-White relations over four centuries.

Atiyah, Edward. *An Arab Tells His Story*. London: John Murray, 1946.
The autobiography of a Syrian Christian, born in Lebanon and educated at English schools. His first-hand reports on the impact of the coming of the Europeans in the Sudan are unique. Photos enhance an understanding of the book's theme.

Awolowo, Obafemi. *AWO: The Autobiography of Chief Obafemi Awolowo*. Cambridge: Cambridge University Press, 1960.
The autobiography of a Nigerian born in 1909 which focuses on life before the arrival of the Europeans and then on efforts to ameliorate the social tensions caused by the clash between the new and traditional.

Awoonor, Kofi. *This Earth, My Brother*. New York: Doubleday & Co., 1971.
Short pieces by a prominent Ghanaian writer illustrating the clash between European and African cultures.

Ballard, Martin. *White Man's God*. Westport, CT: Greenwood World Publishing, 2008.
    The account of European missionary activity in Africa for over 200 years. The book makes clear that the missionaries' impact went far beyond that of religion to include education, exploration, medicine, and colonizing.

Beasley, W. S., ed. *Select Documents on Japanese Foreign Policy, 1853–1868*. London: Oxford University Press, 1955.
    Translations of mid-nineteenth-century Japanese documents including those related to the reactions to American Commodore Matthew Perry's aggressive attempts to open up trade with Japan.

Bent, George and George Hyde. *Life of George Bent Written from His Letters*. Norman: University of Oklahoma Press, 1968.
    Using the letters of the mixed-race son of a Cheyenne mother and a white father, the book describes in great detail the life of the Plains Indians and their attempts to fight off the invaders.

Beti, Mongo. *Mission to Kala*. London: Heinemann Educational Publishers, 1964.
    An intriguing novel relating the story of a young man from the Cameroons, who, having failed his examinations in a French college, returns home not in disgrace, but as a fount of knowledge about European culture.

Boorstin, Daniel. *The Discoverers*. New York: Random House, 1983.
    A 745-page tome on the discoverers of the present-day world. Parts 5–8 deal with the bursting forth of Europeans to explore, to engage in trade and in some places, to colonize.

Calloway, Colin G., ed. *The World Turned Upside Down: Indian Voices from Early America*. Boston: St. Martin's Press, 1994.
    The voices of indigenous peoples on Indian history and culture during the colonial period of American history. Included are eyewitness accounts of the clash between cultures as the Europeans arrived.

Clark, Leon E., ed. *Through African Eyes: Cultures in Change*. New York: Praeger Publishers, 1971.
    An extensive anthology of African writings on such topics as tribe to town adjustment, coming of the Europeans, and the colonial experience. Many drawings and photographs enhance the 89 selections.

Connolly, Bob, and Robin Anderson. *First Contact*. New York: Viking Penguin, 1987.
    Unusual accounts of the peaceful encounters between Australian prospectors and pre-technological native dwellers of Papua, New Guinea. Over 100 photographs provide striking views of previously unknown societies.

Conton, William. *The African*. Boston: Little, Brown, 1960.
    A semi-autobiographical novel about an African who returns home after a university education in Britain and assumes leadership in the struggle for independence.

David, Jay and Helise Harrington, ed. *Growing Up African*. New York: William Morrow & Co., 1971.
    An anthology of texts written or told by Africans which deal with a range of topics on African life including the arrival of Europeans.

deBary, Wm. Theodore, ed. *Sources of Chinese Tradition*. New York: Columbia University Press, 1960.
  Extensive collection of historical documents, letters, editorial writing, speeches, and reports that illuminate the civilization of China during the last two millennia.

————. *Sources of Indian Tradition*. New York: Columbia University Press, 1958.
  Extensive collection of historical documents, letters, editorial writing, speeches, and reports that illuminate the civilization of India during the last two millennia.

————, general ed. *Sources of Japanese Tradition*. New York: Columbia University Press, 1958.
  Extensive collection of historical documents, letters, editorial writing, speeches, and reports that illuminate the civilization of Japan during the last two millennia.

————. *Sources of Korean Tradition*. New York: Columbia University Press, 1997.
  Extensive collection of historical documents, letters, editorial writing, speeches, and reports that illuminate the civilization of Korea during the last two millennia.

Duodu, Cameron. *The Gab Boys*. London: Andre Deutsch Ltd., 1967.
  A novel dealing with a young man's coming of age in Ghana, facing the many problems brought about by the clash between western and native cultures.

Eastman, Charles. *Indian Boyhood*. Lincoln: University of Nebraska Press, 1991.
  An autobiography written in 1902 by a Santee Sioux whose eleven books sought to bring Indians and whites together.

Equiano, Olaudah. *The Interesting Narrative of the Life of Olaudah Equiano*. Boston: Bedford/St. Martin's, 1995.
  An autobiography, first published in 1789, recounting his boyhood in Nigeria, capture by slavers, transport across the Atlantic, sale at auction, and purchase by a British officer leading to freedom and a good education.

Garcilaso de la Vega, El Inca. *Royal Commentaries of the Incas, Part II*. Austin: University of Texas Press, 1966.
  Part two of this prodigious 1,500 page history of the Incas concentrates on the conquest of Peru through the accounts of those who witnessed it.

Hasan, Mushirul, ed. *Westward Bound—Travels of Mirza Abu Taleb*. Translated by Charles Stewart. New Delhi: Oxford University Press, 2005.
  Travels of an Indian Muslim scholar from India to Europe and back in the early nineteenth century. His long stay in England resulted in India's first detailed assessment, both pro and con, of British society and life.

Hunefeldt, Christine. *A Brief History of Peru*. New York: Lexington Associates, 2004.
  Includes accounts of building of the Incan empire and its destruction by the invading Conquistadors in the early 1500s.

Jones, Douglas W. *Exploration into Highland New Guinea 1930–1935*. Tuscaloosa: The University of Alabama Press, 1991.
  Uses his diaries and photographs to tell the story of Michael Leahy's explorations in New Guinea where he encountered untouched indigenous people.

Kenyatta, Jomo. *Facing Mount Kenya*. New York: Vintage Books, 1965.
  The classic anthropological study of the Kikuyu tribe of Kenya, first published in 1938. Written by the man who later would become the president of Kenya.

Kiki, Albert Maori. *Kiki: Ten Thousand Years in a Lifetime*. Melbourne: F. W. Cheshire, 1968.
  The unique autobiography of a man who was born into a head-hunter society on the island of Papua New Guinea. He describes how he adjusted to the enormous changes in his life required by the imposition of European culture, ultimately becoming his country's deputy prime minister.

Landes, David. *The Wealth and Poverty of Nations*. New York, New York: W. W. Norton and Co., 1998.
  Preeminent Harvard historian analyzes why the Europeans have been the dominant nations in the world for the last six hundred years.

Lee, Peter H., ed. *Sourcebook of Korean Civilization. Vol. II. From the Seventeenth Century to the Modern Period*. New York: Columbia University Press, 1996.
  Extensive collection of writings related to the development of Korean civilization.

Lee, Peter H. and Wm. Theodore deBary, ed. *Sources of Korean Tradition. Vol. II. From the Seventeenth Century to the Modern Period*. New York: Columbia University Press, 2000.
  An abridgement of *Sourcebook of Korean Civilization Vol. II*, focusing on "the social and civic."

Leon-Portilla, Miguel, ed. *Broken Spears: The Aztec Account of the Conquest of Mexico*. Boston: Beacon Press, 1962.
  An important compilation of indigenous accounts of the conquest of Mexico by Cortés made available in English for the first time.

Lunenfeld, Marvin, ed. *1492: Discovery, Invasion, Encounter*. Lexington, MA: D. C. Heath and Co., 1991.
  A wide range of primary source documents on topics relating to the arrival and conquests of North and South America by Europeans.

Minear, Richard. *Through Japanese Eyes*. New York: CITE, 1994.
  Japanese, speaking for themselves rather than through others, reveal their history, civilization and values through autobiography, diaries, historical documents, magazine articles, poetry, and fiction.

Modupe, Prince. *I Was a Savage*. London: Harcourt, Brace and World Inc., 1958.
  The autobiography of a man growing up in Guinea at a time when confrontation with the intruding Europeans was at the peak. Drawings add reality to the descriptions of daily life.

Moses, Daniel D. and Terry Goldie, ed. *An Anthology of Canadian Native Literature in English*. New York: Oxford University Press, 1998.
  Indigenous Canadian voices on a full range of topics depicting local societies including the recurring theme of the arrival and impact of Europeans.

Nabokov, Peter, ed. *Native American Testimony*. New York: Viking, 1991.
 An extensive anthology of Native American writings on the relationships with the intruding Europeans. The book includes material from Columbus's time up to the twentieth century and includes more than 75 illuminating photographs.

Osborne, Roger. *Civilization—A New History of the Western World*. New York: Pegasus Books, 2006.
 A noted British historian provides a fresh look at the development of Western Culture including first encounters between Europeans and native peoples.

Petrone, Penny. *First People First Voices*. Toronto: University of Toronto Press, 1984.
 Writings in English by Canadian Indians dealing with the full range of culture from 1700 on. The book consists of poems, drama, speeches, songs, letters, and stories.

Restall, Matthew et al. *Mesoamerican Voices*. New York: Cambridge University Press, 2005.
 A collection of indigenous-language writings from Mexico and Guatemala translated into English, dealing with a wide range of topics on changes that came about during the colonial period 1600–1800.

Rutherfoord, Peggy, ed. *African Voices*. New York: Vanguard Press, 1958.
 Probably the very first anthology of native African writing published in the United States. The book consists of stories, poems, recorded oral history, and other folklore from sub-Saharan Africa.

Schiffers, Heinrich. *The Quest for Africa: Two Thousand Years of Exploration*. New York: Putnam's Sons, 1957.
 A German writer's history of European exploration in Africa which, in spite of its title, deals almost entirely with the nineteenth century.

Schwartz, Stuart. *Victors and the Vanquished*. Boston: Bedford/St. Martins, 2000.
 The conquest of Mexico from Spanish and native Nahua perspectives. Many drawings and reproductions of native paintings add interest to the texts.

Síocháin, Séamas Ó., and Michael O'Sullivan, eds. *The Eyes of Another Race: Roger Casement's Congo Report and 1903 Diary*. Dublin: University College Dublin Press, 2003.
 The report to Parliament by Roger Casement, British government's investigator into the Belgium Congo atrocities of 1903. It revealed the infamous cruelty shown to the Congolese peoples.

St. Barbe Baker, Richard. *Kabongo: The Story of a Kikuyu Chief*. New York: A. S. Barnes and Co., 1955.
 The author, a British forester and writer, spent many years in Kenya where he recorded the life story of his good friend, Chief Kabongo. The book is illustrated by outstanding wood cuts.

Stanley, Henry M. *Through the Dark Continent, or, The Sources of the Nile around the Great Lakes of Equatorial Africa*, 2 vols. New York: Harper & Bros. 1878.
 Stanley's lengthy account, in high Victorian prose, of his explorations in Central Africa following the Congo River to the ocean.

Teng, Ssu-yu and John Fairbank. *China's Response to the West*. Cambridge: Harvard University Press, 1954.
  A documentary survey, 1839–1923, which focuses upon China's attempts to deal with the aggressive expansion of the modern West.

Turnbull, Colin M. *The Lonely African*. New York: Simon and Schuster, 1962.
  Based on numerous extended trips to Africa by a British anthropologist. Six autobiographical interviews on the coming of the Europeans are interspersed with six chapters of commentary.

Wachtel, Nathan. *The Vision of the Vanquished: The Spanish Conquest of Peru through Indian Eyes, 1530–1570*. New York: Barnes and Noble, 1977.
  An important analysis of the impact of the conquest using native sources and the tools of history and anthropology. First published in French in 1971.

Wright, Ronald. *Stolen Continents: The Americas through Indian Eyes since 1492*. Boston: Houghton Mifflin Co., 1992.
  Aztec, Maya, Cherokee, Iroquois, and Inca accounts of the invasion by Europeans, resistance and rebirth.

Yupanqui, Titu Cusi. *An Inca Account of the Conquest of Peru*. Translated and edited by Ralph Bauer. Boulder: University Press of Colorado, 2005.
  A vivid narrative of the Incan view of the Spanish invasion. The 56-page introduction places the Incan writers' views into clear historical context.

INDEX

About the Editor

HOWARD B. LEAVITT, now retired and living in Amherst, Massachusetts, spent his early years in Beirut, Lebanon, where his father was an administrator at the American University of Beirut. He is a graduate of Dartmouth College and holds graduate degrees from Columbia University in sociology and education. He was a professor at several universities, including Boston University, and served as visiting professor at the American University of Beirut for two years. He has worked for the U.S. Agency for International Development assessing the effectiveness of foreign aid education programs and has visited Africa and Latin America on numerous occasions, residing in Brazil for three years on a U.S. foreign aid assignment. He served as Assistant Provost and Coordinator of International Programs at Pennsylvania State University and was a long-term educational consultant in residence at the World Bank under Robert McNamara.

His latest publication, *Issues and Problems in Teacher Education: An International Handbook* was published by Greenwood Press.